SYRIA UNDER ASSAD

SYRIA
UNDER
ASSAD

Domestic Constraints and Regional Risks

Edited by MOSHE MA'OZ and AVNER YANIV

ST. MARTIN'S PRESS
New York

© 1986 Moshe Ma'oz and Avner Yaniv.
All rights reserved. For information, write:
St. Martin's Press, Inc., 175 Fifth Avenue, New York, NY 10010.
Printed in Great Britain.
First published in the United States of America in 1986.

Library of Congress Cataloging in Publication Data

Main entry under title:
  Syria under Assad.

  Includes index.
  1. Syria—Politics and government—Addresses, essays,
lectures. 2. Syria—Foreign relations—Addresses,
essays, lectures. I. Ma'oz, Moshe. II. Yaniv, A.
(Avner).
DS98.2.S97   1986   956.91'042   85-18274
ISBN 0-312-78206-3

CONTENTS

Part III: Syria and the Superpowers

Part IV: The Syrian Paradox

NOTES ON CONTRIBUTORS

Amazia Baram is instructor in Middle East History at the University of Haifa.

Yair Evron is Senior Lecturer in Political Science at Tel-Aviv University.

Kais Firro is Lecturer in Middle East History at the University of Haifa.

Robert O. Freedman is Professor of Political Science and Dean of the Peggy Meyerhoff Pearlstone School of Graduate Studies of the Baltimore Hebrew College.

Yair Hirschfeld is Senior Lecturer in Middle East History at the University of Haifa.

David Kushner is Senior Lecturer in Middle East History at the University of Haifa.

Moshe Ma'oz is Professor of Middle East History at the Hebrew University of Jerusalem.

Zeev Ma'oz is Lecturer in Political Science at the University of Haifa.

Joseph Nevo is Lecturer in Middle East History at the University of Haifa.

Itamar Rabinovich is Professor of Middle East History at Tel-Aviv University.

Avner Yaniv is Senior Lecturer in Political Science at the University of Haifa.

PREFACE

This collection of studies is the harvest of a one-day symposium held at the University of Haifa in January 1984. The initiative came from the University's Institute of Middle Eastern Studies. Bearing the name of Gustav Heinemann, the late President of the Federal Republic of Germany, the IMESH is an interdisciplinary meeting ground for researches in Islamic studies, Arab history and culture, politics and international relations in the Middle East, ethnic relations, the social psychology of international conflicts, the political geography of conflict and problems of education in a conflict environment.

Every year, and occasionally more than once a year, the IMESH holds a large symposium. In 1984 it was the turn of the political scientists and area specialists to design a meeting. And since Syria was in the news and there was tremendous public interest in its history, domestic problems and, above all, role as an actor on the Middle Eastern scene, a symposium on it appeared to be a timely and promising idea.

Initially the objectives were rather modest. No one, to put it bluntly, had any intention of going beyond a learned exchange of views for the benefit of the campus audience. But once the conference was held it turned out that the quality of the presentations, the main recurrent themes and the uniquely synoptic panorama of the Syrian scene which the presentations offered had the potential of an interesting book. Concerned to avoid quick outdating of the papers,we requested the contributors to add onto the bones of their analyses as much factual flesh as they could without presenting the publisher with an over-long manuscript. Most of the contributors responded to the challenge with such enthusiasm that we found ourselves inundated with enough material for two volumes. Consequently, we had no alternative but to cut many of the articles to almost half their size in the original form. This was a painful phase and it is a tribute to the patience and generosity of the contributors that we succeeded in completing the task in the same spirit of co-operation and good will which had characterised the enterprise at the very beginning.

But while the creative enthusiasm of scholars is a *sine qua non* for a good book, it is not at all a sufficient condition, especially when the book holds many articles by different authors coming from various scholarly traditions, teaching at different universities, writing in a variety of languages, and either living in three different continents or, worse still, constantly on the move among them. To edit a book under these conditions is a nightmare unless one has the assistance of administrative and editorial staff of the calibre which we were fortunate to have at the IMESH. Among them three individuals deserve a special tribute. The first is Mr. Asher M. Goldstein, the linguistic editor, who tirelessly and with an amazing skill read and re-read the manuscript in pursuit of technical and linguistic perfection. The second is Professor Arnon Soffer, a leading geographer and currently the Director of the IMESH whose support and encouragement made the project possible. The last, but by all accounts not the least, is Mrs. Sarah Tamir, the Executive Secretary of the IMESH who literally carried the project through from the symposium to the edition. Throughout the two years in which the book was in the making she showed ingenuity, tact and charm, a rare combination of qualities without which it would probably take longer to produce a far less gratifying result.

The Editors
Haifa

1 THE STUDY OF SYRIA

Moshe Ma'oz and Avner Yaniv

Research on Syria has evolved in three fairly distinct perspectives. The first, and so far most elaborate, has focused primarily on politics and society within the Syrian state. Scholars in this area have concerned themselves primarily with the power struggle that has dominated Syrian politics since the inception of an independent Syrian polity. What were the traits of the generation of leaders who received the reins of power from the French? What were the causes and the consequences of the succession of *coups d'état* which took place between 1949 and 1963? What were the social bases of the new political and military elites which took over from the *ancien régime* during the 1950s? What were the emerging patterns of relations between the rising military, on the one hand, and the politicians, on the other hand? What were the social, ideological and personal origins of the power struggle among the Sunnis, the Alawis, the Druzes and the Christians and within each one of these religiously distinct communities, both before and after the advent of the Ba'ath? What were the socio-economic and political relations between town and country and among Syria's competing regional centres? Finally, and perhaps most important of all, has a genuine political community emerged in the Syrian state? Or has Syria remained a largely artificial administrative edifice, hopelessly caught between the magnetic attraction of Pan-Arabism, on the one hand, and the even more vigorous attraction of local, particularist loyalties, on the other hand?[1]

The second, but far less significant, focus of attention has been essentially a scholarly response to Syria's growing involvement in Lebanon in the course of the 1970s. Writers on this topic have been concerned with Syria's motives for steadily increasing its visibility in and impact on the troubled Lebanese scene. Specifically they have asked themselves whether Syria was out to fulfil a historic dream of glory or was merely acting in a strategic, damage-limiting fashion, responding to challenges as they presented themselves and ultimately more disposed to avoiding than to expanding intervention and making it permanent. In addition some writing in this area has also attempted to assess the viability, endurance, capabilities and operational reflexes within crisis contexts of the ever-growing Syrian state machinery.[2]

1

By shifting the emphasis of inquiry from the Syrian domestic scene to Syria's external posture, this second perspective in the study of Syria has formed a necessary link between the domestic-political perspective and a third perspective, whose main concern is Syria's foreign and security policies. This last trend, the most recent, clearly reflects the visible ascent of Syria as a regional actor. The roots of the foreign-policy perspective can be found in two larger assumptions. The first is that a 'normal' (as the term is employed by Kuhn[3]) Arab state system is rapidly emerging from the debris of the fading myth of Pan-Arabism. Once the most powerful force in the life of Arab individuals and Arab communities alike, a source of hope and inspiration, a blueprint for an Arab *risorgimento*, a welcome challenge to an illegitimate internal and wider regional order foisted upon the Arabs by European colonialism, a source of wars, revolutions, writings and ultimate despair, this myth has become, some writers argue forcefully, a spent force. It has led the Arabs to an abyss of internecine fighting, spectacular defeats at the hands of the Israelis and neo-colonial control by the superpowers.[4] Inevitably, therefore, it led to the rise of a new reference point: namely, the individual Arab state, which by developing capabilities and dispensing extensive services is gradually and successfully turning itself into a focal point of enduring loyalty.

The process, to be sure, is not complete. Pan-Arabism remains officially a sacrosanct, overriding purpose. Arab nations in the European sense, connoting both internal and international legitimacy, have not yet fully emerged. Indeed, Arab state particularism is still formally a partially legitimate, but essentially transient phenomenon. But a notion of 'stateness' — i.e. a legitimate, enduring intermediary between specific Arab communities and the larger Arab nation — has already, some argue, become a preponderant fact.[5] The second source of the foreign-policy perspective on Syrian politics follows logically from the first. If Arab 'stateness' has become a reality, then one can speak of the political process in the Middle East, not as a special case, but rather in the same terms employed for the analysis of international politics elsewhere. Some may invoke the European concept of a balance of power.[6] Others may prefer to view the foreign relations of an Arab state as a test case of 'linkage theory'.[7] A third group of specialists prefer decision-making theory as the primary tool with which to analyse Arab foreign-policy-making in general and the Syrian case in particular.[8]

Assuming implicitly that the emergence of Syrian 'stateness' has led to a Syrian foreign policy in this 'normal' sense, and tending to de-emphasise the question of whether or not Syria is a fully integrated political community, this third perspective in the study of Syria, especially its decision-making variant, focuses on the foreign policy of the Assad regime as the enactment by a small group of decision-makers of a more or less distinct state policy, with goals, capabilities and apparatus. What these studies ask themselves more specifically are questions such as the following: What is the Syrian foreign-policy environment? What is the structure of the Syrian government that makes foreign policy? How does the Syrian political system operate, and how do internal interest groups and parties affect the government's external behaviour? What are the main issue areas on the Syrian foreign-policy agenda? What foreign relations does Syria have? What are the *objectives* of its foreign policy, and what *strategies* and *instruments* does it employ to realise these objectives? Finally, how successful has Syria been in attaining these goals?[9]

Broadly speaking, such questions have guided the editors of this book, and it, therefore, falls squarely into the foreign-policy rather than in either of the two other perspectives. Yet by its very emphasis on decision-making, this approach raises an important general question that is particularly pertinent in the case of a polity as 'closed' as Syria. The foreign-policy perspective having its emphasis on decision-making makes two general assumptions: first, that foreign-policy-making is what de Gaulle defined as a *domain reservé*, the exclusive prerogative of a small, especially knowledgeable elite; second, that there is no way of understanding a country's foreign policy without penetrating the decision-making 'black box', that secret nerve centre in which critical decisions are made. If this is the case, how does one collect sufficient evidence to account for Syria's foreign policy? Is this at all possible? And if not, are we not advocating a research strategy whose requirements are totally beyond fulfilment?

The answer is both 'yes' and 'no'. 'Yes', because literally penetrating the Syrian 'black box' is, indeed, impossible. 'No', because there are ways of circumventing this seemingly insurmountable obstacle. Specifically it is arguable that the guiding principles, premises, preoccupations, techniques and objectives of any foreign-policy decision-making body will tend to fall into discernible patterns; the longer this body remains in power, the easier it should become to decipher its operational code as a functioning collectivity.[10]

The Assads — both Hafez and Rif'at — Abdal-Halim Khaddam, Mustafa Tlas, Hikmat Shihabi and their colleagues have been in power for a long time. When they first emerged, King Idris was still ruling Libya, Nasser was still President of Egypt, Faisal King of Saudi

Arabia, Golda Meir Prime Minister of Israel. Brezhnev then ruled supreme in Moscow and Nixon was making his first steps as President of the United States. The Ba'ath regime in Syria, more or less in its present configuration, is thus close to breaking not only Syria's (unimpressive) record of ruling longevity, but also that of the Middle East as a whole (with the notable exceptions of Hussein in Jordan and the Taqritis in Iraq). It is, therefore, becoming increasingly easier, though not yet easy, to identify long-term patterns in the conduct of the Syrian regime even without penetrating the thick veil of secrecy in which Syria's foreign-policy-making is shrouded. In practical terms, what this implies is a simple research strategy. The starting point is an investigation of the broader Syrian domestic scene, with a view to tracing emerging patterns. This entails two separate investigations. The first emphasises the political aspects, the second focuses on the main features of the Syrian economy. Decoupled for research purposes and then reintegrated again, such analyses (offered in this volume by Moshe Ma'oz and Kais Firro, respectively) should yield a sound evaluation of strengths, weaknesses, problems, prospects and critical trade-offs faced by the Syrian system.

But this is surely not enough. If the elements of Syrian power — the most important domestic 'givens' affecting its foreign policy — are to be soundly appraised, they should be accompanied by a measurement of the evolution of Syria's power over time *relative* to the international environment in which Syria operates. This methodologically demanding exercise calls for the participation, side by side with economic and social historians, of an international relations specialist. Zeev Ma'oz offers an interesting example of what this entails in Chapter 4.

Part I of the volume seeks to identify patterns in the evolution of Syrian power. The intention of Part II is to underline patterns in Syria's relations with its neighbours. The growth and the limits of Syria's accommodation with its powerful neighbour to the north, Turkey, are discussed in Chapter 5 by David Kushner from the Turkish perspective. The steadfast, though somewhat incongruous alliance between Ba'athist Syria and Khomeini's Iran is analysed by Yair Hirschfeld in Chapter 6. Syria's feud with its ideological twin to the east, Ba'athist Iraq, is appraised by Amazia Baram in Chapter 7. The significance and causes of Syria's severely fluctuating relations with the Hashemite Kingdom of Jordan are studied in Chapter 8 by Joseph Nevo. Syria's strategic behaviour in the context of its ever-escalating conflict with Israel is explored in Chapter 9 by Avner Yaniv. To complete the circle, Chapters 10 and 11 by, respectively, Itamar Rabinovich, Moshe Maoz and Avner Yaniv shift attention to Syria's role in Lebanon and to its puzzling attitude to the PLO.

The discussion now moves to Part III, in which Yair Evron and Robert O. Freedman each discuss relations between the Ba'athist republic, on the one hand, and one of the two superpowers, on the other hand.

Most of the contributors to this volume are country specialists or, at least, area specialists. Most of them look at Syrian policy from the perspective of one of the other countries that have frequently been at the receiving end of Syrian policy. Consequently these various authors contribute not only to the identification of patterns in Syria's behaviour, but also to the understanding of the far wider canvas of Middle East politics over the past decade and a half. The blend of historical survey and contemporary analysis which runs throughout the book provides the basis of the editors' conclusion which addresses the primary questions: Where is Syria, especially as an actor on the Middle East scene, heading? What makes it such a seemingly restless, dangerous and obstinate entity? What, ultimately, makes Syria tick?

Notes

1. Kamel S. Abu Jaber, *The Arab Ba'ath Socialist Party* (Syracuse University Press, Syracuse, 1966); I. Ben-Tzur, 'The Neo-Ba'ath Party of Syria', *Journal of Contemporary History* vol. 3, no. 3 (July 1968), pp. 161-81; John Devlin, *The Ba'ath Party* (Hoover Institute Press, Stanford, 1976); William E. Hazen, *Selected Minority Groups of the Middle East: The Alawis, Berbers, Druze and Kurds* (American Institute for Research, Kensington, MD, 1973); Raymond A. Hinnenbusch, 'Local Politics in Syria: Organization and Mobilization in Four Village Cases', *Middle East Journal* vol. 30, no. 1 (Winter 1976), pp. 1-24; Malcolm H. Kerr, 'Hafez Assad and the Changing Patterns of Syrian Politics', *International Journal* vol. 28, no. 4 (Autumn 1973), pp. 689-706; Thomas Koszinowski, 'Die Innenpolitische Entwicklung in Syrien seit der Machtergriefung des Ba'ath im Marz 1963', *Orient* vol. 13, no. 3 (September 1972), pp. 95-100; Avigdor Levi, 'The Syrian Communists and the Ba'ath Power Struggle, 1966-70', in Michael Confino and Shimon Shamir (eds.), *The USSR and the Middle East* (Israel Universities Press, Jerusalem, 1973), pp. 395-417; Moshe Ma'oz, 'Alawi Military Officers in Syrian Politics', in H.Z. Schiffrin (ed.), *The Military and State in Modern Asia* (Academic Press, Jerusalem, 1976), pp. 277-97; Moshe Ma'oz, Attempts at Creating a Political Community in Modern Syria', *Middle East Journal*, vol. 26, no. 4 (Autumn 1972), pp. 389-404; Tabitha Petran, *Syria* (Praeger, New York, 1972): Itamar Rabinovich, *Syria Under the Ba'ath, 1963-6; The Army-Party Symbiosis* (Halsted Press, New York, 1972); Patrick Seale, *The Struggle for Syria* (Oxford University Press, New York, 1965): Martin Seymour; 'The Dynamics of Power in Syria Since the Break with Egypt', *Middle Eastern Studies* vol. 6, no. 1 (January 1970), pp. 35-47; Gad Soffer, 'The Role of the Officers Class in Syrian Politics and Society', PhD dissertation, American University, Washington DC, 1968; Michael D. Suleiman, 'Syria: Disunity in Diversity', in Tareq Ismael (ed.), *Governments and Politics of the Contemporary Middle East* (Dorsey Press, Homewood, Ill., 1970), pp. 213-30; Gordon H. Torrey,

'Aspects of the Political Elite in Syria', in George H. Lenczowski (ed.), *Political Elites in the Middle East,* (American Enterprise Institute, Washington, DC, 1975), pp.151-61; George H. Torrey, 'The Ba'ath: Ideology and Practice', *Middle East Journal* vol. 23, no. 4 (1969), pp. 445-70; N. Van Dam, *The Struggle for Power in Syria* (Croom Helm, London, 1979); Michael H. Van Dusen, 'Syria: The Downfall of a Traditional Elite', in Frank Tachau (ed.), *Political Elites and Political Development in the Middle East* (Shenkman, Cambridge, MA, 1975), pp. 115-55; Michael H. Van Dusen, 'Political Integration and Regionalism in Syria', *Middle East Journal* vol. 26, no. 2, (Spring 1972), pp. 123-36.

2. The most typical example of writing in this vein is Adeed I. Dawisha, *Syria and the Lebanese Crisis* (MacMillan, London, 1980). Also relevant are studies of the Lebanese tragedy which devote an extensive attention to the Syrian role. See Walid Khalidi, *Conflict and Violence in Lebanon* (Harvard Studies in International Affairs, Harvard University, Cambridge, MA 1979); Itamar Rabinovich, 'Syria, The Limits of Military Power: Syria's Role', in P. Edward Haley and Lewis W. Snider (eds.), *Lebanon in Crisis* (Syracuse University Press, Syracuse, 1979); Itamar Rabinovich, *The War for Lebanon* (Cornell University Press, Ithaca, 1984).

3. Thomas S. Kuhn, *The Structure of Scientific Revolutions* (University of Chicago Press, Chicago, 1962). Kuhn, of course, does not speak about states, but his definition of the 'normal' seems to apply, by implication, in this context, too.

4. The most forceful proponent of this view is Fuad Ajami. See 'The End of Pan Arabism', *Foreign Affairs,* vol. 57, no. 2 (Winter 1978-9)

5. See Gabriel Ben-Dor, *State and Conflict in the Middle East* (Praeger, New York, 1983).

6. See Alan Taylor, *The Arab Balance of Power* (Syracuse University Press, Syracuse, 1982).

7. See Robert Burrows and Bertram Spector, 'The Strength and Direction of Relationships Between Domestic and External Conflict and Cooperation: Syria, 1961-7', in Jonathan Wilkenfeld (ed.), *Conflict Behavior and Linkage Politics* (McKay, New York, 1973); Yaakov Bar-Siman-Tov, *Linkage Politics in the Middle East: Syria Between Domestic and External Conflict 1961-70* (Westview Press, Boulder, 1983).

8. See Richard C. Snyder, W.H. Bruck and Burton Sapin, 'The Decision Making Approach to the Study of International Politics', in James N. Rosenau (ed.), *International Politics and Foreign Policy* (The Free Press, New York, 1969), pp. 199-206.

9. Paul Y. Hammond and Sidney S. Alexander, *Political Dynamics in the Middle East* (Elsevier, New York, 1971), ch. 7 (by P.J. Vatikiotis); R.D. McLaurin, Mohammed Mughisudin and Abraham Wagner, *Foreign Policy Making in the Middle East* (Praeger, New York, 1977), esp. ch. 6, 'Syrian Foreign Policy'; Itamar Rabinovich, 'Syria', in Edward A. Kolodziej and Robert E. Harkavi (eds.), *Security Policies of Developing Countries* (D C Heath and Co., Lexington, MA, 1982), pp. 267-83; Raymond A. Hinnenbusch, 'Revolutionary Dreams, Realist Strategies: The Foreign Policy of Syria', in Bahgat Korani and Ali H. Dessouki (eds.), *The Foreign Policies of Arab States,* (Westview Press, Boulder, 1984), pp. 283-322.

10. This is an adaptation of the collective body of Alexander George's concept, which was applied originally to individuals. See Alexander George, 'The Operational Code: A Neglected Approach to the Study of Political Leaders and Decision Making', *International Studies Quarterly,* (June 1969).

PART I

THE ELEMENTS OF SYRIAN POWER

2 THE EMERGENCE OF MODERN SYRIA

Moshe Ma'oz

Introduction

Under the leadership of President Hafez al-Assad, Syria has been transformed from a weak, shaky and vulnerable country into an apparently strong and stable state, a regional power in the Middle East. Indeed, in a country which for generations had been torn by vigorous centrifugal forces and jolted by military *coups* and countercoups, the Ba'ath Party has been able during the last decade or two to establish an unchallenged, highly centralised reign in Damascus. Similarly, Syria, which for decades had been an object of annexationist tendencies from several of its Arab neighbours and threatened by Israeli military might, has become under Assad's leadership one of the most influential, assertive powers in the region. Not only has Damascus managed to turn part of Lebanon into its protectorate and part of the PLO into its instrument, Syria has also challenged Egypt's Arab policy, Iraq's Fertile Crescent ascendancy, and Israel's military superiority, and it has threatened Jordan's *rapprochement* with Arafat's PLO. Finally, while securing massive Soviet military and strategic guarantees, but without becoming a Soviet client, Damascus has caused the USA to acknowledge its powerful position in the region.

What are the forces, developments and processes which have brought about this remarkable transformation of Syria? Does Syria's domestic stability and regional ascendancy stem from deep structural changes? Or, are they rather superficial and transient phenomena, having been effected by an Alawi sectarian military dictatorship using its instruments of coercion against the Sunni Muslim majority?

This work will attempt to review and analyse the major socio-political developments that have occurred in Syria during the last several generations. In particular, it will examine the changes that have taken place in Syrian politics and society under the leadership of Hafez al-Assad.

The Historical Background

Under Ottoman rule (1516-1918). Syria was not a unified, separate political entity. It was subdivided into several provinces that were loosely governed for long periods of time by the central authority in Istanbul. Within these provinces there developed local centrifugal or autonomous forces, such as mountain chiefs, tribal shaikhs, feudal overlords and urban notables. Distinct among these were two heterodox Islamic minority sects, the Alawis of the Ansariyya mountains (near Lattakia), and the Druzes of Jabal Hauran. Drawing upon their topographical and geographical vantage points, as well as upon their social and communal solidarity, these two groups, but particularly the Druzes, virtually secured semi-independent positions vis-à-vis the central government. Finally among the Sunni Muslim majority population, a small urban oligarchy of *ulama* (religious seculars) and *ayan* (notables) possessed great social prestige, economic wealth and, periodically, military power — and thus managed to wield local political power, which the central government was forced to acknowledge and come to terms with.

It is true that during the era of reform and modernisation, which started with Ibrahim Pasha in the early 1830s under the Egyptian occupation and continued under the Ottomans, successive governments attempted to destroy both the local centrifugal forces and the urban oligarchies and to establish strong centralised rule in Syria.[1] Although Egypt's powerful government during the 1830s was able to accomplish most of its aims, the Ottoman *Tanzimat* regime was too weak to pursue the Egyptian policies. It failed during most of the nineteenth century to subdue completely the Alawis and the Druzes, and to undermine the socio-political power of the Muslim urban notables. The Alawis were first overpowered by the Ottoman government only in the late 1850s, and the Druzes at the end of the century. These two war-like minorites soon revived and further enhanced their autonomy under the French mandatory administration of Syria (1920-46). Indeed, in consonance with their tactic of divide and rule, the French authorities established Alawi and Druze 'states', and granted them full domestic autonomy, independent of the central Syrian government. This autonomous status, although subsequently diminished in name, effectively continued until the end of the French Mandate. Similarly, under Ottoman rule, the Sunni Muslim urban elite not only escaped any decrease in its local authority, it also succeeded in augmenting its wealth and in strengthening its political power. The Ottoman administration did not possess sufficient authority in the country and needed the help of indigenous notables to enforce its unpopular reforms. Members of the urban elite were, thus, allowed to man and control the provincial councils *(majlis)*, which were set up to assist in the implementation of the reforms. These notables received from the councils extensive administrative, fiscal and judicial powers. Consequently, they were able not only to increase their economic strength but also to dominate, with the help of relatives, the various local governments and municipal institutions that were established in the second half of the nineteenth century.

Under the French mandatory government,[2] this socio-economic and political status among the Muslim population was maintained, affording the notables, particularly those who co-operated with the French, economic opportunities as well as political and administrative positions in the government machinery. Consequently, the Syrian urban elite — some hundred Sunni Muslim families, owners of vast tracts of land, big businesses and the like — continued to control the institutions of self-rule in the country, and to maintain the socio-economic gap between them and the lower classes of peasants and workers.

Another schism among the Syrian population that developed during the Ottoman period and persisted in certain respects under French rule was of a sectarian-religious nature. In addition to encouraging Alawi and Druze autonomies, the French also recruited a comparatively large number of soldiers from among these sects and periodically employed them to put down demonstrations and riots by Sunni Muslims. The French authorities, similarly, cultivated the autonomous status of various Christian communities, notably Catholics, Armenians and Assyrians, and granted them preferential positions in the government administration as well as in the economy. These policies contributed to the fostering of communal separatism, while further widening the sectarian-religious and socio-economic gaps between the Sunni majority population and the various minorities of the Syrian population.

If all these developments were not sufficient to maintain division and conflict, other important factors, both external and internal, also contributed to hampering the emergence of a coherent Syrian national community: namely, the absence of territorial unity, central authority and ideological consensus.

Obstacles on the Road to National Community[3]

Until the middle of the twentieth century, Syria lacked any exclusive central authority, capable of serving as a focus of identity and loyalty for the masses. For generations the Ottoman sultans had constituted a centre of religio-political allegiance for the Sunni majority. This centre was geographically distant. It became a mere abstraction for lack of governmental authority and the inability to maintain internal security. Nearer and more concrete were the family, tribe and village, which provided security and held their basic loyalty, although weakening political — if not religious — identification with the sultan. Members of the non-Sunni communities and sects apparently felt no loyalty, whether political or religious, to the Ottoman regime. The only social groups in Syria that identified themselves with the sultan and the Ottoman empire in both aspects were members of the religious and administrative establishment, which were fully integrated in the Ottoman Muslim community.

The aim of the Ottoman modernisation movement (Tanzimat) in the nineteenth century was to extend the sphere of identification with the state, to include, also, the members of non-Muslim communities. The Tanzimat leaders and the Young Ottomans strove to establish a framework for a new political community. The basis of its identity was to be Ottoman patriotism and all the sultan's subjects were to participate in it without difference of religion. In order to achieve this end, the reform movement attempted to re-establish the sultan's authority in the provinces, to improve the general standard of living and to grant equal status to the non-Muslim inhabitants. Although the political control of the sultan gained strength in the Syrian provinces, his spiritual authority declined among the Muslim population because of his secular policy. Obviously, Turkish linguistic and cultural values could not have any attraction for the Syrian population, the majority of which was Arab.

The elements of Arabic language and culture and of Syrian territorial identity — which the idea of Ottoman community lacked — formed the basis of a small cultural-ideological circle that originated in Syria in the middle of the nineteenth century. Professing Syrian supra-communal patriotism, this circle was founded in Beirut by a handful of Christian intellectuals, mainly Orthodox and Protestant, following massacres of Christians in Lebanon and Damascus in 1860. The members of this circle believed that the communal and religious loyalties splitting the Syrian population could be replaced by a secular patriotism based on a common homeland, language and culture. Christian men of letters, such as Butrus al-Bustani, Faris al-Shidyaq, Khalil al-Khuri and Marun al-Naqqash, contributed to the revival of the Arabic language. In writings of these intellectuals — al-Bustani in particular — there appeared for the first time the concepts of 'homeland' *(watan)*, 'love of homeland' *(hubb al-watan)* and land *(bilad)* of Syria'. They preached the initiation of 'a new era for Syria within the limits of the Ottoman Empire'.[4]

Nevertheless, it should be emphasised that until the end of the nineteenth century, the sense of Syrian territorial patriotism or the feeling of Ottoman identification did not affect the majority of the Syrian population. These concepts remained confined to small groups of Christian intellectuals. An experienced observer visiting Syria at the end of the 1850s described the situation as follows:

> Patriotism is unknown .... there is not a man in the country whether Turk or Arab, Mohammedan or Christian who would give a para (penny) to save the Empire from ruin. The patriotism of the Syrian is confined to the four walls of his own house; anything beyond them does not concern him.[5]

Even at the beginning of the twentieth century, no change in this situation was evident. According to a contemporary Christian Syrian intellectual and senior government official, 'the patriotic bond *(irtibat watani)* is weak and concerns only a few members of the upper class.'[6]

In the second half of the nineteenth century, however, there did occur a conceptual change not only among Christian intellectuals, but also among the local Muslim spiritual leadership. On the other hand, the entire political and religious Muslim elite rejected the secular reform policy of Sultan Abd al-Majid (1839-61) which provoked doubts among traditional Muslim circles in Syria, who questioned his right (in fact, they labelled the sultan *'al-kha'in'*, the betrayer of Islam, to lead the Muslim world. In these circles, Ottoman reform appears to have fanned latent feelings of difference between Arabs and Turks and re-emphasised the special role of the Arabs in Islam. In some Syrian towns during the 1860s and 1870s hopes of 'separation from the Ottoman Empire and the formation of a new Arabian state under the sovereignty of the Shereef of Mecca'[7] were expressed — as was the aim of independence for *'bilad al-sham'* (the land of Syria) under the Amir Abd al-Qadir, a Damascus notable of Algerian origin.[8] Later, under the tyrannical rule of Sultan Abd al-Hamid, Muslim intellectual leaders of Syrian origin, such as Abd al-Rahman al-Kawakibi and Rashid Rida, pleaded for the return of the caliphate to the Arabs.

All these expressions of Arab consciousness were weak and sporadic during the second half of the nineteenth century. They became a major trend only at the beginning of the twentieth century — as a reaction to the secular nationalism of the Young Turks — particularly following the Arab revolt against the Turks. Indeed, only after World War I did the sense of an Arab-Syrian identity gradually become more widespread. This was mainly due to the establishment of a separate political-territorial entity by the great powers and Amir Faysal. This entity was first formed during Faysal's rule in Syria (1918-20). Though short-lived it gave rise to semi-independent Syrian Arab government as well as to local political parties. The names given to those bodies indicate the emerging sense of a Syrian identity. The government of Faysal was called the 'Arab-Syrian Government' and the 'Kingdom of Syria'. The institution that was to serve as a kind of national assembly was called the 'National Congress' and also the 'Syrian Congress'. The parties represented in that institution called themselves the 'Independent Pan-Arab Party' and the 'United Syrian Party'.[9] Faysal also sought to attract the loyalties of the minorities of the new Syrian state under the motto, 'Religion to God, the homeland to all'. He appointed leaders of the Muslim heterodox communities to the regional administration and allocated seats in the Syrian congress and government to Christians. Faysal also acted towards the Arabisation of state institutions and the educational system and founded an academy for the Arabic language in Damascus.

The abolition by the French in 1920 of Faysal's Syrian Arab Kingdom caused a crucial setback in the process of the creation of a political community in Syria. Nevertheless, feelings of Syrian identity did not slacken among members of the Syrian-Arab national movement. Under the French Mandate these feelings were in fact fostered with the formation by the French of a separate Syrian political unit and local government institutions — cabinet, parliament, etc. These feelings were also enhanced by the Arab national movement's struggle for Syria's independence.

The joint struggle of various Syrian personalities and groups against the mandatory rule undoubtedly contributed to the fostering of Syrian-Arab national consciousness among large circles of the population, in particular, among the Muslim and Christian urban intelligentsia. This consciousness, however, was not as crystallised and extensive as in

Egypt or Iraq, and it could not have constituted a sufficient basis for a political community. Unlike the developments in those two countries, the mandatory regime in Syria greatly damaged the process of creating a local political community. The French interrupted the first steps of Syria towards independence and unity by putting an end to Faysal's reign. They reduced the areas of the historic Syrian *vilayets* by incorporating into Lebanon the Tripoli, Beqaa, and Sidon districts in 1920 and by surrendering the *Sanjaq* of Alexandretta to Turkey in 1938. The mandatory government also weakened the political centrality of Damascus and the territorial unity of the country by reviving, and even enlarging, regional divisions and strengthening marginal centrifugal forces. Thus at the beginning of the 1920s, the French divided Syria into four 'states': Damascus, Aleppo, and the Alawi and Druze 'states'. The Jazira region was also administered separately, and Alexandretta enjoyed broad autonomy until its annexation. The French also foiled any tendencies towards Syrian national unity and increased intercommunal contrasts by encouraging, for example, polarisation in the educational system. In 1938, for instance, only 31 per cent (mostly Muslims) of all Syrian students attended government schools, compared to 38 per cent (mainly Christians) who attended private communal schools, and 20 per cent (again mainly Christians) who attended foreign schools. Thus Christian pupils, about one-third of the total, received a largely communal or foreign education, compared to the 'national' education of Muslim pupils in the towns or traditional Islamic education in the rural regions.[10]

The national leadership of mandatory Syria was itself also responsible for retarding the crystallisation of the Syrian people into one political community. The national parties, centred on personalities and families controlling vast properties, represented narrow class interests. Mainly interested in sustaining the *status quo* created during the Ottoman period, they refrained from drawing up any long-range plans for socio-economic reform among the rural and urban masses. Similarly, the nationalist leaders also refrained from taking radical measures to change and improve the educational system. Nor did they act to weaken Muslim religious zeal and foster intercommunal tolerance. For example, certain clauses of the Syrian constitution, composed in 1930 under the direction of nationalist representatives, mentioned freedom of conscience and religion, as well as equal rights for all citizens (Nos. 6, 15, 28); but these were not wholly implemented because of objections from senior officials and Muslim ulama.[11] A subcommittee of the Permanent Mandates' Commission, which investigated this matter in 1934, stated:

'The commission regretted to note that the application of the Syrian legislation prescribing equality before the law is still sometimes impeded through the absence of a spirit of tolerance on the part of the autochthonous authorities.' In 1938, the law of personal status, which expressed the constitutional principle of freedom of conscience and religion, was annulled under pressure from the ulama.[12] As in the Ottoman past, the Muslim masses continued to express their objections to intercommunal equality through acts of violence against Christians. During the uprising of 1925, for example, Christians suspected of collaboration with the French were attacked in Damascus; in Homs, the local Christian governor was assassinated by Muslims. In 1936, clashes occurred between Muslims and Christians in Aleppo, and in the Jazira such clashes were even more frequent.

Some of these intercommunal clashes certainly resulted from Christian or French provocation, such as the use of Armenian troops against Muslim rebels and the arming of the Christian population of Damascus during the 1925 revolt. Nevertheless, the Syrian national leadership cannot be exempt from its responsibility. Plainly, the leadership did not use its political status and prestige to educate the masses in the values of patriotic brotherhood and Syrian national identity.

The challenge of national identity was, indeed, enormous, as most of the population in mandatory Syria did not identify itself as Syrian Arabs. The minority communities — both Muslim heterodox and Christian, but with the exception of the Orthodox and Protestant intelligentsia — continued to rely on the French mandatory government. The rural and tribal masses and a considerable portion of the urban lower classes continued to live within the limits of family and regional loyalties. They considered themselves Sunni Muslim Arabs — rather than Syrian Arabs. Even among the more advanced urban members of the national movement, the feeling of nation-state identity was not as strong as it was in neighbouring Arab countries. Among these circles, regional tendencies and/or a Pan-Arab orientation were still strong, owing to the continuing tradition of the past (Damascus versus Aleppo) or to the persisting belief in Arab unity (which originated in Syria). Another reason for the lack of feeling of national unity was the absence of a strong centre or a great leader who could have served as a focus of authority, unity and identificaiton — like Zaghlul in Egypt or even Faysal and the monarchy in Baghdad.

The leadership of the Syrian National Bloc (*Kutla*) consisted of personalities with regional, rather than national, influence. Ibrahim Hananu, who possessed national prestige, died in 1935 — Hashim al-

Atasi, the other national leader, was too old and lacked political stature. This leadership had the semblance of a united body as long as the struggle against the French predominated. Following the agreement of 1936, however, the 'Bloc' and its leaders split along personal-family and regional-local lines; political differences additionally enhanced disunity. After, for example, the Damascene Shukri al-Quwatli became leader of the 'Bloc' and President of Syria in 1943, he was unable to maintain unity for long. In 1947 Jamil Mardam, another Damascus leader, resigned from the Kutla and established the 'Republican Party'; and in 1948, young leaders of the Kutla in Aleppo rebelled and founded the People's Party, with an Iraqi orientation. The remnant of the Kutla survived under al-Quwatli's sole leadership, changed its name to the 'National Party' and opened Syria to Saudi and Egyptian influence. Thus, when Syria was at last freed from the French and became an independent republic in 1946, it had neither a crystallised political community nor a unified society. Attempts at establishing a Syrian entity had failed; and socio-political developments in the course of one hundred years of modernisation had not mitigated the religious, regional and social contrasts among the Syrian population. Yet, once the French were gone, a new generation of young Syrian leaders were in a better position to embark upon the difficult task of achieving national unity and bringing about socio-political change.

Socio-political Changes since Independence

The seeds of socio-political change that developed in Syria from independence had already been sown in the middle of the mandatory period. It was then that the beginnings of an urban bourgeoisie class — consisting of lawyers, teachers, students, public employees and skilled workers — were created. The basis for a national army, in which the lower and middle classes and a considerable portion of the minority communities served, was also laid. These two social groups, which were able to grow beyond the control of the traditional elite, later carried out changes in independent Syria by means of the several organisations which they had founded: namely, modern political parties and young officer groups.

During the 1930s political parties advocating progressive political or social changes were established in Syria. The most prominent among them were the Syrian Nationalist Party (PPS) and the Syrian Communist Party both founded in 1930; the League for National Action in 1935; and the Arab Resurrection Party (Ba'ath) in 1940 (which merged in 1953 with the Arab Socialist Party). All these parties shared common principles: national independence, social (or socialist) and economic reform, and secularisation of public life. They disagreed, however, on the question of national territorial identity: whereas the League for National Action and the Arab Resurrection Party strove for an all-Arab unity, the Syrian Nationalist Party and the Communist Party preferred the territorial limits of Syria.

None of these parties, however, could realise its aims during the 1930s and 1940s. Parliaments and government were in the hands of the nationalist conservative leaders, who represented the upper class and opposed any change. The new parties were small, weak, operated separately and were harassed at times by the regime in power. Furthermore, they were not always permitted to participate in elections.

The only group that could effect any change in the political and social system was that of the army officers. Coming from middle- and lower-class origins, many members of this group shared the social grievances of the new middle class. They were also disappointed by the incompetence of the veteran civilian leadership. Some of the officers possessed social consciousness, and were influenced by the new parties; others were motivated by a sheer lust for power. There were underlying motivations for the actions of the Syrian military officers who seized power in 1949, particularly Adib Shishaqli (1949-54), who for the first time in Syria's modern history imposed socio-economic reforms on the country. With the help of Akram Haurani, the leader of the Arab Socialist Party (and since 1953, one of the Ba'ath Party leaders), Shishaqli reduced large land ownership while distributing state lands to poor *fellahin*. He also attempted to weaken the autonomous power of the minorities, being able to subdue the Druze community to central control. Shishaqli's actions contributed to the jolting of the old socio-political *status quo* and, perhaps more significantly, to cultivating new forces and tendencies in Syrian society.

The new political parties, notably the Ba'ath, utilised the socio-economic unrest among peasants and workers, as well as the political grievances and aspirations of the middle class, to increase its ranks and its seats in the Syrian parliament. In the 1954 parliamentary elections, for example, the Ba'ath Party emerged as the third largest, with 16 out of the 142 seats (which were mostly retained by the veteran 'People's' and 'National' parties).

By that time, Syria's political parties, both old and new, realised that neither the parliament nor the electorate served as the main source of political authority, but that the new core of power was the military. Consequently, following Shishaqli's removal in 1954, the major scene of the ensuing power struggle became the ranks of army officers, with rival military groups affiliated with the various political parties. For several years, pro-Ba'ath officers managed to gain the upper hand. Aiming at preventing a Communist ascendancy in the government, as well as withstanding external pressures (from Turkey, Iraq and Israel), in 1958 the Ba'athist civilian and military leaders initiated a union with Egypt.[13]

The Syrian-Egyptian union, termed the United Arab Republic (UAR), lasted until 1961 and greatly enhanced the shift in the balance of power between the old and the new socio-political forces. The veteran conservative upper class suffered deadly blows. Their political leaders were removed, their parties dissolved and their economic assets reduced in a series of socialist reforms: appropriation of large tracts of land, nationalisation of big private enterprises and strict supervision over and restriction on commercial and financial transactions. By contrast, the economic and social conditions of the lower and middle classes improved. Many thousands of fellahin received land under the new agrarian reform, while urban workers benefited from improved social services, low-cost housing and a progressive tax system. Simultaneously, the socio-political status of the middle class was further enhanced. Young intellectuals were absorbed into the new government administration and the expanding educational system. Young army officers were promoted to senior positions, thus replacing the veteran conservative officers. Among these young officers, a significant number were members of the Druze and Alawi minorities, thus indicating the growing integration of the minority communities in Syrian politics.

These important socio-economic changes received further impetus under the Ba'ath regime that first came to power in March 1963 and was followed by the so-called new Ba'ath rule, in February 1966.[14] Ba'athist policies were essentially a continuation of the socialist reforms carried out in the UAR period. In the domains of industry, commerce, services and finance, the Ba'ath leaders completed state ownership and control over the main basic enterprises. Hundreds of large plants, export and import companies, banks and insurance companies, and the network of wholesale commerce were nationalised. On the other hand, medium and small plants, companies and shops were allowed to operate privately. The Ba'athist tendency was to refrain from total violation of private enterprise, which in the past had always been the driving force in the Syrian economy. Thus, even enterprises which had been nationalised in the UAR period were now returned to their original owners, compensation was paid, and measures were undertaken to encourage small- and medium-scale private capital investment and the establishment of joint private-state enterprises.

Alongside these measures, working conditions and social benefits (compulsory vacations with full pay, social and medical insurance, etc.) were continuously improved. Simultaneously, efforts were made to increase worker output by, *inter alia*, linking wages to productivity.

The socio-economic reforms of the Ba'athists were not confined to the cities and the urban workers; they were in fact primarily directed at the rural regions and peasant masses, who formed some 70 per cent of the population. Agrarian reform was obviously the major event. It enlarged and complemented the reforms carried out in the UAR period that were designed to limit private land ownership and distribute the requisitioned surplus among the peasants and tenants. Thus the new law of agrarian reform published in June 1963 was more extensive than that of 1958 under the UAR. The reform law of 1963 limited ownership of land from 150 to 500 dunams of irrigated or 800 to 2000 dunams of unirrigated land (according to the rainfall in the region) as against 800 dunams of irrigated and 3000 dunams of unirrigated land during the UAR period. The law also limited the quota of land which could be given to a landowner's spouse and sons. On the other hand, this law, like that of 1958, granted every farmer 8 dunams of irrigated or 300 dunams of unirrigated land in exchange for payment of one-quarter of the land's value over twenty years. The payments were allocated to the regional co-operation fund (during the UAR period, they went to the state treasury) in order to finance agricultural development and establish social institutions for the members of co-operatives. By law, every co-operative would receive 15,000 to 30,000 dunams of irrigated or 60,000 to 80,000 dunams of unirrigated land and would be equipped with modern machinery and tools.

These radical, extensive reforms, which have now been carried out for almost a generation, are undoubtedly leading Syria towards a social-political revolution — for the first time in its modern history. Agrarian reforms and other measures destroyed the economic base of the traditional elite, the big landowners, merchants, and the like, and reserved their social status. The political power of this class was then shattered completely with the dissolution of its parties and the arrest or deportation of its veteran leadership. In its place, a new elite, consisting of army officers and young politicians, mainly from provincial towns and villages and many of them members of the minorities, has emerged.

Integration and Ascendancy of the Minorities

One of the major socio-political developments that took place in Syria following independence was the weakening of the autonomous status and sectarian tendencies of the country's minority groups and their integration in its political life. The territorial communities — of Druzes, Alawis, and to a lesser extent Kurds and other minorities in the Jazira — had a tradition of extensive self-government and posed a challenge to the newly independent Syria. These minorities and the various Christian communities had also enjoyed communal-religious and/or educational-cultural autonomy. Tending towards communal isolation, they thus constituted an obstacle to the formation of a cohesive society and unified political community.

One of the first steps taken by the Syrian government after independence as part of the trend towards national integration was to reduce or abolish communal representation in parliament. Between 1947 and 1949, the parliamentary representation of the Christian communities was reduced from nineteen to fourteen delegates, the Alawi from seven to four and the Druze from five to three delegates. The Jewish representation — one delegate — was abolished, as was that of the Kurds, Turkomans, and Circassians, the latter three being included in the Arab Sunni majority. Under Shishaqli, communal representation was further reduced, and in 1953 a bill completely abolishing the communal system in parliament was passed. Further legislation did away with separate jurisdictional rights in matters of personal status, which the French had granted the Alawis and the Druzes. These communities, like the Shi'ites and Ismai'ilis, were now subject to Syrian law, though the Druzes were granted some special rights, similar to those enjoyed by their brethren in Lebanon.[15]

In addition to the Arabisation of public life, Shishaqli also fostered the Islamic character of the state and its public institutions. In a draft constitution prepared under his supervision in 1950, Islam was named the state religion — in contrast to the 1930 mandatory constitution, in which Islam was merely the Syrian president's religion. These measures sparked agitation among the minorities. The various Christian communities, including the Greek Orthodox, protested against the infringement of their parliamentary representation and the intention to declare Islam the official religion. This pressure resulted in the declaration in the 1950 constitution — and later also in the 1953 constitution — that Islam was the president's religion.

The Syrian authorities also made great efforts to destroy the military strength of the Druzes and Alawis and to impose the authority of central government. In the summer of 1946, for example, the government sent a large force to Jabal Ansariyya to fight an Alawi uprising headed by Suleiman al-Murshid; the rebels were defeated and al-Murshid was later sentenced to death and executed. In 1952, another uprising followed the dismissal of Alawi officers and the assassination of Muhammad Hasan Nasir, an Alawi colonel who commanded the Syrian air force. Groups of Alawis, under the command of Mujib al-Murshid, son of Suleiman, attacked government forces, but were quickly subdued, and Mujib himself was shot and killed.

Likewise, the Za'im and Shishaqli military dictatorships could not tolerate the centrifugal Druze minority. Za'im sent the army to Jabal Druze to enforce conscription and to disarm and subdue the inhabitants. The Druzes later reacted by participating energetically in the *coup* against Za'im. Shishaqli ordered the dismissal and arrest of Druze officers for taking part in an alleged pro-Hashemite plot; among those taken were the sons of Sultan al-Atrash, the Druze chief, who were charged with conspiring with foreign elements and with activities against the regime. Their arrest led to a big uprising in Jabal Druze at the beginning of 1954 that was crushed by the Syrian army using tanks and aircraft.

The smashing of the 1954 Druze revolt became a turning point in the balance of power between the central government and the mountain-dwelling heterodox communities. For the first time, the government in Damascus achieved decisive military superiority over these centrifugal forces through the use of sophisticated weapons and a large, well-trained army. The seclusion and political autonomy of these elements was terminated. From then on, the heterodox communities began to take an increasing part in Syrian political life, including the struggles for power within the parties — mainly the Ba'ath Party — and the army. The Druzes and Alawis now became involved in a process that had begun earlier among the Orthodox and Protestant Christian communities and the Kurdish urban elements: the process of political integration. In the 1954 elections, for example, 16 Christians had been elected to the parliament representing the People's Party, the National Party and as independent candidates. Such Christian personalities as Faris al-Khuri, Mikha'il llyan and Michel Aflaq held foremost positions on the political scene of the 1950s, whether as party leaders, ministers and even prime ministers. Personalities of Kurdish origin, too — notably Husni al-Za'im, Mushin al-Barazi, Sami Hinnawi, Fawzi Silu, and Khalid Baqdash — played important roles in Syrian politics of that period. Druze and Alawi personages began to participate in the political life of Syria through the military groups and the political parties. Alawi officers, for instance, commanded the Syrian air force: Muhammad Hasan Nasir in 1950 and Aziz Abd al-Karim in 1952. The Druze officers, Amin Abu Assaf and Fadl Allh Abu Mansur, were actively involved in the *coups* against Za'im and Shishaqli.

It should be stressed that along with their political involvement, the minority-group politicians and officers, especially the Druzes and Alawis, still retained strong affinity with their own communities. They tended to hire members of their communities as assistants and preferred to nominate such individuals as officers under their supervision. Some even gave preference to communal interests when these were at odds with those of the state. The communities themselves, on the other hand, strongly identified with their representatives in the army and the government; when the latter required help in power struggles, members of these communities would normally render their active support, both politically and militarily. With the solid backing of their respective communities, Druze and Alawi army officers and politicians not only were able to integrate into the new Syrian political community; they also managed in the course of one generation to ascend to positions of influence and authority in Syria. The channels for this ascendancy were the Ba'ath Party and the Syrian army.

The Arab Socialist Resurrection Party (Ba'ath), originally established at the end of 1953, consisted of members with a heterogeneous social background and communal affiliation. On the one hand, these members came from the new middle class, the intelligentsia and the young bourgeoisie; most resided in the big cities, especially Damascus; in part, they were Sunni Muslims and, in part, Christian Orthodox, Protestant, and others. By and large, they hailed from the 'Resurrection Party' of Michel Aflaq and Salah al-Din al-Bitar. On the other hand, the party absorbed Sunni peasants and soldiers from the Syrian lowlands who were originally members of Akram Haurani's Arab Socialist Party, as well as Alawi, Druze and Ismai'ili soldiers.

Ba'ath membership, which was drawn from people of village and provincial origin, increased during the 1950s, not exclusively on account of the party's socialist leanings, but also because of its efficient organisation in areas outside the big cities. In spite of the growing number of members from the lower strata, the party was mainly run by the new urban middle class intelligentsia, who had been pioneers in the struggle against the traditional ruling elite. These Ba'ath activists, however, wore themselves out in the political struggles of 1954-8 and lost power altogether during the period of the union with Egypt. The rural and minority elements in the party, on the other hand, gained strength through the central focus of power — the army. Young people from the provinces and from the minorities were drawn to the army in increasing numbers, hoping to improve their social and economic status. Some of them were sent to officers' courses or were promoted by senior Ba'ath officers seeking to strengthen their influence by increasing their followers — members of their community or party — in the officers' corps. The new officers, many of them Alawis and Druzes, quickly rose in the military hierarchy. The cadre of veteran officers, mostly Sunni Muslims, was shattered after the many military *coups* between 1949 and 1954, the struggle for power in the army from 1954-8, and the big purges among officers during the union with Egypt and in 1961-2.[16]

The young officers of provincial and minority origin formed the backbone of the March 1963 Ba'ath revolution. They established a new regime in the name of the Ba'ath, since most of them were party members or sympathisers and considered themselves bound by its mission — though in many ways they deviated from the original Ba'ath course. They exploited the party and its veteran leadership. Namely, they sought to use the party apparatus to strengthen their hold in the state and to take over the party leadership. At the end of 1964, they completely excluded the veteran leadership from the political life of Syria: Salah al-Din al-Bitar was removed, Michel Aflaq went into exile voluntarily. Amin al-Hafiz, the leader of the young officers, established himself as ruler of Syria. But then a fierce struggle took place among the new Ba'ath rulers. This struggle continued, with climaxes in February 1966 and November 1970, between communal groups and personalities, as well as between military and civilian factions.

Thus, for example, in 1965 there developed a power struggle between Amin al-Hafiz, and Salah Jedid, the chief-of-staff and former ally of al-Hafiz in their joint struggle against the veteran Ba'ath civilian leadership. Jedid, an Alawi, surrounded himself with officers of Alawi and Druze origin and strove to seize power. Hafiz, a Sunni Muslim, forced to defend himself, relied upon his former rivals, the civilian leadership, who were also mostly Sunni Muslims. The Jedid faction, however, controlled the centres of power in the army, air force, armoured corps and commandos. In February 1966, Jedid seized power and unseated his rivals by means of a *coup d'état*.[17]

Following the *coup*, the temporary, and unprecedented, co-operation between Alawi and Druze officers was terminated. The Druzes, led by Salim Hatum, chief of commando unit, demanded a larger share in power and tried to mobilise the support of certain elements in the army and the party. The Alawi officers, led by Jedid and Hafez al-Assad, commander of the air force, enjoyed clear numerical and tactical superiority in the army command and the party leadership. They overcame the Druze faction and removed its members from key positions. Druze officers, headed by General Fahad al-Sha'ir, were dismissed, and Salim Hatum, who had escaped to Jordan, was executed upon his return to Syria in 1967.

Communal affiliation was not the only factor in the struggle for power among the Syrian top ranks in the 1960s, however. Other factors of weight were personal and factional interests, the manifestation of which was the struggle for power between Jedid and Assad, the two leaders of the ruling Alawi faction. This contest, which began behind the scenes in 1966, erupted in September 1969 and concluded with Assad's victory in November 1970. Once Assad had established his authority in the army, in the party and indeed in the country, the majority of Alawis, both soldiers and civilians, transferred their support and allegiance to him. The Alawis have continued under Assad's leadership to form the backbone of the Ba'ath regime in Syria.[18]

Assad in Power: the Consolidation of Alawi-Ba'athist Rule

Judging from his background, it would seem that Assad's drive for power has stemmed partly from his Alawi minority background and his desire to integrate into the Syrian-Arab community and play an active role in it; partly from his patriotic and nationalistic feelings and his sense of mission for country and nation; and partly from his personal lust for power. This last motivation was encouraged by the example of many of his army colleagues during the 1950s and the 1960s, who also cared for their state and society. Whereas most of them failed to reach the top or were soon ousted by their rivals, Assad is the first Syrian army officer who achieved authority and whose rule has lasted for almost a decade and a half as of this writing. He is, moreover, the first member of a minority to have become president of Syria.

There is no doubt that Assad's personal qualities and political skills largely account for the preservation of his position. His appearance, tall and grave, his conduct, calm and cool, and his dignified bearing all bespeak a strong personality, which is manifested, *inter alia*, in his determination, consistency and stubbornness. He possesses an air of authority and confidence, acquired during his military career. These qualities make him a natural leader; and with his traits of modesty and honesty, also make him a popular idol with whom ordinary people readily identify. In addition, Assad is a shrewd politician, with an instinctive cautiousness, patience and realism — which possibly stem from his peasant-minority background. He is a systematic, though slow, thinker and has the rare habit of listening to others and of learning from his own mistakes. These characteristics, together with this deep and intimate knowledge of the Syrian political scene and his keen interest in inter-Arab and global politics, have made Assad a politician and statesman of national, regional and, to some extent, international standing.

In this chapter, we are primarily concerned with Assad's role in the national politics of Syria, which he has controlled, almost single-handedly, since November 1970. Unlike his predecessor Salah Jedid, Assad has neither shared authority with his comrades in a collective leadership nor held the reins of power from a modest position, such as Assistant Secretary General of the Ba'ath Party. Once he determined to assume control, Assad worked systematically to realise full authority. After a brief transitional period of holding the dual positions of Prime Minister and Defence Minister, Assad formed a new presidential system early in 1971. In doing so he apparently was influenced by the Egyptian model which he tailored to his own conception of government. Under Syria's Permanent Constitution, promulgated on 31 January 1973, the president (Assad) was bestowed with extensive political and military powers as well as substantial legislative authority.[19] For example, being elected for a seven-year term (article 85), the president establishes the general policy of the state and supervises its application (article 94). He nominates one or more vice-presidents, the president of the Council of Ministers, the ministers and assistant ministers. Moreover, he undertakes responsibility for receiving their resignation, or for dismissing them (article 85). 'The President of the Republic declares war or calls for general mobilisation' (article 100); he is the 'supreme leader of the army and armed forces....' (article 103); he 'appoints civil and military functionaries and ends their services in conformity with the law' (article 109). 'The President of the Republic promulgates the laws passed by the Council of People. He has the right to oppose those laws by a reasonable resolution ...' (article 98). He is entitled to 'dissolve the council by a justified resolution he promulgates' (article 107); he 'exercises the legislative authority during periods of prorogation in the intervals between... two councils...' and 'during sessions in cases of necessity pertinent to the national interest of the country' (article 111) and he 'has the right to refer important questions, related to the interests of the country, to citizens. The results of the referendum are obligatory...' (article 113).

The constitution gives the president almost unlimited control of the country. Assad exercises this control through the formal institutions of the state: the presidency, the cabinet, the government machinery, the armed command, as well as the Council of People. To these one should add Assad's leadership of the Ba'ath Party — which is, according to the constitution (article 7), 'the leading party of the society and state' — as Secretary General of both its regional and national commands. He also dominates the 'National Progressive Front', the coalition of the Ba'ath and three left-wing and national parties or groups. Not content with exercising his authority through the official government institutions and the party machinery, Assad exerts his power simultaneously through other channels as well. One of these is the team of advisors in the presidential office who are separately assigned to political, military, security and economic affairs, and who apply certain supervisory functions over the government machinery. A more important, pivotal body is an unofficial group, called the *Jama'a* (Company), which is mainly composed of the founding members of Assad's regime and his current core-team.

The major tasks of the Jama'a are to assist Assad in safeguarding the regime against its enemies, in exercising effective control in the country and in tackling critical issues in Syria's domestic and foreign policies from a level above the regular government machinery. Although there have been rivalries and rifts between certain members of the Jama'a, notably between the president's younger brother, Rif'at Assad, and Mustafa Tlas, the Defence Minister, most if not all members have been completely loyal to Hafez al-Assad. Among those of special importance in the Jama'a are the commanders of elite army units assigned to protect the nerve centres of the regime, such as the presidential palace, radio and television stations, airports and the like. The conspicuous units are 'Defence Companies' and 'the Special Forces', which are stationed near Damascus and equipped with their own helicopters, planes, artillery and other modern material. One of these units is commanded by Assad's brother, who was elected in 1975 to the Ba'ath National Command. In 1984, Rif'at was appointed a vice-president, one of three, in an attempt to contain his ambition to succeed his then ailing brother. Other weighty members of the Jama'a are officers in charge of the major combat divisions of the Syrian army and the various military intelligence services, notably Air Force Intelligence, which has greatly helped Assad in both his ascendancy and rule.

What also helped Assad, 'the supreme commander of the army', wield a power that is most crucial to the regime's stability is that he personally appointed a large number of officers as commanders, or to other key positions, of the select combat units. The criterion for their selection, as for the choice of the top government ministers, is that they are personal, Alawi-communal and Ba'ath-partisan friends, relatives or comrades. Among these are a number of Sunni-Muslim personalities, such as Defence Minister Mustafa Tlas and Chief-of-Staff Hikmat Shihabi, whose loyalty to Assad is beyond doubt. Many more Sunni Muslim functionaries serve in the cabinet positions and other government posts and in the army. Within the officer corps, however, the number of Alawis holding various command positions — the substructure of Assad's regime — greatly exceeds the proportion of Alawis (twelve per cent) in the total population. This phenomenon is particularly conspicuous among the officers and NCOs of the 'Defence Companies' and the 'Special Forces'. This situation is essentially not different from that during Salah Jedid's regime, when commanding ranks were heavily staffed by Alawi officers.[20] The famous 70th Armoured Brigade, assigned to protect the regime's centres, was under the command of Izzat Jedid, a close relative. The Jedid regime was criticised, even by certain veteran Ba'ath leaders, as a ruthless military government with an Alawi sectarian grouping within its officers' corps.

The prolonged Alawi military grouping raises the question of how Assad has tackled the Achilles' heel of his regime's national policies. It is a latent dilemma caused by Assad's vital need to build his rule on the narrow base of Alawi military support in order to stay in power, while attempting to achieve his genuine ambition of establishing a regime on a solid foundation of national consensus and legitimacy as well as on sound constitutional and political institutions.

From the outset, Assad has systematically endeavoured to avoid an image of his regime as being based on confessional-military support, or a junta of Alawi army officers. He has sought to bring legitimisation and consensus to his rule and to project himself as a national-popular leader with the interests of the Syrian people at heart. Thus Assad has described his *coup* against Jedid as a 'corrective movement' which 'came to light in response to our people's demands and aspirations ...' The people, he said, 'are the chief concern, the organ and the goal of the revolution'; they have been 'registering the bright pages in the history of this homeland'. Assad has described himself as a citizen of Syria, a member of the people, with whom he shares an 'unprecedented identification'. He was not just an 'ordinary soldier', he has stressed, but joined the army in order to serve the people, not by means of military coups, but through a 'positive struggle', hand in hand with the pioneers of the enlightened citizens, who 'have faith in the nation'.[21]

Alongside these statements, Assad adopted measures to emphasise the people's participation in shaping his regime. In May 1973 (and again in August 1977), Syrian citizens elected their first National Council (parliament), which previously had been an appointed body. Representatives of several parties as well as 'independent' delegates have successively been elected to the National Council. With the Ba'ath Party, these other parties — the Communist Party, the 'Socialist Arab Union' and the 'Arab Socialists' — formed in 1972 a 'National Progressive Front' under the initiative and direction of Assad.

By taking these actions, Assad obviously aimed at expanding the public base of his regime in order to underline its legitimacy and democracy. He has tried, also, to demonstrate the national consensus behind his leadership, which he projects as standing above party allegiances. In certain respects, Assad's national orientation has diminished the exclusive position of the Ba'ath Party, which under Jedid had been the supreme authority in the state with powers to appoint and impeach the president. Nevertheless, the Ba'ath Party has continued to be the leading party of the society and the state, rendering the ideological infrastructure and legitimisation to the Assad regime. As Secretary General of the party, Assad has utilised its organisational apparatus to mobilise greater support for his rule and to facilitate his control. Simultaneously, however, he has made great efforts to enlist the backing, or at least neutralise the opposition, of large sections of the Syrian population that had been antagonistic to the political and economic system of the neo-Ba'ath under Jedid.

Thus Assad has tried to conciliate the traditional upper middle classes, who had been affected by the economic policies of Jedid's regime. He modified the socialist measures of his predecessor, encouraged economic activity and private initiative and lifted restrictions on the import of consumer goods. Assad's goal of improving the standard of living of the common people and bringing them closer to the regime has been expressed through creating jobs, lowering taxes, raising salaries and improving services. As in Jedid's time, special attention has been given to improving the lot of peasants and the urban working class.

The outstanding moves made by Assad since his ascendancy have been directed at appeasing or neutralising the conservative Sunni Muslim circles, particularly the religious leadership. In June 1971, Assad restored to the Syrian constitution the previous formulation of the presidential oath, 'I swear by Allah Akbar', which had been replaced by a secular format ('I swear on my honour and my faith') in the 1969 constitution.[22] In the Permanent Constitution of March 1973, he reinstated the paragraph establishing the religion of the president as Islam; this had previously been deleted from both the 1969 constitution and the draft Permanent Constitution. Assad has made other gestures to underscore his public image as a faithful Muslim, such as publicly participating in prayers and religious ceremonies at various mosques, distributing honours among Muslim religious leaders (ulama), raising them in rank and salary, and nominating the prominent *alim* as Minister of Waqf in the government. Assad's own authenticity as a Muslim was verified by Sunni Muslim ulama, including the Mufti of Damascus, Ahmad Kaftaru; and he succeeded in having the leader of the Shi'ites in Lebanon, the late Imam Musa al-Sadr, certify that the Alawis are Shi'ite Muslims. Thus Assad has shown his awareness of the importance of Islam as the majority religion and as a value shared by the entire Syrian population.

Parallel to these activites, Assad has sought to strengthen two other central values which serve as common denominators for most Syrian citizens and as a foundation for national and cultural identity, Arabism and Syrian patriotism. In order to indoctrinate all segments of the Syrian public with these values, the mass media and the national educational system have been mobilised to stress constantly the importance of the unity of the Arab-Syrian nation behind the leader-president, Hafez al-Assad.[23]

Conclusion: Can Ba'athism Persist in the Face of the Muslim Opposition?

The crucial question is: has Assad succeeded during the long years of his presidency in crystallising a Syrian national community which would grant his rule legitimacy and consensus and serve as a solid foundation for his regime? Has he managed to solve the crucial dilemma of the Ba'ath system, namely the indispensability of Alawi military support versus the need for establishing supra-communal political institutions that would ensure the future of Ba'athism in Syria?

Assad's role has been marked by three characteristics: (a) his ability to master the foci of power, notably the army, and to set up a centralised presidential system; (b) his success in curbing opposition to the regime, particularly from the Muslim fundamentalists; (c) his emergence as a supreme leader and as a focus of identification for growing sections of the population, including the young intelligentsia, urban workers and peasants. His leadership may indeed serve to foster the emergence of a new political community. His tendency, however, is still nascent, since the process of building a supra-confessional political community in Syria is, as we know, painstaking and beset with formidable difficulties. It must involve radical changes in both the traditional social structures and the religious conceptual frameworks of the population; and these changes, in turn, require systematic socio-political reforms and educational-indoctrinational efforts by a strong and popular government in order to be carried out.

Here lies the 'Gordian knot' of Ba'athism in Syria: the strength of the Syrian government derives from two inter-related factors: Hafez al-Assad and Alawi military support. While the Alawi factor constitutes a serious liability in the process of nation-building, Assad's leadership, although an important asset in this process, is neither lasting nor sufficient in itself to create a new Syrian national community. The stability and strength of Assad's regime rest largely upon his personal authority and centralised rule, not on deep-rooted political traditions; thus Assad's disappearance is likely to cause a total disintegration of the regime, as well as a serious setback in the process of nation-building in Syria.

Yet, even under Assad, the accomplishments in the policy of national integration have been partial and superficial, since this policy has neither revolved around the majority Sunni Muslim population nor embraced Islam as the cornerstone of the new national ideology. Indeed, it appears that the appointment of Sunni Muslim personalities to senior positions in the Syrian government does not alter the fact or the awareness of the majority of the population that Alawi army officers control the centres of power in the country. Similarly, the public gestures and tributes which have been made by Assad towards Muslim ulama and Islamic values have apparently failed to satisfy misgivings in conservative circles lest Islam be divorced from the Syrian state and society.

By contrast, it seems that the educational efforts as well as the nationalist and socialist measures that have been taken by Assad since 1970, and previously by the Ba'ath regime since 1963, have not transformed the traditional Islamic belief system of the majority population into a new supra-communal, or secular, national ideology. To be sure, large sections among the Sunni population have manifested fierce opposition or strong reservations concerning both the anti- or non-Islamic ideology of the Ba'ath regime and Alawi military rule, by Jedid and Assad alike. Thus, for example, there have been several violent demonstrations in the major Syrian towns carried out by large, conservative Sunni groups against well-equipped army troops.

Such demonstrations were held before Assad's time, in March and April 1965 and again in January 1966, under the slogan 'Allah Akbar' — either Islam or Ba'ath; and in May 1967, riots broke out in reaction to an article by a young Alawi officer who stated that God and religion are 'but mummies in the museum of history'.[24] Similarly, under Assad's government, a series of violent popular protests erupted between February and May 1973 against the abolition of the 'Islamic clause' in the Permanent Constitution; in the summer of 1976, grave disturbances broke out again that were instigated *inter alia* by *fatwas* (religious opinions), whose leaflets denounced 'secularism and sectarianism' and called for the overthrow of the 'fanatical Alawi regime'; Assad was labelled an 'Alawi' and a 'Christian', while Alawis and Christians were attacked in some places by Sunni Muslims.[25]

Muslim opposition to the Alawi sectarian regime continued during the late 1970s and early 1980s and was manifested in political assassinations of Alawi military officers as well as of governmental and Ba'athist officials. This guerrilla struggle culminated in February 1982, when a large group of 'Muslim Brotherhood' initiated an armed rebellion in the city of Hama and took control of the city after killing tens of government and military personnel. In reaction, elite units of the Syrian army fiercely shelled the city, destroying large parts of it and killing an estimated 30,000 inhabitants, men, women and children. It can be assumed that the brutal suppression of the Hama revolt, as well as other harsh measures employed by the government, would serve to deter the Muslim Brotherhood and their followers from organising another such uprising in the near future.

The violent suppression of the Hama rebellion by no means reflects the destruction of the Muslim opposition to the Alawi regime. The opposition movement, guided and led by the Muslim Brotherhood underground organisation, represents not only the conservative and fundamentalist elements, who have struggled since 1963 against the allegedly secularist, anti-Islamic, sectarian Alawi regime. This opposition has also represented in the last decade or so other sections of the population, mostly city dwellers, whose socio-economic interests and/ or political-civil rights and beliefs have been hurt or violated by the Ba'ath regime. Among these are many members of the traditional urban middle class of merchants and artisans, many of them conservative Muslims, who resent both the socialist, secularist measures of the regime as well as its disposition to develop the rural areas, allegedly at the expense of the cities. The latter grievance is also shared by not a few urban intellectuals, professionals and other members of the intelligentsia, who complain bitterly about the suppression of their basic political and civil liberties.

The crucial question is whether or not the Muslim opposition stands a chance of toppling the Ba'ath regime and of changing the character of the state and of its political community. Although it is almost impossible to predict future developments in Syria, it can nevertheless be assumed that in the foreseeable future, as long as Hafez al-Assad remains in power, the chances are slim that the Ba'ath regime will be overthrown by either a military *coup* or a popular Muslim uprising (as occurred in Iran). For, as we have seen above, Assad is in full control of the army, government and state, while his instruments of supervision and compulsion are efficient and effective.

As for the long-term prospects following Assad's death, various scenarios may be predicted: (a) the establishment of an Alawi-Sunni collective leadership resting on the common vested interests of the present ruling elite in continuing the Ba'ath rule in Syria; (b) the eruption of a power struggle among the ruling elite: i.e., between Rif'at Assad and other Alawi officers, on the one hand, and senior Sunni officers, on the other hand, or between coalitions of mixed Alawi-Sunni groups. The results of such may then influence the character of the new regime and render it a more Syrian-national image. In such a case, particularly in the event of an Alawi-Sunni collective leadership, let alone the ascendancy of Rif'at Assad, the prospects of a takeover by the Sunni Muslim opposition will presumably still be slim. Not only will the military balance of power in Syria continue to favour the ruling elite; this elite also possesses both political interests and ideological motivations to carry on the Ba'ath mission. Ultimately, the Ba'ath derives its power and support from large sectors of the Syrian population that have benefited from the regime or that share the Ba'ath concepts. Besides the Alawi and Druze minorities, many thousands of Sunni peasants and urban workers have significantly improved their socio-economic conditions under the Ba'ath regime. In addition, there are thousands of Ba'ath Party members and their families, government officials and members of the intelligentsia, who support the regime out of interest or belief. Finally, for the last two decades, many thousands of youngsters have been educated and indoctrinated in Ba'athist ideology, and many of them are ardent supporters of the regime. All these groups and sectors may in the long run constitute the new and cohesive political society and a solid basis for the Ba'ath regime. In a future struggle between such socio-political forces and the conservative urban Sunni Muslim sections of the population, the former are likely to have the upper hand.

Notes

1. For references see Moshe Ma'oz, *Ottoman Reforms in Syria and Palestine* (Oxford University Press, Oxford, 1968); A.L. Tibawi. *A Modern History of Syria,* (London, 1969).

2. On French rule in Syria see A.H. Hourani, *Syria and Lebanon* (Oxford University Press, Oxford, 1954); S.H. Longrigg, *Syria and Lebanon Under French Mandate* (Oxford University Press, London, 1958).

3. For a detailed survey and analysis see Moshe Maoz, 'Attempts at Creating a Political Community in Modern Syria', *Middle East Journal,* (Autumn 1972).

4. *Nafir Suriyya,* 25 October 1860; see A.H. Hourani, *Arabic Thought in the Liberal Age* (Oxford University Press, London, 1962), pp. 101, 274-5.

5. J. Murray, *A Handbook for Travellers in Syria and Palestine* (London, 1858), p. xlvi.

6. Yusuf al-Hakim, *Suriyya wa'l-ahd al uthmani* (Beirut, 1966) vol. 1, p. 84 (in Arabic).

7. Public Records Office, London, F.O. 78/1389 No. 33, Aleppo, August 7, 1858; see Ma'oz, *Ottoman Reform,* pp. 246-7.

8. Adil al-Sulh, *Sutur min al-risala* (Beirut, 1966), pp. 98-100 (in Arabic).

9. Sati al-Husri, *Yawm maysalun* (Beirut, 1947), p.229 (in Arabic).

10. Haurani, *Syria and Lebanon,* pp. 93-5.

11. League of Nations, Report of the Permanent Mandate Commission, 27th Session (1955).

12. A. Hourani, *Minorities in the Arab World* (Oxford University Press, Oxford, 1947), p. 77.

13. On the period 1945-58 see P. Seale, *The Struggle for Syria* (Oxford University Press, Oxford, 1965).

14. On the Ba'ath regime in Syria during the years 1963-6 see I. Rabinovich, *Syria Under the Ba'ath, 1963-1966* (Tel-Aviv University, Tel Aviv, 1972); regarding the Ba'ath Party see J.G. Devlin, *The Ba'ath Party* (Hoover Institute Press, Stanford, 1976).

15. J.N.D. Anderson, 'The Syrian Law of Personal Status', *Bulletin of the School of Oriental and African Studies* (London University) vol. 17 (1955), pp. 34-5.

16. See Munif al-Razzaz, *al-Tajriba al-murra* (Beirut, 1967), p. 159 (in Arabic).

17. On the power struggle in Syria since 1961 see N. Van Dam, *The Struggle for Power in Syria* (Croom Helm, London, 1979).

18. Moshe Maoz, 'Alawi Military Officers in Syrian Politics', in H.Z. Schiffrin (ed.), *Military and State in Modern Asia* (The Truman Research Institute, Jerusalem, 1975).

19. The Permanent Constitution of the Syrian Arab Republic, 31 January 1973, Damascus. On Assad's personality and rule see M. Ma'oz, 'Hafez Assad – A Political Profile', *Jerusalem Quarterly* (Summer 1978).

20. Razzaz, *al-Tajriba al-murra*, pp. 158-60.

21. Radio Damascus, 8 March 1972.

22. See the provisional Syrian Constitution, 1 May 1969, in *Al-Thawra, 3 May 1969.*

23. For details see M. Ma'oz, *Syria under Hafez Assad: New Domestic and Foreign Policies* (Davis Institute, Jerusalem, 1975).

24. *Al-Nahar* (Lebanon), 9 May 1967.

25. See H. Batatu, 'Syria's Muslim Brethren', *MERIP Reports,* November/ December 1982; U.F. Abd-Allah, *The Islamic Struggle in Syria*, (Mizan Press, Berkeley, 1984).

3 THE SYRIAN ECONOMY UNDER THE ASSAD REGIME

Kais Firro

Introduction

Since the 1982 war in Lebanon, in which the Syrians suffered a military defeat and had to withdraw from Beirut, from the Shouf mountains and from parts of the Beqaa valley, Syria has emerged as a regional super power endeavouring to achieve 'strategic balance' with Israel. Towards this end, Syria has made great efforts to increase its standing armed forces to more than half a million soldiers and to supply this army with the most sophisticated weapons. Can the Syrian economy sustain the immense outlays that such a military ambition entails — spending on a scale which creates economic vulnerability even among the strongest economies of the world?

Despite the evolution of the Syrian economy over the past decade and a half, marked by real growth, most of the country's economic features reveal themselves as still too backward to meet its burgeoning defence requirements. The low level of structural differentiation of both the economy and the society, moreover, exacerbated the difficulties involved in absorbing sophisticated technologies. The emergence of new industrial activities, expanding agricultural production and increasing oil exports have not been sufficient to eliminate the type of structural dualism characterising the Syrian economy. The consequence is that the gap between military power and economic capacity, on the one hand, and between aspirations for economic development and the ability to fulfill these plans, on the other hand, have forced Syria into a state of dependence on those industrialised economies — whether of the East or West — supplying it with arms and technologies.

Nominally Syria is considered one of the non-aligned nations; however, its military dependency, coupled with the political orientation of the ruling Ba'ath Party, link Syria to the Soviet Union in a special relationship. Nevertheless, economic considerations and, in particular, the need for Western technology in a number of critical sectors, such as oil, preserve Syria's ties with the West.

As in many other developing countries, Syria's internal political situation plays an important part in economic development. With the state being the main force in the development of the economy and with

36

the country experiencing continuous political turbulence from its inception as an independent country in 1946 until 1970, any constant economic policy was effectively prevented. The year 1970, however, in which Hafez al-Assad seized power, represents the beginning of a new era, not only in the political life of Syria, but also in its national economy. The main purpose of this study is to evaluate the impact of the new policies on the state of the Syrian economy.

Population and Manpower

In 1970 the Syrian population was estimated at 6.3 million. By 1982 it had increased to 9.66 million. Thus Syria has exhibited one of the highest population growth rates in the world, about 3.4 per cent a year. Until 1950, most of the population was concentrated along the fertile coastal strip and in the district which begins around Damascus in the south and stretches towards the Turkish border, north of Aleppo.

Since 1950, great transformations have taken place in the regional distribution of the population. With, however, the expansion of industry in the cities and the construction of dams coupled with agricultural expansion in the north-east, notably in the Euphrates valley, the geographic shiftings became relatively modified. The migration towards the north-eastern provinces of Al-Hassakah, Rakkah, and Deir al-Zor had the effect of creating a relative equilibrium in the distribution of the rural population. By 1960, about 33 per cent of the population of Rakkah and about 18 per cent of that of Al-Hassakah were immigrants from other provinces.[1] The migration process to these districts, and especially to the large cities, though weakened after 1960, has continued even into recent years. In 1972, the provinces of Damascus and Aleppo together represented about 44 per cent of the total population, or 2.9 million inhabitants of Syria's 6.7 million.[2] In 1980, these districts accounted for only 40 per cent, or 3.6 million persons of the total population of 8.98 million.[3]

In most Middle Eastern countries, as in the Third World as a whole, two main phenomena characterise population movements: the first relates to the imbalance in the development of the rural and the urban population in favour of the latter; the second, to the immense migration towards the capital and other big cities. Although Syria shares this general trend, as we have seen, its population development also exhibits certain manifestations of its own. The exodus from the rural districts in Syria has been more feeble than in Iraq, Saudi Arabia and Lebanon.

Syria has more than five large cities that pull immigrants; in three other Middle Eastern countries — Jordan, Egypt, and Lebanon — the pressure of the rural exodus is on the capitals only. These variations between Syria and its Arab neighbours are reflected in the process of urbanisation, as seen in Table 3.1.

An interesting comparision can be made with Egypt, where large demographic pressures on resources exist in the rural regions as well as in the cities. The ratio of land to rural inhabitants in Egypt dropped from 1.310 hectares per family of five in 1947 to 0.840 hectares in 1971.[4] This ratio continued to worsen right through the early 1980s. Meanwhile, the resources in the cities have not progressed fast enough to make up for the population pressure. In Syria, by contrast, the land under cultivation expanded from 1.75 million hectares in 1953,[5] to 5.9 million in 1969,[6] and to 6.2 million in 1980.[7] Without worsening its situation, the rural sector has been able to absorb part of the country's population growth. This is not true of the cities, however, to which a steady migration continues. Of the approximately 40,000 persons who migrate every year from villages to cities, only 17,000 can find employment.[8]

The economic development of Syria has changed the distribution of the country's religious communities, particularly of its major minorities: Alawis, Druzes, Kurds and Armenians. The first two groups, which in 1981 constituted about 15-20 per cent of Syria's population, were previously concentrated in the mountains. Although no official data concerning the religious and communal features of the rural exodus are available, it has been observed that the Alawis are migrating towards Hama, Lattakia, Tartous and Damascus. Until the middle 1960s, Hama was mainly a Sunni city,[9] but in the past two decades many Alawis have immigrated to it. Lattakia, now considered the capital of the Alawi region, was up to 1945 a city of Sunnis (18,500) and Christians (6,400).[10] The Druzes, who were concentrated in Hauran and Golan, have been migrating towards Damascus, notably the Jaramanah, Sihnaiah and Ashrafiah quarters. Indeed, Damascus and its environs now probably contain about one-third of the entire Syrian Druze community.[11]

The nomadic phenomenon has been disappearing from Syria. The Bedouins, who in 1930 represented 12.8 per cent of the total population, or 360,000 persons, numbered only 211,670 in 1960.[12] Their number continues to drop in both absolute and relative terms because of economic projects in the north-east and centre of the country. As a regime that mainly depends on the country's minorities, the Assad

Table 3.1: Distribution of Urban Population in Representative Arab Countries 1960 to 1980

Country	Urban population as percentage of total population			Average annual growth rate (%) of urban population		Percentage of urban population in large cities			Percentage of urban population in cities over 500,000		Number of cities with over 500,000 population	
	1960	1975	1980	1960-70	1970-80	1960	1975	1980	1960	1980	1960	1980
Iraq	43	66	72	6.2	5.4	35	53	55	35	70	1	3
Saudi Arabia	30	59	67	8.4	7.6	15	17	18	0	33	0	2
Jordan	45	53	56	4.5	4.7	31	36	37	0	37	1	1
Lebanon	44	70	76	6.2	2.8	64	77	79	64	79	1	1
Egypt	38	44	45	3.3	2.8	38	39	39	53	53	2	2
Syria	37	47	50	4.8	5.0	35	33	33	35	55	1	2

Source: World Bank, *World Development Report 1979*, pp. 164-5; *1981*, p. 170.

government has probably used the changes in the old distribution pattern of the Syrian population in order to strengthen its control in certain areas, such as Damascus, the north-east, and the coastal cities of Lattakia and Tartous.

Another demographic process has paradoxically strengthened the central government while imposing difficulties on the economy. This concerns the structure of the labour force and its distribution among the economic sectors. According to the draft economic plan of 1960/1-1964/5, the labour force constituted 33.6 per cent of Syria's estimated population of 4.55 million.[13] Within two decades, however, the proportion of the labour force dropped to about 24 per cent. If we take 1979 as a representative year of the 1970-83 period, we can observe the features of the changes in the labour force. From 1970 until 1979, the total population of Syria increased 38.4 per cent, from 6,304,685 to 8,723,468.[14] In 1979, children up to and including age ten represented 32.6 per cent of the population; those age fifteen and younger, 49 per cent.[15] This large non-active population percentage was due to the rise in the rate of population growth. Whereas the annual average growth rate was 3.2 per cent in the decade 1960-9, it rose to 3.6 per cent in 1970-9. The increase was more a consequence of a significant decline in the crude death rate, from 18 per thousand in 1960 to 8 per thousand in 1979, as the crude birth rate dropped slightly from 47 to 45 per thousand over these years.[16] Thus the proportion of actives in the total Syrian population decreased from 52 per cent in 1960 to 49 per cent in 1979.[17] If those from 16-19 years old are also excluded, the active population was less than 45 per cent of the total population.

The female population constitutes another problem because three-quarters of all Syrian women are excluded from the labour force.[18] The small labour-force proportion of the active population is shown in Table 3.2. The fact that the labour force represents only about 50 per cent of the active Syrian population reflects the difficulties the country faces in capital formation and, ultimately, in creating economic prosperity. It might be noted that Syria's small labour-force percentage is characteristic of the Third World as a whole; in the West, by contrast, the labour force represents about 42 per cent of the active population[19]

Examining the distribution of the Syrian labour force among the various economic sectors and the change in the distribution over time, we find a radical development. Agriculture, which prior to 1970 absorbed more than 60 per cent of the labour force[20], only gave employment to 31 per cent by 1979. This transformation was due not only to urbanisation and the concomitant rise of industry, construction, and notably the service sectors, as Table 3.3 demonstrates, but also to the technical development of the agricultural sector.

Syria is desperately short of professionals, technicians and other skilled manpower, whose number in 1979 constituted about 9 per cent of the total labour force, or about 190,000.[21] In fact, Syria suffers from the emigration of the skilled. There are about one and a half million Syrian citizens who work abroad, most of them professionals or skilled workers.[22]

Two significant obstacles to the country's long-term economic and social progress are the shortage of technical manpower and the absence of effective administration institutions. From 1956 to 1978, some 61 per cent of Syria's engineers, 59 per cent of its scientific specialists and 65 per cent of its physicians emigrated.[23] In order to solve the problem of the shortage of technical manpower, Syrian governments since 1946 have allocated increasing amounts to education. Allocations rose from 13.4 per cent of the total budget in 1946-9, 14.5 per cent in 1956-9,[24] a high of 18.6 per cent in 1975-6,[25] and 18 per cent in 1981-2.[26] In absolute terms, the education budget increased from L. Syr. 266 million in 1972 to L. Syr. 2,968 million in 1981.[27] The results of these efforts were a considerable growth in the number of pupils, including female pupils, whose education was encouraged, the establishment of adult vocational training centres and the expansion of the technical secondary schooling systems.[28] The number of pupils at all educational levels increased from 741,369 in 1963 to 2,209,736 in 1981. The number of third-level pupils rose from some 43,000 students in 1970 to about 120,000 in 1982.[29] Table 3.4 provides details of the number of institutions, staff, and enrolment in the 1970s.

Table 3.2: The Syrian Labour Force in 1979

Sex	Labour Employed	Force Unemployed	Total labour force	Total population
Male	1,762,169	69,174	1,831,343	4,446,896
Female	329,934	12,921	342,855	4,276,572
Total	2,092,103	82,095	2,174,198	8,723,468
% of total population	24%	0.9%	24.9%	100%

Source: *Syrie et le Monde Arabe,* 25 February 1981, p. 14.

Table 3.3: Breakdown of Labour Force by Sectors, 1971 to 1979 (in 000 and %)

Sector	1971	%	1972	%	1973	%	1974	%	1975	%	1976	%	1977	%	1978	%	1979	%
Agriculture, forestry, hunting, fishing	926	56.2	926	54.0	858	50.8	874	50.8	916	49.7	578	31.6	754	37.7	671	34.7	693	31.8
Mining and quarrying	2	0.1	3	0.2	15	0.9	14	0.8	12	0.7	13	0.7	8	0.4	14	0.7	—	—
Manufacturing	182	11.1	185	10.8	166	9.8	190	11.1	211	11.5	276	15.1	265	13.3	264	13.7	339	15.6
Electricity, gas and water	7	0.4	19	1.1	8	0.5	7	0.4	10	0.6	12	0.9	13	0.9	14	0.7	32	1.5
Building and construction	78	4.7	106	6.2	96	5.6	110	6.4	130	7.0	204	11.2	178	8.9	233	12.1	298	13.7
Wholesale and retail trade, restaurants and hotels	148	9.0	141	8.2	158	9.4	164	9.5	189	10.3	186	10.2	203	10.2	205	10.6	221	10.2
Transport and communications	48	3.0	65	3.8	67	4.0	68	4.0	78	4.2	114	6.2	119	6.0	102	5.3	98	4.5
Finance, insurance, real estate	11	0.7	9	0.5	10	0.6	11	0.6	10	0.6	15	0.8	13	0.7	27	1.4	22	1.0
Social and personal services	190	11.5	219	12.8	270	16.0	228	13.3	236	12.8	355	19.5	381	19.0	404	20.9	422	19.5
Miscellaneous	54	3.3	42	2.5	41	2.4	53	3.1	45	2.5	70	3.8	57	2.9	—	—	49	2.2
Total	1646	100	1715	100	1686	100	1719	100	1839	100	1828	100	1995	100	1934	100	2174	100

Sources: 1971-5: Syrian Central Bureau of Statistics. *Statistical Abstracts* (Annual), 1972-76; 1976-9: Central Bank of Syria, *Quarterly Bulletin*, No. 1-2, 1981.

Table 3.4: Educational Institutions, Teachers and Pupils, 1970 to 1979

Level	Educational Institutions		Teaching Staff				Pupils Enrolled			
			Total		Females		Total		Females	
	1970	1979	1970	1979	1970	1979	1970	1979	1970	1979
First	5,500	8,189	25,134	50,327	9,949	26,561	924,969	1,481,496	335,940	626,912
Second			15,045	31,466	3,374	7,119	327,639	588,865	85,206	211,208
Third							42,667	112,172*	8,464	31,066*

Note: *refers to 1978.
Source: *UN Statistical Yearbook* 1981, pp. 328-91.

Table 3.5: Syria's Gross Domestic Product, 1970 to 1983 (L. Syr Billion — 1980 prices)

	1970	1971	1972	1973	1974	1975	1976	1977	1978	1979	1980	1981	1982	1983
GDP	23,383	25,480	27,955	28,581	34,006	38,703	41,588	42,678	46,232	47,793	51,799	57,107	61,042	65,498
Real Growth (%)		9.0	9.7	2.2	19.0	13.8	7.4	2.6	8.3	3.4	8.3	10.2	6.9	7.3

Source: IMF *International Financial Statistics.*

The advances made in the areas of education and technical training account for part of the economic development achieved by Syria in the last decade. At the same time, advances were also manifested strikingly in the areas of health and life expectancy. As mentioned above, the crude death rate per thousand underwent a significant decline between 1960 and 1980 as a result of positive developments in the health field. For example, the number of people served by one physician dropped from 4,630 persons in 1960 to 2,570 in 1977.[30] Similarly, the number of patients served by one nurse declined from 6,660 to 3,890 over this period.[31] Finally life expectancy rose, from 50 years in 1960 to 65 in 1979.[32]

On the basis of the indicators discussed above — internal migration, labour force, education, and health — it may be said that the Syrian economy underwent in the last two decades a process of development that changed the traditional structure of the population. Although the Syrian economy still suffers from certain handicaps, notably shortages of skilled manpower and technically trained personnel, the quantitative and qualitative changes are clearly reflected in the economic growth of the country.

Economic Growth

Syria's average rate of economic growth of about 7.5 per cent per year in terms of gross domestic product from 1960-79 covers a differentiation between the decade of the 1960s, when its growth was lower than this average, and that of the 1970s when it was higher, as well as fluctuations from year to year. Although the several estimates of Syrian economic growth frequently differ, all of them indicate that the growth rate in the 1970s was higher than that of the 1960s by at least half. Thus the World Bank reports that Syria's annual growth from 1960-70 was 5.7 per cent; and from 1970-9 it was 9 per cent.[33] According to the United Nations, however, Syria's annual growth in GDP from 1963-70 averaged 3.6 per cent, but from 1970-9 it averaged 10 per cent.[34]

Two factors have combined to bring about the relatively high rates of growth in the 1970s. The first factor consisted of the economic steps taken by the Assad government to revitalise private enterprise and to form links with Western economies. Assad's policy encouraged the investment of foreign capital and the repatriation of Syrian capital that was abroad. Although the 1973 war with Israel cost Syria an estimated US $1 billion, over the next three years Assad received large amounts of Arab aid as well as favourable loans and grants to expedite economic development. The second reason for the 1970s growth rate was the vast increase in oil production and oil exports, particularly in the period of the oil boom of 1973-6. The expanded revenues from oil, which became Syria's largest export item, permitted the undertaking of very large development programmes during these years.

Average annual growth during the 1970s was not consistent, as it slackened from 7.4 per cent in the first half of the decade to 6 per cent after 1976 (although it later rose to 8.1 per cent in the early 1980s). Moreover, the rate of growth also fluctuated from year to year, mainly because agriculture, once one of the most important contributors to the country's national product, was often exposed to poor rainfall and erratic climatic conditions. In fact, for more than two decades from the mid-1950s, the contribution of agriculture to the Syrian economy declined steadily in relative terms, falling from 35.1 per cent in the 1953-9 period to 26.6 per cent in 1960-73[35] and to 19.9 per cent in 1974-80.[36]

Until 1970, Syria had been an agricultural country; but from 1973 onwards, agriculture lost its leading position in the economy in favour of commercial, mining and manufacturing sectors. Trade rose from a 20 per cent contribution to GDP in 1970 to 23.7 per cent in 1977-80. Mining and industry increased from 12.6 per cent in 1963[37] to more than 18 per cent by 1980.[38] The government sector also made advances, from 10.2 per cent in 1963[39] to more than 16 per cent in the decade 1970-80.[40] The expansion of trade, mining, industry and public services was related to the change in Syria's socio-economic system with the Assad regime, which encouraged private commercial activities, on the one hand, and expanded the economic role of the state, on the other hand. As Table 3.6 demonstrates, however, the relative contribution of the commodity sectors to Syrian GDP has declined while the service sectors have gained.

Agriculture

Although the contribution of agriculture to GDP fell in the course of two decades from about 35 per cent to about 20 per cent, the value of agricultural production at current prices rose about 225 per cent during the 1970s. A comparison with its neighbours shows that Syria registered the highest rate of agricultural production (Table 3.7).

Table 3.6: Syria's Gross Domestic Product, by Sectors, 1976 to 1980 (L. Syr. Million, at constant 1975 prices)

	1976	1977	1978	1979	1980
Agriculture	4,359	3,710	4,921	3,985	5,466
Mining, manufacturing	4,456	4,182	4,469	4,138	4,555
Building and construction	1,499	1,532	1,588	2,072	1,887
Wholesale and retail trade	5,196	5,457	5,626	5,704	6,349
Transport and communications	1,771	1,582	1,735	2,085	2,150
Finance and insurance	1,646	1,744	1,899	2,140	2,248
Social and personal services	410	475	547	598	584
Government services	3,036	3,128	3,424	4,288	4,153
Non-profit private services	20	22	24	26	29
Total	22,393	21,832	23,733	24,991	27,420

Source: Syria, Central Bureau of Statistics, *Statistical Abstracts,* 1977-81

Table 3.7: Indices of Agricultural Production for Syria and Neighbouring Countries, 1977 to 1981 (1969-71 = 100)

	Food					All Agricultural Commodities				
	1977	1978	1979	1980	1981	1977	1978	1979	1980	1981
Syria	169	203	190	261	257	156	183	171	227	224
Israel	134	135	140	139	130	137	140	144	144	138
Jordan	97	110	80	135	102	97	111	81	135	102
Iraq	107	110	125	126	127	106	109	123	124	125

Source: *UN Statistical Yearbook,* 1981.

Syria's renewed interest in the agricultural sector gained impetus in the late 1970s with the decline in oil revenues and the awareness of the need for food security as well as the important role of agriculture in the balance of trade. Indicative of the attention being paid to this sector was the government's proclamation of 1983 as the year of agriculture.[41]

Syria has four principal agricultural regions. One is the narrow coastal strip extending from the border of Lebanon in the south to the Turkish border in the north. This region produces fruits, olives, tobacco and cotton. The second is the valley of the Orontes river, whose marshes have been drained. Called Al-Ghab, this region is one of the most fertile of the country. The third, which produces cereals, fruits and cotton, is the central plain stretching northwards from Jordan and joining with the narrow Euphrates valley. Most of the Syrian population is concentrated in its main cities: Damascus, Homs, Hama and Aleppo. The fourth region is Jazira in the north-east of the country, where cotton and cereals are grown.[42]

Despite the government's efforts to expand the cultivable land, the most recent data suggest that only a small expansion took place from 1961-80. Much of the so-called new area put under cultivation in the Deir al-Zor and Al-Hassakah districts had been done so in the immediate post-war period by groups of merchants from Hama, Homs and notably Aleppo, who shifted huge investments into mechanised agriculture.[43] Irrigated land, too, had been greatly expanded in the 1945-60 period, by more than 58 per cent. From 1961 onwards, there was nearly a cessation in the expansion of lands under irrigation. As Table 3.8 shows, total cultivated land has fluctuated from year to year, owing to the level of rain. Table 3.8 also shows that Syria has noticeable potential for agricultural expansion. Until 1980, the amount of land

Table 3.8: Syrian Land Utilisation, 1945 to 1980 (000 Hectares)

Type of Land	1945	1961	1969	1974	1977	1980
Irrigated	324	558	546	578	531	539
Non-irrigated		3,256	2,936	2,956	3,336	3,354
Crop lands		3,814	3,480	3,534	3,867	3,893
Fallow		2,567	2,395	2,493	1,642	1,791
Cultivated		6,381	5,875	6,027	5,509	5,684
Uncultivated cultivable			2,839	2,025	355	470
Cultivable			8,714	8,052	5,864	6,154
Uncultivable			3,748	3,627	3,671	3,520
Forests		402	440	446	452	466
Pasture		6,463	5,445	6,393	8,531	8,378
Total		18,448	18,347	18,518	18,518	18,518

Sources: 1945-61: Sayigh, p. 245;
1969: *Syrie et le Monde Arabe*, 25 May 1971;
1974, 1977, 1980: Syria, Central Bureau of Statistics, *Statistical Abstracts.*

under cultivation represented only 31 per cent of the country's total area; crop lands constituted about 20 per cent of the total, irrigated land about 3 per cent and cultivable land 8.8 per cent. The government had hoped to increase the percentage of irrigated lands with the construction of the Euphrates Dam, completed in 1978. The expectation was that this project would irrigate, in the long term, about 640,000 hectares, of which 500,000 would be ready for cultivation in 1990.[44] The improvement of the land in the Euphrates valley, however, has been disturbed by the appearance of quantities of chalks and by the saltiness of the Euphrates water.

Wheat and barley together make up approximately two-thirds of the cultivated areas, and cotton about 26 per cent of the irrigated lands. Table 3.9 provides a breakdown of the amount of cultivated area devoted to Syria's main crops.

Table 3.9: Distribution of Cultivated Surface of Syrian Land, 1978 to 1982 (000 Hectares)

Crop	1978	1979	1980	1981	1982
Wheat	1,555	1,445	1,600	1,255	1,213
Barley	1,033	1,102	1,210	1,347	1,587
Lentil	136	89	85	72	57
Millet	19	13	16	15	n.d.
Cotton	169	154	139	143	155
Sugar beet	12	18	23	22	26
Tobacco	16	13	13	13	13
Olive	234	241	245	258	n.d.
Others	988	620	562	751	n.d.
Total area cultivated	4,162	3,695	3,893	3,876	n.d.

Source: *Syrie et le Monde Arabe*, 25 August 1983, p. 5.

Although Syria is a self-sufficient in cereals, it remains largely dependent on other sources of food. Thus its imports of fruits, vegetables and meats represent about 20 per cent of its total imports.[45] Efforts have been made to increase the production of sugar beet, fruits, milk, eggs and meat. Similarly, livestock farming has received considerable attention. Thus, the number of sheep- and cattle-raising units, model farms, and veterinary and artificial insemination centres has grown considerably since 1975.[46] Between 1963 and 1980, Syria's livestock herds more than doubled to over 10 million animals, the growth being due principally to the increase in lactiferous animals.[47] In terms of value, too, animal production increased from L. Syr. 782 million in 1974 to L. Syr. 2,033 million in 1980,[48] the latter figure constituting about 35 per cent of the total value of Syria's agricultural output.[49] Until 1972, agricultural products contributed more than half of Syria's export earnings, with cotton accounting for the largest proportion or about 33 per cent of the total.[50] From 1974 onwards, oil took over as Syria's largest export item; by 1980, the share of agriculture had fallen to 13 per cent.[51]

In recent years, Syria's oil exports have faced serious problems, the fall in world oil prices cutting their value and, at the same time, domestic consumption taking an increasing proportion of production. Between 1975 and 1980 the domestic consumption of oil products increased 45 per cent and the forecast to 1990 is for an increase of 140 per cent over the 1980 figure.[52]

The decrease in oil earnings coincided with difficulties caused by a deficit in Syria's balance of payments and the intervention in Lebanon, the economic cost of which has been very heavy. Syrian officials are now trying to compensate for the balance of payments and oil export difficulties, as mentioned earlier, by encouraging and developing agricultural cash crops. The main item in this category is, once again, cotton. In 1983, the annual cotton conference, held in Aleppo, suggested an allocation of L. Syr. 17,200 million (US $4,380 million) for agriculture in order to increase cotton output.[53], which since 1975 had greatly dropped off. Between 1968 and 1973, the production of ginned cotton amounted to between 200,000 and 250,000 tons; it dropped to 155,000 tons in 1976-7 and to 117,800 tons in 1980-1.[54] The fall in output had been due to the relatively low prices brought by cotton in the international market, which led farmers to turn instead to wheat and sugar beet production.[55] Thus in 1963, Syria had had 292,000 hectares under cotton cultivation; in 1980-1, the total was only 138,000 hectares.

The drive to reverse this trend, however, began in 1981, when prices were raised 44 per cent. Cotton ginning capacity was expanded. Syria now has 21 processing factories.[56] In addition, plans were introduced to expand the cotton-growing area both by re-exploiting land sown in the 1960s and 1970s, but since either abandoned or turned over to cereals, and by increasing irrigation through major schemes on the Euphrates and Khabour rivers. In 1983-4, production increased as about 172,000 hectares were seeded.[57] The government has also tried to modernise the system of crop gathering by offering ten-year, soft loans to farmers wanting to buy new machinery. The farmers, however, feel that the incentive interest of 3 per cent is not sufficient, because cotton prices still remain relatively low in world terms.[58]

Syria has one of the highest cotton yields in the world. In 1983-4, the seed cotton yield from each hectare was 2,980 kilos, about 1,000 kilos higher than the yields of the mid-1970s. The higher yields increased production, and expanded ginning capacity was expected to provide Syria with 125,000 tons of cotton lint for export in 1983/4 (see Table 3.10).[59]

Table 3.10: Syria's Cotton Production and Exports, 1968 to 1983 (000 tons)

	1968-73	1976-7	1980-81	1981-82	1982-83	1983-84
Raw cotton	398	402	399			
Ginned cotton	225	155	118	130	157	190
Local consumption of ginned cotton			45	55	65	65
Exported surplus of ginned cotton			73	75	92	125

Sources: *QER, AS,* Syria and Jordan, 1981, p. 8 and 1982, p. 11; *Meed,* 13 January 1984, vol. 8, no. 2, pp. 35-6.

Although the share of cotton in Syria's total export revenue dropped from 43 per cent in 1965 to 33 per cent in 1973 and to only 8 per cent in 1980, the value of cotton exports rose in absolute terms from L. Syr. 314 million in 1971 to L. Syr. 448 million in 1973 and L. Syr. 665 million in 1980.[60] The potential for greatly increased cotton production and exports is certainly considerable; however, this commodity alone is insufficient to plug the gap in the country's trade balance and to compensate for the decline in oil revenues. Syria remains dependent on oil income for its foreign exchange. Even in decline, oil products still represent more than 60 per cent of the total value of Syrian exports.

Oil

Syrian oil was first struck at Suweidia in 1959 by the West German firm Concordia, a subsidiary of Deutsche Erdöl AG, but was not exported until 1968, when the pipeline from the north-eastern oil fields to Tartous was finally completed. Output then increased, reaching a peak of over 9.6 million tons in 1976. Annual production has since hovered around 8 million tons (See Table 3.11), the relative decrease in production coinciding with the fall in world oil prices, the rise in domestic consumption, and the increase in oil imports. In fact, in 1981 Syria became a net importer of petroleum, the value of its oil imports totalling L. Syr. 6,783.8 million compared to oil exports L. Syr. 6,521.5 million. In 1982 oil imports fell to L. Syr. 5,931.5 million, though exports also fell, to L. Syr. 5,939.6 million, the country's status as a net exporter of fuel was restored, albeit by a narrow margin. Syrian officials believe that Syria can continue to be a net oil exporter until 1990. It is also suggested that its oil reserves in the north-eastern part of the country could enable Syria to remain a net exporter until 2005.[61]

Syria nationalised its petroleum sector in 1964, placing all oil activities under the control of the General Petroleum Authority. Four separate companies were created, each responsible for a different function. In 1975, the Syrian government reversed its attitude towards foreign firms and opened up 50,000 sq km for service contract agreements with foreign companies. The change in attitude was a result of Syrian efforts to increase production when recoverable reserves were expected to last for two decades. Agreements were concluded with Rompetrol of Romania, INA Nattiplin of Yugoslavia, Bureau d'Etudes Industrielles et de Cooperation d'Institut Français du Petrole of France, Tripco and Marathon Company of the United States, Challenger Oil Company of Canada, and two Shell subsidiaries, Pecten Syria Company, and Syria Shell Petroleum Development. In 1977, a Syrian-American consortium, SAMOCO, was established, the enterprise taking a concession in the region of Dier al-Zor.[62] As a result of these activities, four new oil fields were opened — at Derrik, Saida, Wahab and Safeh[63] — and the country's known oil reserves in 1983 were put at 1,400 million tons.[64] Nevertheless, domestic output is not expected to improve significantly; because of the fact that Syrian oil has both high extraction costs and a high sulphur content, only 25 per cent to 40 per cent of the reserves will be commercial.[65]

The oil sector was also affected by Syria's loss of transit fees from Iraqi oil carried via a pipeline from northern Iraq across Syria to a point beyond Homs, and branching there to the Syrian terminal of Banias and the Lebanese terminal of Tripoli. Negotiations between Syria and Iraq over fees broke down in April 1976 and Syria lost an annual income that was then estimated at US $136 million.[66] A new agreement was

Table 3.11: Syrian Oil Production and Earnings, 1972 to 1983

	Crude oil production (000 tons)	Value of crude oil exports (L. Syr. Million)	Value of all oil product exports (L. Syr. Million)	Share of oil in total exports (%)	Value of oil imports (US$ Million)
1972	4,197	200	200	17.6	52
1973	4,325	291	291	21.7	76.5
1974	6,160	1,608	1,608	55.2	434
1975	9,530	2,377	2,377	63.1	642
1976	9,662	2,586	2,586	62.4	664.9
1977	7,949	2,436	2,436	58.0	620.6
1978	8,106	2,553	2,553	61.3	650
1979	7,697	4,449	4,722	69.9	1,203
1980	8,300	5,235	6,585	63.3	1,677.7
1981	8,100	5,044	6,521	58.2	1,661
1982	8,150	4,082	5,939	74.6	1,513
1983	8,400				
				830	1,069	1,728	1,511

Sources: 1972-79: Central Bank of Syria, *Quarterly Bulletin*, No. 4, 1980.
1980-81: *Syrie et le Monde Arabe*, 25 August 1983, pp. 8, 16.
1982-83: *MEED*, 13 January 1984, vol. 28, no. 2, p. 22.

reached in February 1979, but in April 1982, the pipeline was again closed because of Syria's support of Iran in the Iran-Iraq war.[67] In sum, the relative decline of oil production, the increasing oil imports, and the loss of transit fees greatly lessened the economic importance that the oil sector had known in the 1970s.

Natural gas, however, could probably compensate for part of the loss suffered by the oil sector. In 1982, proven gas reserves were officially put at 3,539 billion cu ft, with associated reserves of an additional 1,190 billion cu ft. That year, moreover, Marathon Company discovered a pool of gas in the centre of the country.[68] In addition, a new collection scheme for the associated reserves was introduced in 1982-3 to increase gas exports.[69]

In terms of all forms of energy, Syria produced in 1979 14,634,000 tons, coal equivalent, consuming 8,162,000 tons, coal equivalent. Its total energy imports that year came to 3,338 tons, coal equivalent, while exports amounted to 7,703,000 tons.[70]. Doubtless the consumption of energy will increase in the 1980s, but production will also increase owing to increasing electric power production. The production of electric power rose from 116 million kwh in 1950 to 1,366 million kwh in 1974, and as a result of the construction of the Euphrates Dam, to 4,020 million kwh in 1980. Electrification of all Syrian villages with more than 100 inhabitants (5,400 villages in all) is planned for completion by 1990.[71] The consumption of electric power by industry, which used 52 per cent of the total in 1977, is also rising.[72]

Industry

The expansion of electric power coupled with the increase in the consumption of oil products resulted in part from Syria's endeavours to develop its industrial base. The resources directed to that purpose were accompanied by a belief in the value of industry as an instrument of societal development and of 'economic independence'. Syria's industrialisation began in the 1950s. Until 1970, however, industrial development was limited mainly to the establishment of factories producing a range of light consumer goods, such as textiles, processed foods, soaps, matches, glass and cement.[73] Nationalisation of the industrial sector in 1964 and the first half of 1965 caused a certain amount of stagnation after years of slow but steady growth.

The year 1970 marked a new stage in the industrialisation of Syria. Although the industrial sector was nationalised, the liberalisation introduced by the Assad government included encouragement of foreign investment. Foreign companies were allowed either to take an equity participation in state-controlled industries or to invest directly in one of various free zones created in the early 1970s. Syria's third five-year plan (1971-5) gave priority to industry, with 46.3 per cent of total public investments allotted to this sector.[74] The fourth five-year plan (1976-80) was formulated in the light of the massive injections of Arab capital and the increasing earnings from oil exports. Thus public investments in industry came to only 20.8 per cent. Thereafter, however, the cut-off of Saudi and other Gulf aid, the military intervention in Lebanon, and the loss of Iraqi pipeline-transit fees caused several industrial projects to be abandoned.[75] Preliminary figures for the fifth five-year plan (1981-5) show that industry has lost its priority status, as public investments in this sector amounted to 26.6 per cent without the complementary capital that marked the previous plan.[76]

None the less, significant change has taken place in the country's industrial structure. Besides the increase in production, the number of industrial workers grew and diversification was introduced in the sector. From 1970-8 annual growth in industrial output remained high, 13.6 per cent at constant prices; then it fluctuated wildly: dropping to only 0.9 per cent in 1979, bouncing back to 10.1 per cent in 1980,[77] but halving to 5 per cent in 1981.[78] The major industries cover five main areas: textiles, food, chemicals, engineering and cement. Until 1980, food and textiles represented two-thirds of the added value of Syrian industry. The building in the early 1980s of new enterprises in industries such as oil refineries, fertilizers, cement and paper will alter this percentage.[79]

In 1970, the textile industry numbered 13 different enterprises, each with its array of factories. Between 1970 and 1983, the industry added another 12 firms.[80] In 1970, the total capital of the textile industry amounted to L. Syr. 16,460 million. Table 3.12 shows how the industry expanded in the decade that followed.

In order to attain 'food security', the government increased its investments in food industries from L. Syr. 14 million during the third five-year plan (1971-5) to L. Syr. 187 million during the fourth plan. In the 1981-5 plan, however, the investments in this sector are expected to decrease to L. Syr. 80 million. These amounts do not include investments in sugar refining. If they were to, then public investments in the food industry in the 1976-80 plan would amount to L. Syr. 974 million because sugar refining was allocated L. Syr. 787 million.[81] Until 1975, the sugar sector was administered by the General Union of Food Indus-

Table 3.12: Expansion of the Syrian Textile Industry, 1970 to 1980

	1971-1975 (3rd Plan)		1976-1980 (4th Plan)
Investments (L. Syr. Million)	481		1,755
	1970	1975	1980
Production (L. Syr. Million)	250	496	882
Number of workers	19,445	24,777	29,133
Production per worker (L. Syr.)	14,495	20,108	

Source: *Syrie et le Monde Arabe* 25 January, 1984, pp. 2-3.

tries. With the creation of the General Sugar Establishment in 1976, the three old sugar refineries of Homs, Ghab and Adra began to receive important capital. Sugar allocations in the fourth five-year plan also enabled the establishment of four other refineries, in Deir al-Zor, Rakkah, Mashanah and Salhab, each with a production capacity of 4,000 tons per day of beet sugar. The overall value of output in the sugar sector rose from L. Syr. 142 million in 1976 to L. Syr. 307 million in 1980.[82] At the beginning of 1984, plans were made to improve the refineries at Homs, with some L. Syr. 15 million being allocated to this end.[83]

Although Syria increased its raw sugar production from 210,000 tons in 1978 to 505,000 tons in 1980,[84] it still had to import about 80,000 tons of raw Cuban sugar in 1982 for local processing.[85] In the 1970s annual sugar refining production actually decreased on average, dropping from 132,000 tons in 1971-5 to 108,000 tons in 1976-80.[86] Governmental attention to this condition led to an upsurge in production, to 143,000 tons in 1981 and 180,000 tons in 1983.[87]

In order both to respond to local demand and to contribute to future export revenue, Syria has been placing special emphasis on engineering, chemicals (including fertilizers) and the cement industry. The capital invested in these sectors during the third five-year plan (1971-5) amounted to L. Syr. 1,179 million; but the fourth plan (1976-80) increased these investments considerably to L. Syr. 9,585.5 million,[88] which figure represents about 57 per cent of the total investment in the industrial sector. The value of the total output of the three industrial

Table 3.13: Expansion of the Engineering, Chemicals and Cement
Sectors in Syria, 1970 to 1980

	1971-5 (3rd Plan)		1976-80 (4th Plan)
Investments (L. Syr. Million)	1,179		9,585.5
	1971	1975	1980
Production (L. Syr. Million)	171	577	1,664
Number of workers	7,493	11,673	
Production per worker (L. Syr.)	6,176	8,829	

Source: *Syrie et le Monde Arabe,* 25 January 1984, pp. 6-7.

sectors almost tripled between 1975 and 1980, as Table 3.13
shows.

In terms of production value, engineering is the most important of the
three, having risen from L.Syr. 313 million in 1975 to L. Syr. 953
million in 1980, or to some 55 per cent of the total production value of
the three industries. In 1970, Syria possessed three large cement factories, two in Aleppo and one in Hama. Between 1978 and 1982, two
other factories were constructed, in Adra and Tartous. The capacity of
cement production rose from about 970,000 tons in 1970-5 to about 2
million tons in 1980.[89] As for chemicals, the phosphate plants opened
near Homs in 1971, and which started operation in 1974, contributed
significantly to the development of the chemical industry. Phosphate
output increased gradually from 425,000 tons in 1977, 747,000 tons in
1978, 1,170,000 tons in 1979 to 1,300,000 tons in 1980.[90] Their
export value grew concomitantly, from L. Syr. 55 million in 1975, L.
Syr. 89 million in 1980, to L. Syr. 129 million in 1981.[91] In 1982,
expansion projects were carried out at the three existing mines and
storage facilities constructed at Tartous port. Earlier, in 1980, production of new triple-super-phosphates began at Homs, with annual figures
of 450,000 tons of fertilizers and 300,000 tons of urea.[92]

Although Syria still imports a large proportion of its consumer goods,
local efforts have been made in recent years to meet domestic demand
for various items, such as refrigerators, furniture, paper, glass, plastic,
tractors and television sets. Altogether, the index of national industries
registered a real growth of 43 per cent during the seven years from

1968-74, but of 37 per cent during the following seven years, 1975-81. Since 1970, large industrial projects have been carried out in the urban centres — Damascus, Aleppo, Homs and Hama — mostly by foreign contractors working under government supervision.[93] The foundries, the chemical, ceramic, phosphate and textile factories, and the oil and sugar refineries constructed in these regions have had the effect of strengthening the public sector. The state emerged as a major owner of the means of production and the controller of economic power. At the same time, however, these activities weakened the position of economic agents in the large cities of the centre and north of the country. At least one opinion ascribes the events of 1982 in Hama as a result of the hostility of the small artisans and small manufacturers towards the large-scale industrialisation which began in 1970.[94]

Table 3.14: Index of Syrian Industrial Production, 1975 to 1981 (1975 = 100)

Year	1968	1970	1973	1974	1975	1976	1977	1978	1979	1980	1981
Index	43	58	73	86	100	109	106	115	116	130	137

Source: *UN Statistical Yearbook,* 1981.

In the mid-1970s, new industrial projects were located in small cities and peripheral regions of the south and north-east, especially in greater Damascus. These projects created numerous development possibilities in these areas, but also tended to consolidate the position of the economic elites in Damascus. In Damascus alone, public-sector industrial production rose from L. Syr. 277 million in 1971 to L. Syr. 2,898 million in 1982, or 944 per cent and an annual growth of about 86 per cent.[95] The agents of the state, allied with the bourgeoisies of Damascus, extended the control of the central government to the cities of the north and centre of the country as well as over the south and north-east provinces. Controlling the distribution of credit and equipment, the Assad regime employed economic liberalisation to favour its political allies, the merchants and manufacturers of Damascus. By controlling the industrial sector and creating state-owned shops, the government was able to halt the expansion of private industry. As a result, it strengthened its political influence even in the regions of Aleppo, Homs and Hama, where opposition movements had emerged.[96]

Transport and Communications

In order to facilitate economic development and to relieve bottlenecks in the economy, the Syrian government from 1970 onwards made great efforts to construct roads, railways, ports and telecommunication facilities. In 1968, Syria had only 8,120 km of paved roads, 307 km of narrow-gauge railway track and 545 km of standard-gauge line.[97] By 1980, there were 16,872 km of roads, of which 14,696 km were asphalted, and 2,017 km of railway track,[98] over 100% increases in each case in little more than a decade.

In the early 1970s, three railway lines had been built with aid from the Soviet Union: the Hijaz line from Damascus to Jordan and Saudi Arabia, the Tartous-Akkari-Homs-Aleppo line and the line from Lattakia-Aleppo-Kamishli, with a branch from Aleppo to Rakkah and Deir al-Zor that linked the coast with the north and east of the country.[99] Syria has several other railway lines: the ones from Damascus to Homs via Mehine and from Mehine to Palmyra were completed recently.[100] Another, between Deir al-Zor and Abu Kamal, was nearing completion in 1984.[101] Finally, the blueprints for a 90 km railway between Tartous and Lattakia, to be constructed with Russian aid, were started in 1983.

Several highways and roads were built to link the main cities and villages of the country, especially Damascus with the main cities and with the provinces. In Damascus itself, roads and bridges were constructed to ease traffic congestion in the capital and to improve the links of the capital with its environs as well as with the other Syrian provinces.[102]

In essence, the railways and roads that were constructed in the past decade gave Syria's main towns and industrial centres fast communication with its main ports, Lattakia and Tartous. The building of the port of Lattakia started in 1952. It was intended to become the main outlet for Syria's exports of agricultural and industrial commodities as well as to serve imports that previously had arrived overland via Beirut. In 1971, the port handled 1,630,000 tons of cargo.[103] During the 1970s, the port was expanded; and in 1981, it handled 3,539,000 tons of imported goods and 759,000 tons of exports.[104] The port of Tartous was opened in 1970 in order to handle the growing exports of oil products, phosphates and other goods. With its harbour later deepened and improved, Tartous became Syria's largest port. In 1981, it received 2,272 ships with 3,157,000 tons of merchandise and saw 2,100 ships sail with 5,799,000 tons of exports.[105] A third Syrian port, at Banias, was completed at the end of the 1970s and was meant to facilitate the export of oil products, whether Syrian, Iraqi or Saudi Arabian.[106] In 1980, an oil refinery was built there which increased Syrian capacity to 11 million tons per year: five million at Homs and six million at Banias.[107]

Until the beginning of the 1980s, the number of telephones in Syria was very low: 111,000 in 1970 and 287,000 in 1980 (or only a slight increase per hundred inhabitants from 1.8 in 1970 to 3.2 in 1980).[108] Then in 1979, Syria signed a contract with a Japanese firm for installing what was claimed to be 'the world's largest local telephone exchange'.[109] The first results of the system were achieved in August and September 1983, when 20,000 lines were changed to a new electronic switching system in Damascus and a further 40,000 lines were introduced. The Japanese telecommunications system was also installed in Aleppo that year.[110]

Finance and the Balance of Payments

Expanding and improving the communications network and executing large-scale projects in both the agricultural and industrial sectors required Syria to seek foreign aid, financial and technological.

The Eastern-bloc countries are traditionally the most important contributors to Syria's economic plans. The Soviet Union, East Germany, Czechoslovakia, Romania and Bulgaria have supplied the experts and equipment for most of the irrigation, agriculture and transport projects. Russian and East German aid is enabling Syria to carry out its programme of rural electrification. With Soviet assistance, as has been mentioned, dams and railway lines have been constructed.

The Western countries, particularly France, Italy and the USA, have engaged more in the construction of Syria's heavy industries and in developing its oil production. Balance of payments difficulties, however, have obliged the Syrian government to reduce expenditures for heavy industry. At the same time, the expansion of the oil industry has run into problems, affecting Western involvement in the Syrian economy.[111] A further blow to the economy came in late 1983, when the United States decided to halt its aid.[112]

In spite of accelerated investments and rising capital imports, Syria did not suffer balance of payments difficulties to any appreciable extent before 1976. At the end of that year, however, Syria's account with the rest of the world began to show a deficit, which affected its economy.

Table 3.15: Syria's Balance of Payments, 1972 to 1982 (in US$ million: minus sign indicates debit)

	1972	1973	1974	1975	1976	1977	1978	1979	1980	1981	1982
Merchandise: exports fob	299	356	783	930	1066	1070	1061	1648	2112	2230	2052
Merchandise: imports fob	-445	-569	-1039	-1425	-2102	-2402	-2204	-3055	-4010	-4843	-3738
Other goods, services and income: credit	173	275	360	385	314	383	349	470	456	591	437
Other goods, services and income: debit	-81	-125	-397	-503	-505	-451	-590	-684	-855	-888	-832
Private unrequited transfers	39	37	44	52	53	92	636	901	774	582	140
Official unrequited transfers nie	45	364	416	654	402	1143	782	1627	1520	1819	1446
Total of current account	30	338	167	93	-772	-167	35	907	-4	-510	-495
Direct investments and other long-term capital nie	14	25	—	-10	270	228	359	75	-25	48	205
Total	44	363	167	83	-502	61	394	982	-29	-462	-290

Other short-term capital nie	388	531	431	28	−7	150	135	158	−49	314	30
Net errors and omissions	2	−50	−661	−836	−522	−7	13	−6	−8	−50	−43
Total	*100*	*19*	*−258*	*174*	*−135*	*218*	*−354*	*235*	*110*	*327*	*31*
Counterpart to mon/demon of gold	—	—	—	—	—	—	—	—	—	—	—
Counterpart to SDR allocation	—	8	9	8	—	—	—	—	—	—	5
Counterpart to valuation changes	—	−72	6	17	33	−28	—	—	—	—	—
Exceptional financing	−195	—	—	—	—	—	—	—	—	—	—
Total changes in reserves	*95*	*45*	*243*	*−199*	*102*	*−190*	*354*	*−235*	*−110*	*−327*	*−36*

Source: IMF, *International Financial Statistics*, December 1979, p. 411 and June 1984, p.445.

The difficulty stemmed from being cut off from (Western) foreign aid, a decline in agricultural production that was due to bad harvests and a decrease in oil revenues from both local production and pipeline transit fees. The balance of payments crisis became worse at the beginning of the 1980s. In February 1983, the Prime Minister, Abdul Raauf al-Kassim, demanded a partial suspension of imports of industrial equipment for all economic sectors in order to alleviate the problem.[113]

Syria's current accounts for the years 1972-84 may be divided into four periods: the first, 1972-5, in which it ran a surplus; the second, 1976-7, when deficits totalled US $772 million in 1976 and US $167 million in 1977; the third, 1978-9, in which surpluses were registered of US $35 million in 1978 and US $907 million in 1979; the fourth, 1980-4, which began with a slight deficit of US $4 million in 1980, increased to about US $500 million in 1981-2 (see Table 3.15) and apparently reduced to US $300 million in 1983 and US $225 million in 1984.[114]

Although in 1982 observers expected that Syria's ability to provide foreign exchange to pay for its imports was deteriorating,[115] recent political achievements in Lebanon enhanced Syria's prospects for assuring a generous flow of Arab aid, particularly from Saudi Arabia. The levels of this aid, though, remain somewhat unclear. According to pledges made at the Baghdad Summit of 1978, Syria was to receive US $1.8 billion per year; however, it is thought that a maximum of US $1.2 billion was received in 1983, with as much as US $800 million to have come from Saudi Arabia alone. Nevertheless, adding the aid received from Libya after the war in Lebanon in 1982-3, total Arab aid to Syria may have reached US $2.3 billion in 1983, compared with US $2 billion in 1982. Moreover, Iran has provided at least US $1 billion each year; and substantial economic assistance is likely to continue to flow from that country, with which Syria sides in the Iran-Iraq war.[116] Although the Gulf war imposed difficulties on its own economy, Iran became an important backer of Syria to the extent that, according to some Western diplomatic sources, it now gives Syria at least as much economic aid as does Saudi Arabia.[117]

Financing will be the key factor when Syria undertakes a major review of the economic performance of its fifth five-year plan (1981-5), considers proposals for the next plan (1986-90), and at the same time tries to meet its huge military budget. Although part of the country's financial difficulties may be solved by foreign aid, Syria's balance of trade affects any solution. Trade trends, however, show a deficit that has risen from year to year, going from L. Syr. 920 million (US $240 million) in 1972 to L. Syr. 11,527 million (US $2,936 million) in 1981.

This deficit was cut in 1982 by nearly 50 per cent, but the reduction was the result of a fall in imports rather than an increase in exports and reflected the government's strenuous, even harsh, measures to curb the import bill (see Table 3.16).

The year 1982 also marked a change in the direction of trade. Although the Western countries remain the largest partners in its commercial exchanges,[118] Syria began to enforce its commercial and economic co-operation agreements with the Eastern countries as well as with Iran and Libya. In the 1980 treaty of friendship between Syria and the Soviet Union, the two countries had decided to increase their bilateral trade in 1981-5 to 2,000 million roubles.[119] The first result of this treaty was the increase in Syrian exports to Russia from about L. Syr. 320 million in 1980 to about L. Syr. 450 million per year in 1981-2.[120] Syria's close relationship with Iran found expression in trade in addition to direct economic aid. Even before the signing of a formal trade pact in February 1984, Syria had dramatically increased its Iranian imports from L. Syr. 13.7 million (US $3.5 million) in 1981 to L. Syr. 3,094 million (US $788 million) in 1982.[121]

The Arab and Iranian aid and the increasing share of Syrian exports taken by the Eastern-bloc countries do not sufficiently meet Syria's foreign-exchange shortage, which continues to hamper the economy. Efforts to curb imports have not offset the decline in exports. Meanwhile, military costs, notably after 1982, have increased considerably and perhaps account for Syria's present economic recession. Between 1975 and 1979, the Syrian arms bill from the Soviet Union totalled US $3,600 million, which represented 13 per cent of all Soviet arms bought by Third World countries.[122] Since the Israeli invasion of Lebanon in 1982, Syria has spent a further US $2,000 million on Soviet arms. It is thought that Syria's overall military debt to the Soviet Union is in the region of US $14,000 million.[123]

Syria's military spending has been reflected in the state budget. Although this budget increased from L. Syr. 2,787 million (US $729 million) in 1970 to L. Syr. 33,345 million (US $8,495 million) in 1982, the proportion allocated to defence and national security climbed from 26.5 per cent in 1970 to 29.1 per cent in 1982 (and probably to more than 30 per cent since 1982); at the same time, the proportion of development investment declined from 59 per cent in 1970 to 49 per cent in 1982 (See Table 3.17). The declining pace of growth is also reflected in the Syrian state budget: between 1970 and 1976 (when the budget totalled L. Syr. 16,656 million), it grew by about 598 per cent whereas the increase from 1976 to 1982 was only 200 per cent.

Table 3.16: Syria's Foreign Trade Trends, 1973 to 1982 (L. Syr. Million)

	1972	1973	1974	1975	1976	1977	1978	1979	1980	1981
Exports fob	1,141	1,341	2,914	3,441	4,141	4,199	4,160	6,453	8,273	8,254
Imports cif	2,061	2,341	4,578	6,236	9,203	10,497	9,658	13,067	16,188	19,781
Balance of trade	−920	−1,000	−1,658	−2,795	−5,062	−6,298	−5,498	−6,614	−7,915	−11,527

Source: IMF, *International Financial Statistics*, December 1979, p. 372; June 1984, p. 428.

Table 3.17: Syrian Budget Expenditures on Defence and Investments, 1970 to 1982 (L. Syr. million).

	1970	%	1975	%	1980	%	1982	%
Total expenditures	2,787		10,445		29,350		33,345	
Defence and national security	741	26.5	2,639	25.3	8,450	28.8	9,705	29.1
Investments	1,658	59.5	5,850	56.0	14,622	49.8	16,595	49.8
Others	388	14.0	1,950	18.7	6,278	21.4	7,045	21.1

Sources: QER, AS, Syria, Lebanon and Cyprus, 1973, p. 10, and 1972, p. 14.
Syria and Jordan, 1981, p. 14, and 1982, pp. 20-21.

Conclusion

There is no one conclusion that can be drawn from this study of the Syrian economy over the years of the Assad regime. The country's economic performance between 1970 and 1984 has been both positive and negative. In terms of economic growth, agricultural development, the establishment of new industries and oil revenues, the Syrian economy made relative progress. These achievements, though, were counterbalanced by balance of payments difficulties, budget deficits and certain other negative performances, throwing the country into a period of recession, particularly in the past four years. The recession shows signs, moreover, of affecting the social and political life of the country. In order for Syria to sustain constant growth, it must depend on foreign aid, both financial and technological. This last fact is a key factor in determining Syria's relationship with its neighbours, as well as with the Western and Eastern-bloc countries; and it is no less reflected in its own internal situation.

Notes

1. Hilan Rizkallah, *Culture et développement en Syrie et dans les pays retardés* (Prof. de Maxime Rodinson, Editions Anthropos, Paris, 1969), p. 349.

2. Economist Intelligence Unit (ELU), *Quarterly Economic Review* (hereafter *QER*), Annual Supplement (hereafter *AS*), Syria, Lebanon and Cyprus, 1973, p. 3.

3. *QER, AS,* Syria and Jordan, 1981, p. 5.

4. Yusif A. Sayigh, *The Economies of the Arab World: Developments Since 1945* (Croom Helm, London, 1978), p. 318.

5. Ibid., p. 237.

6. *QER, AS,* Syria, Lebanon and Cyprus, 1973, p. 6.

7. *QER, AS,* Syria and Jordan, 1982, p. 10.

8. *Kifah al-Arabi* (Beirut), 23 April 1979 (in Arabic).

9. No data are available on the number of Alawis in Hama; but according to observers who have visited the city, there are quarters populated mostly by Alawis.

10. See Jacques Weuleresse, *Paysans de Syrie et du Proche Orient* (Gallimard, Paris, 1946), p. 88.

11. In Jaramanah alone, there are 40,000 Druzes, most of whom are immigrants from Hauran and the Golan. See A'talla Salman, 'The Druze Villages in Gotha', *Al-Huda* (Acre), no. 62, (April 1982), pp. 38-42 (in Arabic).

12. Rizkallah, *Culture et développement,* p. 347.

13. Sayigh, *Economies of the Arab World,* p. 234.

14. 'Les Caractéristiques générales de la force ouvrière en Syrie', *Syrie et le Monde Arabe,* (25 February 1981), p. 2.

15. Ibid., p. 3.

16. World Bank, (hereafter WB), 'World Development Report' (hereafter WDR), 1981, p. 66.

17. The ages of the active population in Syria differ from those of Western countries. According to the official division of the Syrian population, the active age begins at fifteen; in the West, it begins at twenty.

18. 'Les Caractéristiques générales', *Syrie et le Monde Arabe*, p. 3.
19. 'Le Bureau International du Travail, Genève, 1964', *Syrie et le Monde Arabe*, p. 5.
20. See Sayigh, *Economies of the Arab World*, p. 234.
21. 'Les Caractéristiques générales', *Syrie et le Monde Arabe*, p. 4.
22. *Tishrin* (Damascus), 14 June 1977 (in Arabic).
23. *Kifah al-Arabi* (Beirut), 23 April 1979 (in Arabic).
24. Sayigh, *Economies of the Arab World*, p. 248.
25. *QER, AS,* Syria, Lebanon and Cyprus, 1977, p. 14.
26. *QER, AS,* Syria and Jordan, 1982, p. 20.
27. *Al-Ba'ath* (Damascus), 7 March 1982 (in Arabic).
28. WB, *Annual Report, 1978,* p. 65.
29. *Al-Ba'ath* (Damascus), 10 March 1982 (in Arabic).
30. WB, WDR, 1981, p. 174.
31. Ibid.
32. Ibid.
33. Ibid.
34. *UN Statistical Year Book 1981,* p. 143.
35. Sayigh, *Economies of the Arab World*, p. 231.
36. Syria Central Bureau of Statistics, *Statistical Abstracts,* from 1975-1981 (in Arabic).
37. Sayigh, *Economies of the Arab World*, p. 232.
38. Syria, *Statistical Abstract*, 1981.
39. Sayigh, *Economies of the Arab World*.
40. Syria *Statistical Abstract*, 1981.
41. 'Evolution of the Industrial and the Agricultural Sectors during 1982', *Syrie et le Monde Arabe,* (25 October 1983), p. 2.
42. 'L'Economie de la Syrie, secteur par secteur', *Syrie et le Monde Arabe,* (25 August 1983), pp. 3-4.
43. Sayigh, *Economies of the Arab World*, pp. 238-9.
44. 'L'Economie de la Syrie', p. 7.
45. Ibid., p. 6.
46. *QER, AS,* Syria and Jordan, 1982, p. 12.
47. The number of cattle rose from 528,000 head in 1970 to 817,000 in 1981, and sheep from 5,886,000 head to 11,738,000. The number of goats increased from 684,000 head in 1974 to 1,000,000 in 1980. Poultry units increased from 19,677 in 1976 to 44,932 in 1979. See *UN Statistical Year Book,* 1981; 'L'Economie de la Syrie', p. 6; and *QER, AS,* Syria and Jordan, 1982, p. 12.
48. 'L'Economie de la Syrie', p. 6.
49. *QER, AS,* Syria and Jordan, 1982, p. 12.
50. *QER, AS,* Syria, Lebanon and Cyprus, 1975, pp. 13-14.
51. *QER, AS,* Syria and Jordan, 1982, p. 11.
52. *MEED,* vol. 28, no. 2, (13 January 1984), p. 22.
53. Ibid.
54. *QER, AS,* Syria and Jordan, 1982, p. 11.
55. 'L'Economie de la Syrie', p. 4.
56. *MEED,* (13 January 1984), pp. 23-4.
57. Ibid., p. 24.
58. Ibid.
59. Ibid., pp. 35-6.
60. *QER, AS,* Syria, Lebanon and Cyprus, 1975, p. 7; and Syria and Jordan, 1982, p. 11.
61. *MEED,* (13 January 1984).
62. 'L'Economie de la Syrie', p. 9; *QER, AS,* Syria and Jordan, 1981, p. 10.

63. *MEED*, (13 January 1984), p. 23.
64. 'L'Economie de la Syrie', p. 8.
65. For instance, oil from the Suweidia field, which accounts for 70 per cent of total national output, has a gravity of 24-5 grades API, with a 3.5 per cent sulphur content, making it difficult to refine. In addition, the low pressure of Syrian oil poses difficulties in getting it out of the ground. See 'L'Economie de la Syrie' and *MEED* (13 January 1984), p. 23.
66. *QER, AS,* Syria, Lebanon and Cyprus, 1977, p. 12.
67. *QER, AS,* Syria and Jordan, 1982, p. 15.
68. It was considered the most promising new hydrocarbon discovery to have been made in Syria in years. Ibid., p. 16.
69. 'L'Economie de la Syrie', p. 10.
70. *QER, AS,* Syria and Jordan, 1981, p. 12; and 1982, p. 16.
71. Ibid.
72. *Tishrin,* 19 December 1979.
73. Sayigh, *Economies of the Arab World,* pp. 241-3.
74. *QER, AS,* Syria and Jordan, 1982, p. 17.
75. Ibid., p. 9.
76. See 'Investment' in the fourth five year plan (1976-80) and in the fifth plan, in *QER, AS,* Syria, Lebanon and Cyprus, 1977, p. 16, and 1982, pp. 10, 17.
77. *QER, AS,* Syria and Jordan, 1982, p. 17.
78. 'L'Economie de la Syrie', p. 12.
79. Ibid., p. 11.
80. 'Le Développement du secteur industriel pendant la dernière decade', *Syrie et le Monde Arabe,* (15 January 1984), p. 3.
81. Ibid., p. 8.
82. Ibid.
83. *MEED*, vol. 28, no. 6, (24 February 1984), p. 61.
84. 'L'Economie de la Syrie', p. 4.
85. *MEED*, (20 January 1984).
86. *QER, AS,* Syria, Lebanon and Cyprus, 1976, p. 10, and Syria and Jordan, 1982, p. 18.
87. *MEED*, (20 January 1984).
88. 'Le Développement du secteur industriel', p. 7.
89. *QER, AS,* Syria, Lebanon and Cyprus, 1975, p. 10, and 1977, p. 12; Syria and Jordan, 1982, p. 17.
90. *QER, AS,* Syria and Jordan, 1981, p. 9 and 1982, p. 13.
91. 'L'Economie de la Syrie', p. 16.
92. Ibid., p. 10.
93. See Michel Chatelur, 'La Croissance économique: mutation des structures et dynamisme de Déséquilibre', *La Syrie d'Aujourd'hui (publié* sous le direction d'André Raymond, C.N.R.S., Paris, 1980)), pp. 242-6.
94. Fred Lawson, 'Social Basis for the Hamah Revolt', *MERIP Reports* (Washington, D.C.), no. 110, November 1982.
95. 'L'essor industriel dans la region de Damas', *Syrie et le Monde Arabe.* (25 February 1984), p. 15.
96. See Fred Lawson, 'Comment le régime du President Al-Assad s'emploie à remodeler l'économie Syrienne', *Le Monde Diplomatique,* no. 358, (January 1984), pp. 12-13.
97. *QER, AS,* Syria, Lebanon and Cyprus, 1973, p. 9.
98. *QER, AS,* Syria and Jordan, 1982, pp. 18-19.
99. *QER, AS,* Syria, Lebanon and Cyprus, 1976, p. 10.
100. *QER, AS,* Syria and Jordan, 1982, pp. 19.
101. *MEED*, vol. 28, no. 4, (27 January 1984), p. 34.

102. *MEED*, vol. 28, no. 14, (6 April 1984), p. 59.

103. *QER, AS*, Syria, Lebanon and Cyprus, 1973, p. 10.

104. 'Les Ports de Lattaquie, Tartous et Banias', *Syrie et le Monde Arabe*, (25 September 1983), p. 1.

105. Ibid., p. 2.

106. Ibid., p. 4.

107. 'L'Economie de la Syrie', p. 9.

108. *UN Statistical Year Book*, 1981.

109. *MEED*, Special Report, (December 1983), p. 42.

110. *MEED*, Special Report, p. 42.

111. Fred Lawson, 'Comment le régime', p. 13.

112. Syria received almost all its US allocation for 1983, the cut-off having come only after President Reagan's ban of this aid in November 1983. According to the US Agency for International Development, more than US $158 million was affected. See *MEED*, vol. 27, no. 48, (2 December 1983) and vol. 28, no. 14, (April 1984), p. 59.

113. 'Les Transformations économiques et les perspectives de développement agricole', *Syrie et le Monde Arabe*, (25 March 1983).

114. The accounts for 1983-4 are from *QER*, Syria and Jordan, June 1984, p. 13.

115. According to John Roberts, Syria's net foreign assets position went into the red in 1980, with a tally of minus L. Syr. 1,668.7 million (US $425 million); in 1981, the figure fell to minus L. Syr. 3,114 million (US $793.1 million); in 1982, to minus L. Syr. 4,079.8 million (US $1,039.1 million); see *MEED*, vol. 27, no. 49 (9 December 1983), p. 47.

116. *QER*, Syria and Jordan, June 1984, pp. 5, 13-14.

117. Ibid., p. 14.

118. The EEC share of Syrian exports rose from 34.7 per cent in 1971 to 61.6 per cent in 1980 and to 80 per cent in 1981; its share of Syria's imports rose from 24.0 per cent in 1971 to more than 30 per cent in 1980-1. Between 1971 and 1980, the Eastern-bloc countries accounted for about 25 per cent per year of the exports and less than 20 per cent of the imports.

119. 'L'Economie de la Syrie', p. 14.

120. Ibid., p. 17.

121. *MEED*, vol. 27, no. 49, (9 December 1983), p. 47.

122. 'Le Rôle de l'Union Soviétique dans les ventes d'équipements militaires au tiers-monde', *Le Monde Diplomatique*, (8 April 1984), p. 8.

123. *QER*, Syria and Jordan, June 1984, p. 13.

4 THE EVOLUTION OF SYRIAN POWER, 1948-1984

Zeev Ma'oz

Introduction

Power is the currency of politics. Yet, unlike other assets of high liquidity, the operational meaning of this concept is extremely elusive, owing probably to the wide variety of definitions and to the ambiguity surrounding its tangible and intangible foundations. Nevertheless, there are three general approaches to the conceptualisation and measurement of power in international relations:[1] (a) control over resources, (b) control over actors, and (c) control over events and outcomes. Whereas the two latter approaches have received wide academic attention, the first conception seems best to represent what the practitioners of politics have in mind when they refer to national power:[2] a combination of tangible and intangible — quantitative and qualitative — resources that define to a large extent a nation's ability to pursue its goals in world affairs. As one of the most prominent theoreticians of power politics phrased it:

> A nation does not necessarily attain the maximum of national power because it is very rich in natural resources, possesses a very large population, or has built an enormous industrial and military establishment. It attains that maximum when it has at its disposal a sufficient quality and quantity *in the right admixture* of those resources of power which would allow it to pursue a given foreign policy with a maximum chance of success.[3] [Emphasis added.]

The centrality of power-related issues among all the considerations underlying the making of a nation's foreign policy is reflected both in theory and in practice. One may insist on attributing unique features to the nation-building and policy-making processes of states, and unique properties to their social and political structures or to their ideologies and national aspirations. The pursuit of power as a means of accomplishing national goals is, however, perhaps the most basic generalisation that the theory of international relations can offer. The accumulation and allocation of resources capture the essence of political behaviour over time and across national boundaries; hence, any account of a nation's domestic and foreign politics must inevitably be concerned with the intimate link between its power and its behaviour.

This study addresses three fundamental questions concerning Syria's history and foreign policy: (1) What are the factors that make up Syria's national power, and how did they account for changes in its power over time? (2) How did this power evolve over time in relative terms, i.e. compared to changes in the power of other states in the Middle East? (3) What is the relationship between the structural evolution of Syria's power and its foreign policy?

The first question requires focusing on Syria as an isolated unit of analysis. Changes in the various dimensions of Syrian power will be discussed in terms of domestic political and social processes — in particular, the nature and stability of its various regimes. The accumulation and allocation of national resources will be discussed independently of foreign-policy calculations, such as those stemming from the Arab-Israeli conflict or inter-Arab political struggles. The second question, which focuses on Syria's relative power-status, discusses processes of resource accumulation and allocation in relation to parallel processes in neighbouring states that were the relevant reference group for Syrian power-related calculi. Here, the relationship between international developments and changes in Syria's capabilities is addressed. The third question requires an integration of the previous perspectives in an attempt to analyse the extent to which Syria's control over resources coincided with its control over external actors and events.

Dimensions of Syrian Power

An analysis of the evolution of Syrian power must take into account three dimensions of resources that have traditionally been considered to compose the main — though not the exclusive — determinants of national power, defined as a combination of resources. These dimensions are as follows: the demographic, the economic and the military. The demographic dimension, defined in terms of population, represents the basic pool of human resources from which a government can extract other forms of resources (such as economic resources in the form of taxes or labour, political resources in the form of legitimacy and public support, and military resources in the form of personnel).[4] Although a brief discussion of demographics as an independent dimension of national power seems adequate, most subsequent analyses in this chapter will use Syria's population as a control variable for both the economic and military dimensions of power.

The economic dimension of power will be represented by Syria's gross national product (GNP), which is seen as the best single indicator of a nation's economic and technological capacity.[5] As mentioned above, the need to control for changes in the population size suggests the use of per-capita GNP as an index of economic power.

Finally, the military dimension of power is represented by two indicators: personnel and expenditures. More specifically, the extent to which a government is capable of extracting human and material resources from the society in its pursuit of national security aims is measured by the size of its military personnel as a proportion of the population and by its financial expenditures on the military as a proportion of GNP. These indices of economic and military power will now be compared for Syria and its neighbours to assess the relative aspect of Syrian power.[6]

The Demographic Dimension

In 1947, the population of Syria was estimated (according to UN figures) to be 3.05 million people. Nearly 20 per cent of the population was considered urban, i.e. residing in towns and cities of 100,000 people or more. Syria's population grew at an average annual rate of 2.7 per cent; its urban population, though, increased at an average annual rate of 4.7 per cent (owing both to natural growth rates and to internal migration). Both the natural growth rate of Syria's population as a whole and the change in the size of its urban population were not significantly different from what took place in Egypt, Iraq or Jordan. Further, some interesting demographic characteristics of the Syrian population exhibited a considerable similarity to other Arab states. For example, in 1975 the infant mortality rate in Syria stood at 93 per 1,000 live births, compared with 100 in Egypt and Iraq and 97 in Jordan; life expectancy was estimated at 57 years, compared with 53 years in Egypt and Iraq and 54 years in Jordan; and the literacy rate was 40 per cent, compared with 40 per cent in Egypt and 50 per cent in Jordan (but only 26 per cent in Iraq).[7] These demographic indicators — namely, high growth rate of the total population, rapid urbanisation rate exceeding the natural growth rate, high rate of infant mortality, relatively low level of life expectancy and low literacy rate — placed Syria in the category of the developing countries.[8] These indicators also suggest that the demographic dimension is a relative constraint on Syrian power because of the fact that Syria's population has been growing at a rate that imposes tremendous resource-allocation and development-related problems for the government in power. This point will become more apparent during the discussion of the economic dimension of Syrian power. At present, Syria's total population is estimated to be 10.4 million, of which nearly 38 per cent reside in cities of 100,000 people or more.

Economic Power

Figures for Syria's gross national product are available for the years 1953-84. In 1953, the Syrian GNP was estimated at US $936 million (at 1974 constant prices); in 1984, at nearly US $9 billion. Figure 4.1 depicts the changes in per-capita GNP over the 32 years for which data are available. As is evident from the figure, Syria clearly did not benefit economically from its 1958-61 union with Egypt. Following its secession from this union, however, Syria's economic power increased at a fairly rapid pace (an average annual growth rate of 6.0 per cent as of 1962). The relative contribution of various sectors to Syria's gross domestic product (GDP) indicates increasing bureaucratisation and institutionalisation of Syrian society over time. For example, nearly 25 per cent of the GDP in 1960 was accounted for by the agricultural sector; this figure declined to 20 per cent in 1978. Twenty-two per cent of the 1960 GDP was accounted for by the industrial sector; this figure also declined to 20 per cent in 1978. The decline in the relative contribution to Syrian economic power of the two sectors was matched by the increase in the services sector, from 54 per cent in 1960 to 60 per cent in 1978.[9] Thus, while Syrian regimes may have been struggling with a multitude of social and economic difficulties over the years, both the absolute and relative amounts of economic resources at their disposal increased markedly. Most noticeable in this regard are the periods of 1968-71 and 1974-80, which were characterised by very steep economic growth rates.

Military Power

The Syrian army has exhibited probably the most dramatic numerical increase compared with any other army in the Middle East. In 1947, it consisted of 10,000 soldiers; in 1984, some 362,000 soldiers (of which nearly 100,000 soldiers were active reservists). In relative terms, Syrian military personnel represented about two-tenths of one per cent of the population in 1947; this climbed to nearly 3.5 per cent in 1984. If

Figure 4.1: Syrian Per-capita GNP, 1953-1984

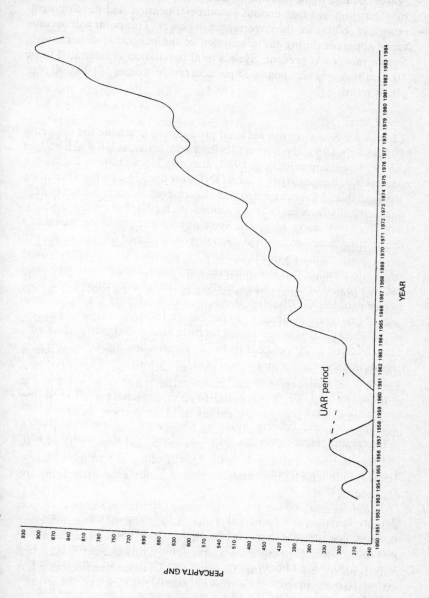

the basis for measuring this rate of growth is the working-age population, these figures then become more impressive. Syrian military personnel increased from 2.3 per cent of the working-age population in 1965 to 6.3 per cent in 1975, an average annual growth rate of 39.7 per cent.[10]

The most dramatic increases in the relative proportion of the Syrian army occurred in the periods immediately following Arab-Israeli wars (1957-8, 1968-72, 1974-6 and 1982-4). Although evidence about the quality of the Syrian army is highly unreliable, several observers have noted the marked improvement in the technical and tactical quality of the average Syrian soldier. Indeed, the performance of the Syrian army as a whole during the 1973 Yom Kippur war and the 1982 Lebanon war reflects this trend.[11] The qualitative improvements can be attributed to sophisticated weapons that can be operated easily and reliably even by non-technically skilled soldiers, as well as to improvements in tactical training and command and control structures.

The investment in the military dimension of power is also exhibited by the rising proportion of Syria's GNP that has been allocated to the military, from about 2.9 per cent in 1953 to about 30 per cent in 1984. When these figures are coupled with the massive military aid in the form of both equipment and advisers that has been provided by the Soviet Union, it is understandable that the Syrian army grew tremendously both in size and quality, especially after 1970. This investment has been due in large measure to the reliance of the Syrian Ba'ath regime on the army as the single most important source of legitimacy and to the high level of military involvement in Syrian domestic politics. There was, however, a price paid for the government's increased military spending: a relative decline in welfare-related spending. Syrian government spending on education as a proportion of the GNP declined at an average annual rate of 3.3 per cent, and on health at an average annual rate of 5.3 per cent over the period from 1970-84,[12] in addition to the sizeable shift in manpower allocation to the military. These trends in human and material resource allocation to the army are depicted in Figure 4.2.

The increasing size of the Syrian army in terms of various weapon systems is shown in Table 4.1 (for four distinct periods). In considering the evolution of Syrian military power, the massive Soviet aid cannot be ignored. Although numerical information on this subject is less than fully reliable, the US Arms Control and Disarmament Agency has estimated the value of Syria's arms imports from the Soviet Union to be US $780 million in 1978 and US $1,325 million in 1984.

Figure 4.2: Syrian Relative Capabilities, 1948-1984

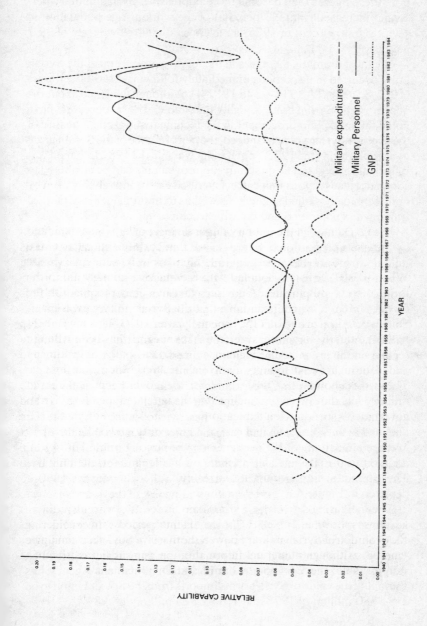

Table 4.1: Syrian Weapon Systems

Year	Tanks	Artillery Regiments	Combat Aircraft	Missile Batteries
1969	470 (25%)	6 (5%)	145 (10%)	6 (3%)
1973	1270 (25%)	7 (5%)	326 (22%)	12 (15%)
1978	2600 (14%)	7 (0%)	392 (9%)	51 (19%)
1984	4700 (15%)	17 (59%)	503 (9%)	102 (27%)

Notes: Numbers in parentheses are average annual rates of change.
Missile batteries include only surface-to-air (SAM 2-3 missiles) up to 1972. From 1973, they include SAM 6 surface-to-air and Frog and squad surface-to-surface missiles. In addition, 1984 missile batteries include Soviet-operated SAM-5 surface-to-air missiles.
Source: International Institute for Strategic Studies, *The Military Balance*, London.

Although the figures shown suggest an increasingly large allocation of human and material resources to the army, this military emphasis seems highly correlated with the amount of overall resources available to the government. (For example, the correlation between military personnel as a proportion of the population and per-capita GNP is $r = 0.904$ (p. 001), while the correlation between military expenditures as a proportion of overall GNP and the per-capita GNP is $r = 0.852$ (p .001)). Yet, the extent to which the Assad regime has been willing to make sacrifices in social welfare expenditures (such as health and education) in order to enhance Syria's military power suggests two important points. First, the intimate political links between the Ba'ath regime and the army are manifested in the latter's rapid rise in size and material resources. Assad's regime has invested in the army more than any other Syrian regime had done, and probably more than have most other military regimes in the contemporary international system. Second, one of the most significant returns of this investment has been Syria's unprecedented political stability, at least during the 1970-80 period. At least in the short term, the willingness of the Assad regime to favour the military in the arms-butter trade-off apparently did not damage its political viability. To the extent that domestic stability has been threatened, the army seems to be both willing and able to suppress the opposition (although friction within the army is more difficult to suppress or relieve by changes in budgetary allocations).[13]

Syria's Relative Power: A Comparative Perspective

This section will discuss the external incentives of Syria's resource-accumulation and resource-allocation processes, and compare the changes in Syrian resources to parallel changes in key Middle Eastern states. Before going into the substance of this comparison two methodological points need to be made: first, the states to be used for this comparison must be specified; second, the method of such a comparison of resources over an extended period of time must be explicated.

The selection of states for a comparative discussion of national power is based on the notion of relevant reference groups. Briefly, a reference group in international relations is a set of states with which a given country interacts on a fairly regular basis. In the case of power-related calculations, a state will consider its relevant reference group to consist of those states with which this interaction is predominantly competitive.[14] In other words, a state will compare its own power to the power of the other states it considers rivals or political opponents. Given this criterion, the relevant reference group for Syria consists of Israel, Jordan, Iraq, Turkey, Egypt and Lebanon. With the exception of Egypt, these states are geographically contiguous to Syria. Egypt, of course, has been Syria's major political rival in inter-Arab politics.

The comparison of Syria's power with that of its relevant reference group will be made by treating each of the indicators of power as a proportion of the total value for all states. For example, in examining the relative change in Syrian military personnel over time, we divided the number of Syrian soldiers by the sum of all soldiers included in the relevant reference group (Syrian soldiers too). This proportional measure allows a comparative assessment of changes regarding each of the indicators discussed in the previous section. In addition, a composite index of national capabilities, which is widely used in the quantitative international relations literature, will be employed to provide an overall summary of Syria's relative power across all indicators.[15]

Distinct Power Indicators

Population: Syria's population growth rate was rapid, not only in terms of the absolute growth of the society, but also in relative terms. In 1947 the Syrian population constituted 6.2 per cent of the (combined) population of its reference group of states. In 1984, its population amounted to 8 per cent of this population. In fact, of these six nations in the set, Syria and Iraq are the only ones that exhibited, in relative terms, significant population growth over the 38-year period compared.

GNP: In contrast, Syria's relative economic power has gone through significant fluctuations. Its relative GNP first declined from 8.2 per cent of the combined GNP in 1953 to 4.6 per cent in 1961, an annual decline rate of nearly 12 per cent. From 1962-73, Syria's relative GNP remained fairly constant at about 5.2 per cent of the combined GNP. The 1974-80 period exhibited a gradual growth to 6.0 per cent; and the most recent period, 1981-4, again suggests a marked decline, to 5 per cent of the combined GNP. Thus, in contrast to the real growth of its national economic resources in historical terms, which was discussed in the previous section, it seems that Syria has not been able to compete successfully with its neighbours in economic terms. Apparently, the reasons for its somewhat abysmal economic performance have, in part, very little to do with Syria's economic policies: its share of the combined GNP is a function of the economic performance of the other states. Yet, as we shall show below, the fluctuations in Syria's relative economic power are not independent of the fluctuations in its military power.

Military Power: The most potent indicator of the change in overall Syrian power is the state's military personnel. In 1947 the Syrian army accounted for 1.3 per cent of the combined military personnel of the reference group; in 1984, this figure had risen to 14.5 per cent, an average annual growth rate of 3.9 per cent. The relative size of the Syrian army has increased markedly since 1970, even when taking into account the parallel relative growth of Israel's army since 1973 and of Iraq's since 1980 (owing to the Iran-Iraq war).

A similar trend is exhibited by Syrian military expenditures, which accounted for 4.4 per cent of the combined total of the reference group in 1947, but 11.6 per cent in 1984, an average annual growth rate of 1.2 per cent. Although in this case the upward trend was not entirely clear-cut, exhibiting some fluctuations over the period, it correlated rather highly with the changes in the relative size of the Syrian armed forces ($r = 0.726$; $p\ 0.01$).

An Integrated Assessment of Syria's Relative Power

The changes in the economic and military dimensions of Syria's relative power suggest that Assad's regime has put a strong emphasis on increasing its military power largely at the expense of its relative economic power. To what extent has this calculus affected Syria's

Figure 4.3: Relative Capabilities of Egypt, Syria and Israel 1948-1984

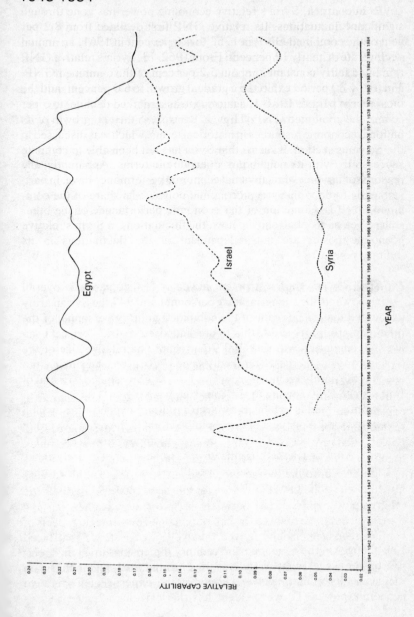

overall power? The answer to this question may be derived from Figure 4.3, which presents the integrated measures of national power for Syria, Egypt and Israel.

Figure 4.3 illustrates that, by and large, the gap in relative power between Syria and its main opponent, Israel, has consistently narrowed since 1970. Although this trend is not very dramatic, it is none the less evident that the heavy military build-up after the 1973 Yom Kippur war and following the 1982 Lebanon war made Syria an important military factor in the Middle East. The trends are evident when Syria's relative power is compared to that of Egypt, Syria's main rival in inter-Arab politics.

The general conclusion stemming from a comparative analysis of Syria's relative power is that the country's heavy emphasis on military resources has brought about a relative stagnation of its economic resources. At the same time, this emphasis on military power has altered the balance of power in the Middle East. In a word, contemporary Syria has become a formidable factor in Middle Eastern power politics.

Conclusion: The Political Implications of Syria's Power

Syria has been involved in 26 inter-state disputes that included the threat, display and use of armed force since 1948. Five of these have been cases of severe levels of violence, namely, inter-state wars.[16] Syria initiated 12 of these disputes (including three wars). Twenty-two of the conflicts were against Israel, and the rest (one each) against Jordan, Turkey, Iraq and Lebanon. It might be imagined that the success rate in these disputes would correlate with Syria's power, if there is indeed a relationship between the notions of power as control over resources and power as control over outcomes. Reality, however, is more complex than this somewhat simplistic theoretical proposition.

With respect to the Syrian-Israeli disputes, Syria's overall success rate has been quite low. The reason for this does not lie primarily in the relative power differentials between the two states. Rather, the low Syrian success rate seems to be better explained by strategic aspects of conflict management and by the relatively higher stakes that faced Israel in these confrontations.[17] None the less, the relatively respectable performances of the Syrian army in the 1973 and 1982 wars suggest a significant improvement in the qualitative aspects of Syrian military power.

The disputes between Syria and other Arab states were contained at relatively low levels, with one notable exception. Thus, the impact of Syria's power on their outcomes was insignificant. In the exceptional case — intervention in the Jordanian civil war of September 1970 — Syria suffered a devastating political and military defeat. Yet, to a large extent, this defeat can be accounted for in terms of self-imposed constraints by Syria.

It seems, therefore, that its heavy investment in military power has had mixed and ambiguous effects on Syria's international performance. Domestically, on the other hand, Syria's investment in military power, though made at the cost of diminishing investments in social welfare, is in large part responsible for the relative stability of the present Ba'ath regime.

Notes

1. Jeffrey Hart, 'Three Approaches to the Measurement of Power in International Relations', *International Organization,* vol. 30, no. 2, (April 1976), pp. 289-305.

2. Intuitively, these three approaches seem to be highly correlated with one other: the more resources a political unit controls, the greater its capacity to influence the behaviour of other units, and the more likely it is to determine the course of events in its external environment. Although such hypotheses underlie much of the conventional thinking of political leaders, there is growing evidence that it is at odds with reality, in many instances. See, for example, Zeev Ma'oz, *Paths to Conflict: International Dispute Initiation, 1816-1976* (Westview Press, Boulder, 1982), pp 161-202; and Frank W. Wayman, J. David Singer and Gary Goerts, 'Capabilities, Allocations and Success in Militarized Disputes and Wars, 1816-1976', *International Studies Quarterly,* vol. 27, no. 4 (December 1983), pp. 497-575.

3. Hans J. Morgenthau, *Politics Among Nations*, 3rd edn (Knopf, New York, 1964), p. 144. On the relationships between quality and quantity in force deployment, see Michael Handel, 'Numbers Do Count: The Question of Quality Versus Quantity', *Journal of Strategic Studies,* vol. 4, no. 3 (September 1981), pp. 225-60.

4. Morgenthau, *Politics Among Nations,* p. 144. Morgenthau notes that a large population can be both a source of strength and a source of weakness for a nation. Thus, one must be careful about treating population as an independent indicator of national power. The idea that a nation's population can be a source of other aspects of national power is discussed by A.F.K. Organski and Jack Kugler, *The War Ledger* (University of Chicago Press, Chicago, 1980), pp. 30-8, 68-86.

5. Organski and Kugler, *The War Ledger, p. 38.*

6. The major sources from which the various figures were derived are the following: International Institute for Strategic Studies, *The Military Balance* (annual publication), London, 1966-84; Stockholm International Peace Research Institute, *SIPRI Yearbook of World Armaments and Disarmament* (annual publication), 1950-84 (Humanities Press, New York); US Arms Control and Disarmament Agency, *World Military Expenditures and Arms Transfers* (occasional publication), 1961-80; International Monetary Fund, *International Financial Statistics* (annual publication), Washington DC, 1948-84; *UN Statistical Yearbook;* Correlates of War Project, *National Capabilities, 1816-1980* (Interuniversity Consortium for Political and Social Research,

Ann Arbor). Both GNP and military expenditure figures were calculated using 1974 constant dollars. Conversion and adjustment procedures are described in US Arms Control and Disarmament Agency, *World Military Expenditures and Arms Transfers, 1966-1975*, pp. 6-11.

7. Bruce Russett and Harvey Starr, *World Politics: The Menu for Choice* (Freeman, San Francisco, 1981), pp. 575-83.

8. On the classification of states into developed and developing countries according to demographic and economic indicators, see, *inter alia*, Gabriel A. Almond and G. Bringham Powell, Jr., *Comparative Politics*, 2nd edn (Little Brown, Boston, 1978), pp. 3-25.

9. See Richard L. Taylor and David A. Jodice, *World Handbook of Political and Social Indicators*, 3rd edn (Yale University Press, New Haven, 1983), vol. 1, pp. 217-25. Also, see the chapter by Kais Firro in this volume.

10. Taylor and Jodice, *World Handbook*, p. 37. This annual growth rate is second only to Israel's. Since the figures for Israel represent only changes in the size of its standing army (excluding reserves), however, the high growth rate of Israeli military personnel reflects only an increasing reliance on standing forces. Thus, the growth rates for Israel are vastly over-estimated and are probably lower than the comparable figures for Syria. This point will be clarified in the following section.

11. See Trevor Dupuy, *Elusive Victory: The Arab-Israeli Wars*, (Westview Press, Boulder, 1977) and Ray Cline, *World Power Trends and US Foreign Policy for the 1980's*, (Westview Press, Boulder, 1980).

12. Taylor and Jodice, *World Handbook*, p. 239.

13. See Moshe Maoz's chapter in this volume.

14. For a more elaborate exposition of this concept, see Zeev Maoz, *Paths to Conflict*, pp. 87-90, 120-2.

15. In general, this index is obtained by averaging the separate relative power indices, and is computed as:

$$RC = \frac{1}{k} \sum_{i=1}^{k} \left[\frac{r_i}{\sum_{j=1}^{n} r_{ij}} \right]$$

Where: k = number of distinct power indicators
r = a given indicator of power
n = number of states

This measure was originally developed in J. David Singer, Stuart Bremer and John Stuckey, 'Capability Distribution, Uncertainty, and Major Power War, 1820-1965', pp. 19-48 in Bruce M. Russett (ed.), *Peace, War and Numbers* (Sage, Beverly Hills, 1972). See also James L. Ray and J. David Singer, 'Measuring the Concentration of Power in the International System', *Sociological Methods and Research*, vol. 1, no. 4 (December 1973), pp. 403-37, and Bruce Bueno de Mesquita, *The War Trap* (Yale University Press, New Haven, 1981), pp. 101-9. The indicators used here are population, GNP, military expenditures and military personnel.

16. For the precise definition of militarised inter-state disputes and wars, see Charles S. Gochman and Zeev Maoz, 'Militarized Interstate Disputes, 1816-1976; Procedures, Patterns, Insights', *Journal of Conflict Resolution*, vol. 28, no. 4 (December 1984), pp. 585-615.

17. See Zeev Maoz and Avner Yaniv, 'Game, Supergame and Compound Escalation: Israel and Syria, 1948-1984', Mimeo, University of Haifa, July 1984.

PART II

SYRIA AND ITS NEIGHBOURS

5 CONFLICT AND ACCOMMODATION IN TURKISH-SYRIAN RELATIONS

David K. Kushner

The Background

Several years following the exchange of diplomatic representatives between Turkey and newly-independent Syria in 1946, relations between these two neighbouring countries remained markedly chilly. Memories of the recent past seemed to have formed this attitude in no small way. Turks remembered the treason of Arab-Syrian nationalist circles during World War I and the stab in the back they suffered from the Arab revolt. Syrians remembered the inimical... of their Ottoman masters and the heavy-handed methods...

5 CONFLICT AND ACCOMMODATION IN TURKISH-SYRIAN RELATIONS

David Kushner

The Background[1]

Several years following the exchange of direct diplomatic representatives between Turkey and newly-independent Syria in 1946, relations between these two neighbouring countries remained markedly chilly. Memories of the recent past seemed to have formed this attitude in no small way: Turks remembered the 'treason' of Arab-Syrian nationalist circles during World War I and the 'stab in the back' they suffered from the Arab revolt; Syrians remembered the misrule of their Ottoman masters and the heavy-handed methods the latter adopted in attempting to suppress the nascent Syrian-Arab nationalist movement. More important, perhaps, Syrians were unable to forget what seemed to them as the arbitrary transfer of the province of Alexandretta by the French mandatory authorities into the hands of the Turks on the eve of World War II. In the eyes of the Syrians, Alexandretta (or Hatay, as it was named by the Turks) was the legal property of the Syrian people, and the Turks were nothing but usurpers.[2]

An unexpected but short interlude of improved relations occurred in 1949, following the rise to power in Syria of Colonel Husni al-Za'im, who pledged himself as an avowed enemy of communism in the area and saw for Turkey an important role in the struggle against Soviet expansionism. Following his overthrow, however, relations between Turkey and Syria deteriorated once again. Syria, for one thing, frowned upon Turkey's recognition of Israel and newly established relations with the Jewish state. Secondly, Syria resisted the sustained efforts made by Turkey to prompt Arab countries into joining the Western system of alliances. When in early 1955, Faris al-Khuri's government, invited Turkish Prime Minister Adnan Menderes for discussions on the matter, public resentment reached such a high point that whatever plans existed for Syria's joining with Turkey had to be abandoned. From then on, relations gradually drifted into confrontation. Internal instability and the growing influence in Syria of radical nationalist and leftist elements, its entry into an alliance with Egypt and its acceptance of military and economic aid from the Soviet Union turned Syria, in Turkish eyes, into a real threat to Turkey's southern border, as well as to Western interests in the Middle East. During the upheavals in Jordan in April 1957, Turkey concentrated troops along the border with Syria as a measure of warning and intimidation. A more serious crisis broke out in August, when new concentrations of Turkish troops (meant to prevent Syria from strengthening its ties with the Soviet Union) led to partial mobilisation in Syria, a Syrian complaint to the United Nations and public warning by the Soviet Union against intervention. Tension subsided only after the gradual withdrawal of the Turkish forces.

Although Turkey welcomed the Egyptian-Syrian union in February 1958 as a possible means of curbing the Soviet and communist influences in its southern neighbour, no significant improvement in relations occurred. The United Arab Republic pursued the radical Pan-Arab and anti-Western policies that were pursued earlier in both Egypt and Syria, while Turkey continued to see itself in the role of guardian of Western interests in the area. Turkish policies did not change significantly even after the military take-over in May 1960, which laid the foundations of the Second Turkish Republic.

Towards Normalisation and Co-operation

Upon the dissolution of the UAR in September 1961, Turkey was the second state after Jordan to recognise the new regime in Damascus, a step leading to an immediate rupture in Turkey's relations with Egypt. Obviously Turkey hoped, as she had on several occasions in the past, that quick recognition of the new regime would help improve relations with its southern neighbour. Also implicit in this step was the displeasure which Turkey felt towards the UAR and its Pan-Arab ideology. It was hoped that Syria, emerging from an unsuccessful experiment, would be more amenable to Turkish overtures.

Circumstances, however, did not support these expectations. With a shaky parliamentary regime desperately seeking to cling to power and with radical Nasserist and Ba'athist elements still exercising strong influence, Syria held out little hope for a drastic reorientation of its foreign policy. In fact, following the ascendancy of the Ba'ath in March 1963, there was renewed emphasis on Arab unity, socialism, and co-operation with the Soviet bloc. These policies, especially socialism and the pro-Soviet orientation, were further accentuated by the rise to power in February 1966 of the extreme Ba'athist faction headed by Salah Jedid. The new ruling group was to give the communists, for the first time in Syrian history, representation in the government.

Despite these developments, there was some positive change in the nature of Turkish-Syrian relations during this period. It consisted of the removal of the *confrontational* element that had characterised these relations for so long. In the world arena, an easing of tensions between the superpowers was accompanied by the first signs of Turkish *rapprochement* with the Soviet bloc. This trend naturally had its effect on Turkey's view of Soviet allies in the Middle East. At the same time, the collapse of the original Baghdad Pact following the Qasim revolution in Iraq in 1958 clearly demonstrated to Turkey (and to the West) the shaky character of regional alliances and significantly weakened its resolve to force Syria or any other Arab state into such a pact, which changing alignments would soon render of less importance anyway. Turkey continued, of course, to see Soviet penetration into the Middle East as a major threat to its security. Rather than attempting to change the *status quo,* however, it now preferred to adapt to the realities of the area and mitigate its differences with its pro-Soviet neighbours. Finally, Turkey's preoccupation during the early 1960s with the question of Cyprus gave further impetus to this partial 'disengagement' from Arab affairs. The combined result of all these factors was that Turkish-Syrian relations, while still cool, no longer revolved around the major question of the 'destiny' of the area, but around several relatively 'simple' bilateral issues. These included, for example, the problems of illegal border crossings and smuggling, the mutual restrictions on the property of citizens of the other country, the apportionment of waters of common rivers, and Syria's possible support for Turkish terrorists. Other issues, such as Alexandretta and Israel, constituted long-standing irritants, but they, too, were not allowed by both countries to get out of hand.

Turkey continued, in fact, to express a desire to set relations with Syria on a healthier basis. Its efforts in this regard, originating in Turkey's interest in mobilising support for its cause in Cyprus, were considerably stepped up with the general reorientation towards the Arab world, beginning in the mid-1960s. Turkey's determination not to repeat the mistakes of the past and to refrain from exhibiting a bias in favour of one Arab country over another was expected to attract the friendship of countries previously alienated by its policies. Similarly, the down-grading of relations with Israel and the adoption of a more pro-Arab stance on the Arab-Israeli conflict would, it was thought, remove a major obstacle in the way of improving relations with the Arab world. The Middle Eastern crisis of 1967 clearly demonstrated this shift in Turkish policy. Before the outbreak of hostilities, Foreign

Minister Ihsan Sabri Caglayangil told Arab ambassadors in Ankara that Turkey still hoped for peace and stability and that 'Turkey would not take any hostile action against her Arab neighbours nor allow NATO bases in Turkey to be used against the Arabs'. He specifically assured Syria that Turkey did not intend to concentrate troops on the frontier.[3] Turkey further showed its sympathy towards the Arab states during the war when it rushed to send food, clothing and medicine to affected civilians, with Syria being the first recipient of such aid.[4]

Following the war, Turkey repeatedly declared its opposition to the acquisition of territory by force (this could also have been a possible reference to Arab irredentism in Turkey). It was imperative for Israel to evacuate the territories it had occupied, Turkey announced, adding that Middle Eastern peace should be re-established in conformity with Arab interests.[5] Positions reflecting an even greater pro-Arab stance were expressed later during the October war of 1973, when Turkey once again pointed out that it had not allowed its military facilities to be used for shipping arms and equipment to Israel; that it had, by contrast, adopted a 'flexible' interpretation of the Montreux Straits Convention to allow Soviet arms shipments and that it had even postponed military manoeuvres on its Syrian borders.[6] By then, Turkey's prescriptions for a solution to the Middle Eastern crisis, while reiterating support for peace in conformity with UN Resolution 242 and demanding a complete evacuation by Israel of the occupied territories, also included the recognition of the 'legitimate rights of the Palestinians'.[7]

Turkey's support of the Arab countries did not escape the attention of Syria. Speaking on 21 August 1967, the Syrian Foreign Minister, Ibrahim Makhus, expressed his appreciation:

> Turkish support of the Arabs during the recent crisis, both in and outside the United Nations, has created feelings of appreciation and gratitude in the Syrian people ... and the continued support of Turkey to the just Arab cause will help to erase the traces of aggression and in consequence will strengthen the friendly and neighbourly relations between the two countries.[8]

A more tangible response, however, was slow to appear. If Turkish overtures towards the Arabs were expected to change their positions on the Cyprus question, then the results, at least with regard to Syria, were clearly disappointing. Preferring, as did other Arab states, the non-aligned Makarios to NATO-member Turkey and its clients on the island, Syria generally voted against Turkish interests in the United

Nations and in other international bodies. This anti-Turkish pattern was manifest even in Islamic conferences, in spite of the common religion shared by Syrians and Turks.[9]

Not until the early 1970s were there any significant signs of a change in Syrian policy towards Turkey. The real turning point in Turkish-Syrian relations, with Syria beginning to demonstrate a readiness to achieve understanding with its northern neighbour,[10] may be linked with the ousting from power in late 1970 of Salah Jedid and his replacement by the Ba'ath faction headed by Hafez al-Assad. Contrary to his predecessor, who had allowed the communists a foothold in the government and increased Syria's dependency upon the Soviet Union, thereby isolating Syria in the Arab world, Assad opted for a more flexible foreign policy. Though he maintained co-operation with the Soviet Union, he sought to bring about a reconciliation between Syria and the Arab states as well as the West. The change was reflected in Syria's internal policy as well through a departure from the strictly socialist policies of the previous regime towards a more open, pragmatic approach. All this was bound to have obvious repercussions on Syria's policy towards Turkey.

The change was expressed in various ways: renewed efforts by the Syrians to bring an end to some of their bilateral conflicts with Turkey, expansion of mutual trade, agreements on co-operation in various fields and a readiness to upgrade the level of contacts between the two countries. This last aspect was perhaps the most visible and dramatic. For years, what contacts there were had largely been held through junior diplomatic officials. Now, a frequent exchange of visits by ministers, including foreign ministers and other high-ranking government officials, began to take place. Although some of these visits were related to tangible difficulties between the two countries, others were concerned with real attempts to foster mutual relations and to effect important steps in co-operation. Whatever the case, the mere existence of high-level dialogue was in itself significant.

First of the foreign ministers 'to break the ice' was Turkey's Haluk Bayulken, who flew to Damascus in December 1972 as guest of his Syrian counterpart, Abd al-Halim Khaddam. According to their closing joint statement, the two ministers covered in their talks the whole range of Turkish-Syrian relations, agreeing to accelerate work on the solution of some of the outstanding problems as well as to further co-operation in such fields as trade, transport, aviation and tourism. In an important move for Turkey, Syria declared in the same statement its support for the independence and sovereignty of Cyprus and a solution based on the rights of both Greeks and Turks.[11] Khaddam reciprocated with a visit to Ankara in July 1973, and various agreements for co-operation were reviewed and apparently decided upon. A cultural exchange agreement was actually signed, and it was further decided to continue high-level contacts. Syria was willing again to express its support for Turkish (as well as Greek) rights in Cyprus. The reported success of the talks was such that a Turkish observer characterised Turkish-Syrian relations as having 'jumped' to the level of real friendship.[12] True to the accord, Khaddam and the new Turkish Foreign Minister, Turan Gunes, exchanged visits, in April and June 1974, respectively; and in May 1975, the foreign ministers of the two countries met briefly at Ankara airport.

Thereafter, no exchange of visits between foreign ministers took place for a number of years, and there was a certain lull in the progress towards co-operation. This hiatus may be explained partially by the preoccupation of both governments with other matters. It may also have been due, however, to some chilly moments in their relations. Turkey was clearly displeased with Syria's welcome to President Makarios in June 1975 and its voting record on the Cyprus issue in international bodies. Syria's occupation of Lebanon in 1976 and its continued intervention in Lebanese affairs were also opposed. In late 1977, Syria closed the railway line with Iraq, a measure, as Syria claimed, that was directed against Iraq, but one that did disrupt important links between Turkey and Iraq until the line was reopened in early 1979. Finally, Syria complained that Turkey was giving refuge to some of the Syrian Muslim Brotherhood and other opposition members at a time of growing agitation in that country against the Ba'ath regime. Turkey, in turn, angrily pointed to the leniency shown towards Turkish anarchists operating from Syrian territory.

Despite these differences, there was little evidence that either Turkey or Syria had given up their determination to retain the level of relations which had already been reached. In June 1981, Khaddam was again in Ankara as guest of Foreign Minister Ilter Turkmen, and the latter returned the visit in March 1983. These meetings seem to have been 'political', largely revolving around the question of terrorism, as well as other bilateral problems, but an atmosphere of good will was reported to have prevailed during the talks. During Turkmen's visit to Damascus, the two countries ratified an extradition agreement and appear to have agreed on 'dynamic co-operation'. Invitations for mutual visits by President Assad and Turkey's Prime Minister Bulent Ulusu were also exchanged.[13] These renewed contacts between foreign ministers were 'supplemented' by other exchanges, more economic in nature. In March 1982, Deputy Prime Minister Turgut Ozal went to Damascus, where he signed no fewer than five different agreements on co-operation as well as a trade protocol. Syria's Deputy Prime Minister, Abd al-Qadir Qaddura, met with a number of Turkish ministers in Ankara in July to discuss mutual projects.

The high-level contacts between the two countries were conducive to reaching agreement on several of the outstanding bilateral issues as well as to furthering co-operation in a number of fields. One such field where progress was particularly evident was trade. Although Syria had been an old-time trade partner of Turkey, with the latter normally enjoying a favourable balance, the volume of trade (or at least the legal part of it) was relatively small and consisted mostly of agricultural produce (including livestock). With its new drive to increase exports and, especially, to find new markets for its expanding industry, Turkey systematically sought to increase trade relations with Syria. A good export opportunity was seen in Syria's fast developing economy and geographical proximity. Syria saw similar prospects for itself. In conse-quence, periodic agreements were signed that envisaged an increasingly rising volume of trade between the two. And indeed, the figures were impressive, especially considering the rise of Turkish exports to Syria. Between 1977 and 1978, for example, their value rose from US $29 million to US $58 million, i.e. by 100 per cent. In 1980 it reached US $102,924,000 and in 1981, US $129,412,000.[14] Turkey's imports from Syria were lower, however. In 1980 they amounted to US $17,290,000 and in 1981, US $19,024,000.[15] It should be noted that among the commodities Turkey imported from Syria were oil and electricity.

Co-operative agreements were reached also in the areas of transport, aviation, tourism and communications. During Ozal's visit to Damascus in March 1982, a long-term economic co-operation agree-ment was signed, as was one on scientific and technological co-operation. A special commission was called for that would meet annually and plan projects for co-operation in all these fields. Of special importance to Turkey was a further agreement on highway transport that was designed to facilitate the passage of people and goods through Syrian territory to other Arab countries with which Turkey maintained strong economic links.[16] Cultural agreements concluded between the two countries were similarly significant in as much as they sought to break the barriers of bias and hostility that existed between the two peo-ples. It is noteworthy that the cultural agreement signed in December

1981 specifically included a paragraph on the need to eliminate expressions of hostility from school textbooks.[17] These agreements and co-operative ventures in fields other than trade seemed, in practice, to lag behind. Nevertheless, by the middle 1980s, both countries seemed eager to explore even more avenues for co-operation, and the effort in itself was significant.

Some Continuous Bones of Contention

The Border

The delineation of the border between Syria and Turkey as agreed upon between Kemalist Turkey and France did not, in itself, give full satisfaction to the two countries. The Syrian claim over Alexandretta may have generated the most tension, but was not the sole problem along the 835-mile-long border that preoccupied the two from the very establishment of relations between them. One perennial problem was — and still is — that of smuggling, not a small amount of which consisted of illegal narcotics. Another was the illegal crossing of people. This latter problem was, in some instances, 'innocent' enough, given the fact that the border in many places cut across areas inhabited by people of common kinship (Turks, Arabs or Kurds) and family, and in some cases even divided farmers and their lands. In other instances, these illegal crossings were effected by refugees or by people deliberately attempting to escape the hand of the law. Whatever the case, Turkish and Syrian authorities normally co-operated in attempting to put a stop to the illegal crossings of both people and goods. They also showed consideration towards farmers with property across the border by issuing local permits allowing them to tend their crops on the other side.

Sometimes, however, the illegal crossings led to serious incidents. This happened, for example, when citizens of one country clashed with border guards of the other or when illegal border-crossers touched off mines, which were particularly used on the Turkish side of the border. These incidents, frequently resulting in death, seemed to increase during times of tension and confrontation between the two countries, when mutual suspicions were on the rise and particular precautions were taken to prevent the crossing of spies or agitators. At the height of the tension caused by the signing of the Baghdad Pact, Syrian authorities imposed strict control over the movement of Kurdish tribes following information that they were spying for Turkey,[18] and the Syrian press carried reports of Turkish propaganda among the Syrian Turkoman:

inhabiting the border areas.[19]

Potentially explosive were incidents involving the armed forces themselves, which greatly increased during military concentrations or manoeuvres on each side of the border. At times, these incidents were spurred by illegal crossings, which were discovered by the border guards of one side, but soon attracted the attention of the armed forces of the other. At other times, confrontations were the result of outright border violations by one of the armed units. At the height of Turkey-UAR tensions, in July 1958, Turkish authorities closed the frontiers for a few months and prevented Syrian farmers from tilling their lands across the border. Syria reacted by prohibiting its citizens from travelling to Turkey;[20] and about a year later, Turkey expelled from the border areas a number of Syrian farmers who held permits to tend their crops.[21]

In November 1961, shortly after the dissolution of the Egyptian-Syrian union, Turkish and Syrian representatives met and, among other things, settled questions relating to crossing permits given to Syrian citizens living along the border.[22] More importantly, with the general easing of tensions between Turkey and Syria in the early 1960s, the number of incidents along the border lessened considerably, further contributing to a better atmosphere between the two countries. Although the upsurge of anarchism in Turkey in the late 1960s and again in the late 1970s increased illegal crossings and arms smuggling by militants either entering Turkey from Syria or escaping the hand of Turkish authorities in the opposite direction, it did not tend to create serious incidents along the border. Syria, in any event, was careful not to show support for the terrorists. The most constant feature of the Turkish-Syrian border remained 'regular' smuggling, which, as estimated for 1981, even surpassed legal trade in value.[23] The subject was discussed at virtually all meetings between officials of both countries, and a special protocol on customs and the prevention of smuggling was included among the agreements signed by Ozal during his visit to Damascus in February 1982. Turkey, probably as part of its drive to increase exports, attempted to 'legalise' the trade that had been going on through smuggling, and by 1983 smuggling was indeed reported to have lessened.[24] At the same time, Turkey and Syria, in line with the desire to see their mutual border reflect peace and co-operation, consented to accelerate work on demining the area, thereby opening new tracts of land for farming.[25]

'Lost Property'

Having lived for many years under the canopy of one state, it was natural for Turks and Arabs to reside and acquire property wherever they wished within the Ottoman empire. The delineation of the border between Turkey and Syria following World War I left large Arab and Turkish populations on the 'wrong' side of the border. Some who had possessed properties away from their homes now found their real estate under control of a country not their own. In some cases, as we have seen, the very lands that farmers had long been cultivating were now situated across the border. Whereas some opted for new citizenship in the place where they lived, others chose to migrate to their 'national homes', selling their properties or leaving them behind. The Treaty of Peace concluded between the great powers and Turkey in Lausanne in July 1923 referred to such cases. It specifically allowed persons who had opted for the citizenship of the state 'in which the majority of the population is of the same race as the person exercising the right to opt' and, accordingly, had to move their place of residence 'to retain their immovable property in the territory of the other state where they had their place of residence before exercising their right to opt'.[26]

In effect, however, this separation between persons and their properties led to numerous legal and practical difficulties. Moreover, friction between the two countries resulted whenever legislation in one country threatened to infringe upon the rights of the other country's citizens. Thus in April 1953, Turkey invoked the Treaty of Lausanne after Syria had legislated to prohibit non-Syrian citizens from purchasing agricultural land.[27] A more serious controversy erupted in September 1958, after the UAR had promulgated a special land reform law for the Syrian region that affected, of course, Turkish landowners as well. Turkey did not lodge a formal protest, but subsequently began to exercise repressive measures against Syrian landowners in Turkey. Syrian farmers with land in Turkey were reported to be pressured to exchange their property with Turks owning land in Syria,[28] and to be prevented from tending their crops on the other side of the border.[29] Matters worsened in 1964 when the Ba'athist government in Syria began to apply in earnest its nationalisation and land expropriation laws, leading to the dispossession of many Turkish (as well as Syrian) landowners. These measures were intensified in 1966, following the ascendancy of the extreme socialist Ba'athist faction under Jedid. This time the Turkish government reacted sharply by ordering the requisition of land and property belonging to Syrian citizens in the Hatay province.[30] In retaliation, Syria froze all movable and immovable assets of Turkish citizens in Syria and curtailed decisions concerning transactions involving Turkish assets.[31]

The 'lost property' issue thus assumed the character of a new crisis between the two countries. Being unwilling during this period to accentuate conflicts needlessly between them, however, Turkey and Syria soon began a joint search for a solution. The talks dragged on for a number of years. Syria, clearly unwilling to forego the stipulations of its land-reform laws, made not very lucrative offers for the compensation of Turkish landowners. Turkey's Foreign Minister Caglayangil was impelled to warn in January 1969 that should an agreement on the matter fail, Turkey would distribute Syrian lands to Turks who had property in Syria.[32] Finally in early 1970, there were reports of a breakthrough — probably connected, as we have seen, with the rise to power of the more moderate Ba'athists, headed by Assad. A more constructive approach then began to mark the continuing talks.[33] In May 1972, a property-compensation agreement was initialled, and was duly signed in December 1972 during Foreign Minister Bayulken's visit to Damascus. A special commission was charged with implementing the agreement.[34] Henceforth the question of property ceased to occupy an important place in bilateral relations between Turkey and Syria. The actual compensation to landowners and the removal of restrictions were destined, however, to be negotiated for many years to come; and as late as early 1983 (when a new protocol was signed), these issues had not yet been fully settled.[35]

The Apportionment of River Waters

National and political divisions superimposed on the realities of nature forced Turkey and Syria to share the benefits of rivers flowing through the territory of both, making one country or the other dependent on the good will of its neighbour. Development projects carried out in one country that aimed at using more river water for either irrigation or hydro-electric power were destined to create uneasiness in the other and did, in fact, intermittently constitute a source of contention between the two.

Chronologically, the Asi (Orontes) river, which flows through Syria in a generally northern direction and then enters the province of Hatay and bears south-west towards the Mediterranean, was the first to cause controversy. In 1956 Syria accelerated planning for the Al-Ghab valley project, which involved drying its swamps and opening new areas for cultivation, the additional water to be made available for irrigation from a new dam on the Asi. Turkey announced its opposition, claiming that the project would inflict losses on Turkish farmers. No serious bilateral talks ensued, and the question remained unsettled.[36] Four years later, General Gursel declared that Turkey was looking into building its own dam on the Asi to help solve the problem, and was hoping at the same time to start negotiations with the UAR on the matter.[37] The issue did come up in later talks, in connection with the utilisation of the waters of the Euphrates river, when Turkey was reported to have demanded an overall settlement that would include the Asi (and also the Tigris), but the demand was rejected.[38]

Of the two other major rivers shared by Turkey and Syria, the Tigris and the Euphrates, the latter, in particular, appears to have been the object of large-scale, highly prestigious development plans in both countries. The Euphrates originates in the eastern highlands of Turkey, flows southward into Syria, and then heads towards Iraq and the Gulf in a south-easterly direction, actually making it the possession of three states. In 1974, Turkey completed a major irrigation and power project, the Keban Dam, on the river and was preparing plans for three more dams to be built in the course of twenty years.[38] Syria's main development project for the Euphrates was the Tabqa Dam, partially completed in 1973 and similarly used for irrigation and power production. Iraq, naturally, had long been a prime benefactor of the Euphrates waters and had its own plans for further exploiting them. Being the third country through which the river flowed, it was primarily Iraq that became concerned at the development projects of the two other countries. Syria's own concern at Turkey's plans, however, was also quite obvious.

Tripartite talks on the proper apportionment of the waters of the Euphrates river were held intermittently during the early 1960s. In 1966, Turkey appears to have committed itself to supplying both Syria and Iraq with 300 cubic metres per second of the waters.[40] The issue, however, came to the foreground in a more serious fashion in the early 1970s, when the Turkish and Syrian dams were nearing completion. Iraq, in particular, voiced its fear of a possible loss of water, and its differences with Syria on this matter accentuated its already existing points of conflict with that country. But, when in March 1974 Turkey began filling the Keban Lake in preparation for the operation of its power plant, both Syria and Iraq complained that Turkey had considerably reduced the flow of the river to well below the agreed quantities. When Turkey informed its neighbours that it could not, for a few months, allow more than 100 cubic metres per second to pass through the dam, Syria and Iraq retorted that they were in equal need for increased supplies to fill their respective lakes at Tabqa and Habaniyya.[41] The issue was included in a message Assad sent President Fahri Koruturk when Foreign Minister Khaddam visited Ankara in April 1974. In fact, it featured at the time in virtually all contacts between the two countries. Only after Turkey resumed the river's normal flow did the controversy largely abate, although Syria continued to demand a tripartite conference for finally determining the apportionment of the Euphrates waters.[42]

With the approaching completion of Karakaya, Turkey's second major dam on the Euphrates, and its preparations for a third in the early 1980s, Syria once again began to voice apprehensions. The second dam alone, it was feared, might reduce by no less than 27 per cent the supply of water to Syria, as well as retain most of the valuable silt in Turkish territory.[43] Turkey, reported to be ready to give assurances to Syria, seems at the same time to have used the Euphrates issue as leverage in discussions over Armenian and Kurdish terrorism.[44] By the middle 1980s, a clear long-term solution to the issue had not yet been found. Given the on-going projects in all three countries for the exploitation of the Euphrates river, the prospects for further friction remain high.

Terrorism

Syria's possible aid to Turkish anarchists has constituted the most recent issue in the bilateral relations between Turkey and Syria. The late 1960s witnessed the rise of various radical, especially leftist, militant groups in Turkey that took more and more to outright terrorist activities. The government, headed at the time by the Justice Party, was unable to control the violence, thereby bringing about its own downfall in March 1971 at the demand of the army. Turkey suspected that many of the anarchists had received training, arms and other means of support in Palestinian installations in Jordan, Syria and Lebanon, or else had found refuge in these camps after fleeing from Turkey. In addition, some of the Palestinian students studying in Turkey who originated from those countries were thought to be involved in one way or another in terrorist activities. Fearful of plots by outsiders (possibly involving the Soviet Union) to overthrow the Turkish regime but careful not to accuse Arab countries directly of co-operating with terrorism, Turkey voiced its concern to the Arab governments and demanded that they not extend their protection to Turkish terrorists.

Much of Turkey's concern was directed at Syria, especially after Jordan had eliminated Palestinian bases on its territory late in 1970 and Syria, together with Lebanon, had become the Palestinians' main base of operations. Following the assassination of Israeli Consul-General Ephraim Elrom in Istanbul in May 1971, Turkey's Prime Minister Nihat Erim explicitly stated that although there was no proof of a link between Turkish terrorists and the Arab countries, it was clear that militants had, in fact, been trained by the Fatah in Syria.[45] Syria rejected all charges of complicity in Turkish terrorist activities, denying even the existence of operation bases on its soil.[46] Reports that Turkish anarchists were operating from Syria and other Arab countries continued, however, to appear in the Turkish press, and the issue was raised in contacts between Turkish and Syrian officials. It was only when Turkish terrorism gradually declined for a time in the mid-1970s that this new strain on Turkish-Syrian relations somewhat abated.

Turkey's growing overtures towards the Palestinians in the mid-1970s, which led eventually (in 1979) to the opening of a PLO office in Ankara, was possibly linked in some way with efforts to draw the Palestinians away from co-operation with Turkish terrorists (in addition, of course, to other considerations). The effort was not without results. When in the late 1970s anarchy became rampant once again in Turkey, this time in an even more serious fashion, reports of Palestinian and Syrian co-operation with the terrorists were much less in evidence than before. This restraint may indeed have reflected the reluctance of the Palestinians, or at least their central organisations, to disrupt their newly-established relations with Turkey.

After the military *coup* in Turkey in September 1980, and particularly during 1982-3, Syria was implicated once again in anti-Turkish activities. Turkey's ruling generals had been fairly successful in eradicating both left- and right-wing terrorist organisations, but now found it difficult to cope with a new wave of Armenian terrorism, which operated mostly abroad and against Turkish diplomats. To a lesser extent the generals also faced growing signs of Kurdish separatism. For the Turks, both movements were not only dangerous as such; they were also remindful of the traditional links both Armenians and Kurds had with the Soviet Union, thus raising once again Turkish fears of an outside plot to upset Turkey's stability and well-being. To the Turks, Syria seemed to play a certain role, at least by turning a blind eye to Armenian and Kurdish activities from Syrian territory (or from Syrian-occupied Lebanon). The Turkish press carried many reports of such activities, some of these accounts implicating official Syrian bodies.[47] In fact, Turkey was not content with protests and warnings, but took care to supply the Syrian government with relevant evidence. Denying again any complicity, Syria responded that it had never allowed, and would never allow, anti-Turkish activities to be conducted in or from its territory. But as Foreign Minister Turkmen put it, 'Syria always promises, but the information is different.'[48]

The two countries did, however, sign an extradition agreement in 1981 that came into force, as has been mentioned, after Turkmen's visit to Damascus in March 1983. Allowing extradition of persons sought for crimes committed against Turkey, the agreement did not, however, cover 'political' cases.[49] Indeed in the mid-1980s, Syria's possible role in facilitating Armenian and Kurdish operations against Turkey came to constitute the greatest strain on Turkish-Syrian relations.[50]

Conclusion

In the 40 years that have elapsed since Turkey and the newly-created Syria first exchanged diplomatic representations, relations between the two have passed through several clearly defined stages. There were, to be sure, ups and downs *within* these periods, but the general pattern is easily discerned. Emerging in the mid-1940s from the trauma of the mandatory period and with memories of contention with the Turks (over Alexandretta and other matters) still fresh in mind, the young nation of Syria found it difficult to establish normal, let alone friendly, relations with Turkey. In the early 1950s, even formal relations between the two deteriorated when Turkey, backed by the West, sought to enrol Syria (and other Arab countries) in a Western-linked regional alliance. By the mid-1950s, relations reached their lowest point as Syria adopted a strongly Pan-Arab doctrine and a policy of close co-operation with the Soviet Union, thereby widening the cleavage of suspicion and hostility between Syria and Western-oriented Turkey. The process of normalisation began in the early 1960s, when Turkey desisted from trying to impose its will on other states and undertook, instead, a policy of *rapprochement* and reconciliation. Relations further developed, from the early 1970s, when Syria began responding to Turkish overtures, finding it expedient to follow the path of closer co-operation with its neighbour. Turkish-Syrian relations still seem to be at this stage.

This outline of the development of Turkish-Syrian relations corresponds to general processes that have left their impact on the modern history of the Middle East. The development was related, first of all, to the changing world situation, moving from cold war politics to *détente* and coexistence. It was related, as well, to the changing prevailing attitudes in Middle Eastern countries towards the major world blocs. From a rather strict political, and sometimes ideological, commitment to either the West or the East (or for that matter, to the Third World non-aligned bloc), Middle Eastern countries moved towards a more flexible, pragmatic approach in forming their international relations. Ideology generally, both in external and in internal affairs, lost much ground: *tharwa* (wealth), not *thawra* (revolution) — as the saying goes — became the motto. These processes inevitably had their repercussions on Turkish-Arab relations and, quite naturally, also affected the course of relations between Turkey and Syria. Turkey moved away from a strict adherence to the Western camp, while Syria was willing to build new bridges of understanding even to countries holding a different world orientation.

The interests which drove Turkey and Syria closer are clear. Turkey, bordered on its other sides by potential enemies, has always been interested in having a friendly Syria on its southern flank. Close alliance was perhaps impossible because of the different world orientation of the two countries; but in the Turkish view, an attempt was called for at least to take the sting out of its neighbour's hostility. In additon, Turkey has viewed the fostering of links with Syria as economically advantageous, its Arab neighbour being regarded, among other things, as an important land link with other Middle Eastern countries with which Turkey sought co-operation. If there existed some 'neighbourly' problems, including a territorial claim, then it was doubly important to attempt their solution by peaceful means. Syria, for its part, has shared similar interests in having good relations with Turkey. It was of vital interest to have a friendly, well-meaning neighbour on its northern border, since Syria could hardly count on the good intentions of its other neighbours. Syria, too, stood to benefit economically from friendly relations with Turkey, on whom it was highly dependent for the regular flow of the Euphrates river.

It is apparent, however, that although much progress has taken place, Turkish-Syrian relations have never really realised their potential and turned into a close friendship. Notwithstanding exchanged invitations, for example, no president or prime minister on either side (with the exception of Turkey's Menderes in the 1950s) has ever paid an official visit to the other. A comparison with Turkish-Iraqi relations may help to explain why.

Iraq, too, has a long border with Turkey, along which incidents and controversy occasionally occur. Often, these involve the strong and rebellious Kurdish minority that in both countries populates areas adjacent to the mutual border. Iraq, furthermore, has a sizeable Turkish community, the treatment of which has at times caused friction between the two countries. Finally, although Iraq shared Turkey's world orientation (as well as its political principles of government) until 1958, it later adopted, as did other revolutionary radical Arab states, a policy of close co-operation with the Soviet Union: for a while, Iraq even allowed communists a foothold in power. Thus, like Syria, Iraq became a grave threat on Turkey's southern border.

The remarkable feature of Turkish-Iraqi relations, however, is that after a period of tension following the Qasim revolution in 1958 and Iraq's withdrawal from the Baghdad Pact, they soon returned to normal and, moreover, were gradually elevated to the level of close co-operation and friendship. Mutual dependency seems to have been the key. For one thing, the existence of a strong Kurdish minority on both sides of the border may have created mutual suspicions; but it also required of both countries a policy of co-ordination and co-operation in order to check the separatist tendencies of the Kurds from threatening the territorial integrity of each state. Second, Iraq's frequent feuds with Syria made it imperative for it to seek alternative routes of communication and trade to the Mediterranean coast; the most obvious solution lay in using Turkish territory. Third, especially after the 1973 energy crisis, Turkey saw in Iraq a nearby supplier of low-priced oil. It also hoped to benefit, through exports, investments and joint development projects, from Iraq's growing revenues. These and other areas of mutual interest, then, have accounted for the frequent and high-level contacts between the two as well as their numerous agreements on co-operation. Turkish-Iraqi relations, even with their ups and downs, were able to develop — if we exclude political and military aspects — to a level that was unattained even during the years of alliance in the 1950s. A strong historical-psychological factor should also not be ruled out: Turkey had long abandoned its claim to the Mosul province, and there were virtually no territorial conflicts between the two countries.

By contrast, there is *relatively* little which binds Turkey and Syria together; conversely, there are some basic elements of friction and controversy tending to draw them apart. Kurdish minorities populate both countries, but the Kurds in Syria constitute a relatively small group and are not as rebellious; consequently, there is much less need for co-operation between the two countries on this point. Also, Syria, being comfortably situated on the Mediterranean coast, does not quite need

Turkey for transit purposes. If, for example, shipments of arms from the Soviet Union do have to cross Turkish territory, then their passage is regulated by the Montreux Straits Convention, and backed by Soviet power. Turkey finds that Syria has relatively few petrol-dollars to take advantage of; and although the Syrian market affords some opportunities for Turkish exports, it is relatively small.

The absence of binding mutual interests is accompanied by some very important differences, foremost among them being Syria's long cooperation with the Soviet Union and Turkey's adherence to the Western alliance. Turkey can and does envisage a simultaneous attack directed at its territory from communist or Soviet-oriented countries lying to both the north and the south. For Turkey, acts of subversion carried out with Syria's co-operation or tacit approval can only mean that Syria is, in fact, harbouring ill intentions against the Turks. Syria, for its part, continuously fears an attack on its northern border. Moreover, for Syria, surrounded by hostile neighbours, Turkey's relations with Israel are not only bad in themselves; they also support latent feeling that co-operation between those two countries could one day extend to a simultaneous encroachment upon Syrian territory. Other irritants — smuggling, confiscated property, the apportionment of river waters — can and do add further obstacles to the development of friendly relations.

Taken together, all these factors partly explain why the drive to improve relations on both sides has not been as strong as that which occurred between Turkey and other Middle Eastern states. It remains to be explained, however, why it was usually Turkey that courted the friendship of Syria, not the other way around, and why Syria remained somewhat cool and aloof, even when ready to respond. The explanation seems to lie in the particular mind-set which has conditioned Syrian attitudes towards Turkey — and towards other countries, as well — and in the way Syrian regimes have exploited this disposition. Regarding itself as the cradle of Arab nationalism and its main torch-bearer, Syria finds it difficult to forget not only the conflicts of the past, but also the very real wound of Alexandretta-Hatay. The province seems to stand as a reminder that accounts between Syria and Turkey, or between Arab nationalism and Turkey, have not yet been fully settled. Although the issue has remained politically dormant, there is no question that psychologically it has exercised a strong impact on Syrian attitudes. Furthermore, the record of modern Syria has shown that most of its regimes have indulged in an almost constant struggle for legitimisation. Syrian regimes have found it of vital importance to promote and uphold strong nationalistic themes, at times preferring to stress existing enmities with the outside world rather than play down such themes. When Za'im in 1949 and Faris al-Khuri in 1955 attempted to bring Syria into close alliance with Turkey, the attempt each time marked the beginning of the end of their respective regimes. It is also this attitude that Turkey's Foreign Minister Caglayangil may have referred to in February 1968, when he said that whereas Turkey was constantly trying to improve its relations with the Syrians, Syria continued to use the question of Hatay for 'political purposes'.[51]

Even without such internal factors, however, there remains little doubt of the genuineness of Syrian sensitivities. Frustrated with Turkey's failure to persuade President Assad to change his position on a particular matter, a Turkish diplomat once commented that there was little that could be done: 'Damascus does not like us.'[52]

Notes

1. There is no major work in a Western language concentrating on Turkish-Arab relations although some relevant chapters on the subject may be found in books which treat Turkish foreign policy; and there are numerous articles which deal with various aspects of these relations. See, in particular, Altemur Kilic, *Turkey and the World* (Public Affairs Press, Washington, DC, 1959), pp. 176-99; Ferenc A. Vali, *Bridge Across the Bosporus: The Foreign Policy of Turkey,* (The Johns Hopkins Press, Baltimore and London, 1971), pp. 271-317; Kemal H. Karpat, 'Turkish and Arab-Israeli Relations', in Kemal H. Karpat (ed.), *Turkey's Foreign Policy in Transition, 1950-1974* (Brill, Leiden, 1975), pp. 108-34. In Turkish, see Omer E. Kurkcuoglu, *Turkiyenin Arap Orta Dogusuna Karsi Politikasi (1950-1970),* (Siyasal Bilgiler Fakultesi, Ankara, 1972); and Hacettepe Universitesi, *Turk-Arap Ilisikler: Gecmiste, Bugun, Gelecekte, I. Uluslararasi Konferansi Bildirileri,* (Ankara, 1979).

2. See Avedis K. Sanjian, 'The Sanjak of Alexandretta (Hatay): Its Impact on Turkish-Syrian Relations (1939-1956)', *The Middle East Journal,* vol. 10, no. 4 (1956), pp. 379-94.

3. *Middle East Record,* vol. 1 (1967), p. 152.

4. Kurkcuoglu, *Turkiyenin Arap,* p. 156.

5. *Middle East Record,* vol. 3 (1967), pp. 152-3.

6. *Pulse* (Ankara), 11 December 1973.

7. Ibid.

8. Kurkcuoglu, *Turkiyenin Arap,* p. 158.

9. For example, *Pulse* 15 November 1976, and 23 June 1975.

10. See, for example, the statements by two Turkish Foreign Ministers, Bayulken in *Pulse,* 19 December 1972 and Turkmen in *Diplomatic Pulse,* 4 April 1983.

11. Radio Damascus, 23 December 1972, quoted in BBC Summary of World Broadcasts, *The Middle East and North Africa'* (hereafter BBC), 28 December 1972.

12. *Pulse,* 28 July 1973.

13. *Milliyet,* 29 March 1983; *Cumhuriyet,* 30 March 1983; *Diplomatic Pulse,* 4 April 1983.

14. *Pulse,* 20 July 1979; *Statistical Yearbook of Turkey, 1983* (Prime Ministry State Institute of Statistics, Ankara, 1983), p. 357. There was a drop in exports in 1982 to US $63,155,000 that reflected Syria's restrictions on the import of cement.

15. *Statistical Yearbook of Turkey, 1983,* p. 356.

16. 'Breakthrough in Turco-Arab Relations', *Briefing* (Ankara), 29 March 1982.

17. *Pulse,* 11 December 1981.

18. *Falastin,* 1 October 1955 — 'Korot ha-Yamim' (Chronology), *Hamizrah Hehadash* (hereafter MH), vol. 7, no. 1 (1957), p. 50.

19. *L'Orient,* 25 August 1955 — MH, vol. 7, no. 7 (1957), p. 50.

20. *Al-Ahram,* 4 July 1958 and 24 September 1958 — MH, vol. 10, no. 1 (1960), p. 70.

21. *Al-Ahram,* 19 July 1959 — MH, vol. 11, no. 1 (1961), p. 67.

22. *Al-Wahda,* 11 November 1961 — MH, vol. 13, no. 1-2 (1963), p. 130.

23. An estimate of US $200 million worth of smuggling as against some US $130 million worth of legal trade is given in 'Evren, Ulusu and Ozal Travel the Arab World', *Briefing,* 22 March 1982.

24. *Diplomatic Pulse,* 4 April 1983.

25. Ibid.

26. J.C. Hurewitz, *The Middle East and North Africa in World Politics,* vol. 2: *1914-1945* (Yale University Press, New Haven and London, 1979), p. 329.

27. *Al-Hayat,* quoted in MH, vol. 4, no. 4 (1953), p. 292.

28. Radio Beirut, 6 April 1959 — MH, vol. 10, no. 4 (1960), p. 361.

29. *Al-Ahram,* 6 June 1959 — MH, vol. 10, no. 4 (1960), p. 361.

30. *Hurriyet,* 26 June 1966; 'Chronology', *Middle East Journal,* vol. 20, no. 4 (1966), p. 513; *Middle East Record,* vol. 3, (1967), p. 152.

31. 'Chronology', *Middle East Journal,* vol. 21, no. 1 (1966), p. 81.

32. *Middle East Record,* vol. 5, (1969-70), pts. 1-4, p. 646.

33. Ibid.; also *Pulse,* 12 July 1971.

34. Radio Damascus, 23 December 1972, quoted in BBC, 28 December 1972.

35. Radio Ankara, 9 February 1983, quoted in BBC, Summary of World Broadcasts, *Weekly Economic Report,* 22 February 1983.

36. *Le Commerce du Levant,* 9 May 1956; MH, vol. 7, no. 4 (1957), p. 303.

37. *Al-Hayat,* 19 October 1960; MH, vol. 12, no. 1-2 (1962), p. 105.

38. *Pulse,* 14 May 1974.

39. See Judith Perera, 'Water Politics', *The Middle East,* no. 76, (February 1981), pp. 48-9.

40. *Pulse,* 1 April 1974.

41. *Pulse,* 14 May 1974.

42. *Pulse,* 9 May 1975.

43. Perera, 'Water Politics', p. 49.

44. *Middle East Contemporary Survey,* vol. 7, (1982-83), p. 860.

45. *Pulse,* 31 May 1971.

46. *Pulse,* 4 June 1971.

47. See for example, a report on the Syrian Secret Services training of Armenian terrorists with the help of the KGB at a camp in Tadmor: *Tercuman,* 15 May 1983; *Diplomatic Pulse,* 20 June 1983. Other reports wrote of services provided by extreme Palestinian organisations; see *Milliyet,* 25 July 1983; *Diplomatic Pulse,* 1 August 1983.

48. *Hurriyet,* 25 August 1983; *Diplomatic Pulse,* 29 August 1983.

49. *Middle East Contemporary Survey,* vol. 5, (1980-81), p. 855.

50. In early 1983 reports circulated of a Turkish military operation against terrorist bases in Lebanon, but were officially denied. See 'Armenian Terror on Damascus Agenda', *Briefing,* 28 March 1983.

51. *Middle East Record,* vol. 4, (1968), p. 197.

52. *Briefing,* 22 February 1978.

6 THE ODD COUPLE: BA'ATHIST SYRIA AND KHOMEINI'S IRAN

Yair Hirschfeld

The Irano-Syrian alliance has remained intact for nearly a decade, in spite of very obvious discrepancies between the two countries: Syria is a socialist republic, Iran a radical Islamic theocracy. Syria is strongly supported by Moscow; Iran is in conflict with the Soviet Union. Syria, by its own claims, is the most devout bearer of Pan-Arabism; Iran opposes the very concept of a nation-state and is at odds with most of the Arab world. Syria is motivated by a powerful drive for social, economic and cultural modernisation; Iran, by contrast, has revived the social, economic, legal and cultural patterns of pre-modern periods. Nevertheless, all signs indicate that both parties have been content with their alliance policies.

Nor has the impact of their relationship on the Middle East been negligible: (1) Syria's decision in early April 1982 to plug the pipeline transiting its territory from Iraq, and thereby prevent Iraq's oil from reaching the Mediterranean, caused a severe blow to Iraq in its war with Iran, helping to tilt the balance in the latter's favour. (2) Syria's support of Iran at a time when Jordan actively supported Iraq contributed, during the early 1980s, to a further deterioration of relations between Damascus and Amman. The outcome so far has been to limit Jordanian rather than Syrian political manoeuvrability. Accordingly, the possibility of achieving a breakthrough in the stagnant Arab-Israeli peace process, although not having been blocked totally, has been diminished. (3) Arab, and particularly Saudi Arabian, pressure against Syrian support of Iran has been ineffective. The fact that Syria has overcome Saudi pressure has strengthened Syrian prestige and added weight to its role in inter-Arab relations. (4) Syrian support of Iranian activities within Lebanon has worked against US, French and Israeli interests in central and south Lebanon, despite the fact that Washington, Paris and Jerusalem have, each in its own way, recognised Syrian supremacy in Lebanon. Finally (5) Syria's continued support of Iran, in spite of worsening relations between Moscow and Teheran, has tended to demonstrate Syria's capability of pursuing its regional policies independently of the Soviet Union.

Has all this been an aberration? Are Iran's relations with Syria only an opportunistic exploitation of a convenient constellation? Or do these relations reflect a more fundamental convergence of interests? The answers to these questions may be summed up as follows:

1. The alliance is asymmetric: it has been of major strategic importance for Iran and only of tactical interest for Syria.
2. Consequently, management of the alliance has been strongly dominated by the Syrians, who have largely determined the extent or limits of co-operation in each sphere of common interest or conflict. Questions of ideology have knowingly been pushed aside. Moreover, the Iranians have asserted a strong degree of self-restraint and discipline in areas in which their political interests potentially clash with those of Syria.
3. This pattern of behaviour has so far secured the longevity of the alliance, and may well continue to preserve it for some time.
4. Egypt's isolation from the Arab world during the late 1970s and early 1980s, the inherent weakness of Saudi Arabia and the oil shaikhdoms, Iraq's total preoccupation with the war with Iran and the failure of Israeli policies in Lebanon have all enhanced Syrian power and influence, and thus added much strength to the Irano-Syrian alliance. The end of Egypt's isolation and the emergence of an Egyptian-Jordanian-Iraqi alliance will tend to decrease Syria's power and influence and, consequently, will necessarily limit the regional importance of the Irano-Syrian connection and in the end may bring about the downfall of the alliance.

For a better understanding of the workings of Irano-Syrian relations, it is necessary to analyse in detail the interests involved on both sides.

Iranian Interests

The Assets of the Alliance

Iran's interest in establishing an alliance with Syria were evident from the very start of Islamic revolutionary rule and became particularly apparent after the outbreak of war with Iraq, in September 1980. Such an alliance offers five major assets for Iran.

Syrian Military Pressure against Iraq. From the very beginning of the Iran-Iraq war, the Iranians have endeavoured to bring Syrian military pressure to bear against Iraq and to tie down as many Iraqi troops as possible along the Iraqi-Syrian frontier. The Iranians hoped for Syrian assistance in three different ways: first, the maintenance of an atmosphere of hostility between Damascus and Baghdad necessarily meant that Iraq's border with Syria could not be kept undefended, which would be an invitation to Syrian military pressure. Second, Syrian support for oppositional forces within Iraq, particularly Kurdish resistance groups, could potentially create far-reaching military consequences. Third, Syria could supply Iran with Soviet arms. Even if the Iranian army was equipped with US and European arms, Soviet equipment was important, at least, for training purposes in order to enable a more adequate military response to the Soviet-equipped Iraqi army.

Syria, in fact, offered assistance to the Iranians in all three spheres. The Syrian media continued its hostile attacks against Iraq, thus reinforcing the sense of insecurity in Baghdad. More concretely, in April 1981, Syria made its airfields available for Iranian strikes against western Iraq. In April 1982, Syrian planes violated Iraq's airspace, thereby enhancing Iraqi fears of Syrian military action.[1] Syria also enlarged its support of military and other resistance operations for the opposition parties within Iraq. Specifically it gave assistance to the National Progressive and Democratic Front in Iraq, which included eight opposition groups, among them the Iraqi Communist Party. Part of this aid was for maintaining a collective military base within Iraq and training camps in other countries.[2] Weapons were supplied to Kurdish insurgents in northern Iraq, with further commitments for both arms and experts given in May 1981 to the Kurdish leader, Galal Talabani.[3] Indirect confirmation of this assistance came from Iraq's Minister of Information, Latif Nasif Jasim, when he accused Syria of reinciting the Kurdish rebellion.[4] Finally, unconfirmed reports have indicated that Syria has been supplying Iran with Soviet arms.[5]

Syrian Economic Warfare against Iraq. Throughout the war with Iraq, a vital Iranian objective has been to cause the Iraqis economic damage. In a situation in which the Iranian army has not been capable of breaking a stalemate on the battlefield through military means, the strategy of economic warfare has become most essential. The Iranians did not spare any effort in attempting to convince the Syrians to cut off Iraqi oil deliveries via Syria to the Mediterranean. The direct economic and indirect psychological effect on Iraq of Syria's turning off the taps early in April 1982 was substantial.[6] The Iraqi-Syrian pipeline, which transferred oil from northern Iraq through Syria to a point beyond Homs, branching there to the Syrian terminal of Banias and the Lebanese terminal of Tripoli, had operated in the early 1970s at a capacity of about 554,000 barrels per day, or 27,700,000 tons annually.[7] Although the exact financial loss to Iraq is difficult to establish, the total capacity of the closed oil pipeline represents a reduction in potential annual income of nearly US $6 billion. The net loss, obviously, is far less, but still significant and with far-reaching repercussions for Iraq's war performance. Iraq's alternative outlets for its oil exports are limited, the only secure carrier being the Iraqi-Turkish pipeline, which has a daily capacity of 650,000 barrels.

The closure of the Syrian pipeline created new needs. First, Iraq took immediate steps to expand the capacity of the Turkish pipeline from 650,000 b/d to 1,000,000 b/d. This work, previously carried out by Turkish firms, obliged Iraq to take out a US $20,000,000 Euroloan. Next, with Saudi help, Iraq started construction of a pipeline to the Saudi Arabian port Yanbu, on the Red Sea. This pipeline is scheduled to be completed by 1986 and to cost an estimated US $2 billion.[8] Finally, work on another pipeline, to Zerqa in Jordan and from there to Aqaba on the Red Sea, has progressed beyond the planning stage. The necessary capital investments for these alternative lines created heavy difficulties for Iraq at a time when its estimated foreign currency reserves have fallen, from US $36 billion in 1980 to US $4.5 billion in 1982. Baghdad did, however, receive about $35 billion in loans from the Arab Gulf states, though it expected additional capital needs of another US $35 billion by 1985[9].

The loss of income and the unproportional growth of Iraqi indebtedness cannot but create certain limits on Iraqi arms purchases. Moreover, this critical economic and financial burden has forced President Saddam Hussein to introduce a policy of austerity. The Iranians hope that such measures will gradually decrease the loyalty of the Iraqi population to its present regime, and thus contribute to Hussein's fall. The combination of military pressure and economic warfare should, according to (optimistic) Iranian calculations, bring an end to the war, without forcing the Iranian army actually to conquer Iraqi territory.

Preventing a Hostile Arab Union against Iran. Another reason for the importance to the Islamic regime in Teheran of Syrian support is to prevent the formation of a united Arab bloc against Iran. This objective is of ideological value to the Iranian Islamic fundamentalists, but is of even greater political and diplomatic importance. Ideologically, Khomeini and his followers have always looked towards Mecca and Medina as the origin and centre of Islam. In his theoretical writings and teachings Khomeini has never made a distinction between Iranian and Arab nationalism; for him, nationalism *per se* is a negative concept, derived from Western thinking. The political framework that is relevant and legitimate for Khomeini is *ummat al-muminin,* the 'community of believers', which comprises all Muslims in the world. Because of this religio-political concept, Khomeini has always had Pan-Islamic ambitions and repeatedly stressed the need to bridge the gap between Sunni and Shi'ite Islam.[10] The occurrence of a united Arab opposition against Iran could not but undermine Khomeini's credibility at home and underscore the fact that his political ideas are cut off from reality.

Related to the ideological question is the political aspect of Iranian isolation in the face of a united, hostile Arab front. The fear of total political isolation is a clearly prevailing feature of Iranian political thinking. In this century, Iran's fate has twice been decided by the intervention of outside powers. On 30 August 1907, the British and Russians agreed upon a partition plan for Iran; and on 25 August 1941, the British and Soviets jointly conquered Iran. These events created traumatic feelings among Iranians and instilled a great fear of the consequences of isolation. The resultant political awareness of the Iranian public has induced the present regime in Teheran to make enormous efforts to present Iran as playing a leading role in a united, powerful, worldwide radical front. For this reason, the coverage of activities of radical Islamic groupings in the Arab world (particularly in Egypt), the fight for 'Palestine', the battles in Nicaragua and El Salvador and the struggle between the poor 'southern' nations of the world and the rich 'northern' nations occupy a disproportional place in the Iranian mass media. By reporting these issues, the impression is created that Iran under Khomeini has been elevated to the pinnacle of all revolutionary movements of the world. The alliance with Syria lends some credibility to this otherwise unrealistic claim.

As for its diplomatic aspect, the prevention of hostile Arab unity and the ability of Teheran to play one Arab state against the other is essential to Iran's standing. The alliance with Syria has been a major asset in the achievement of this diplomatic goal.

In November 1980, shortly after the outbreak of the Iran-Iraq war, the conservative Arab powers, led by Saudi Arabia and Jordan, arranged an Arab summit conference in Amman. The main aim was to mobilise Arab support for Iraq. The conference, however, was boycotted by Syria, Algeria, Libya, the People's Democratic Republic of Yemen and the PLO.[11] Syria was not strong enough by itself to prevent the convening of the summit conference, but its opposition combined with that of other Arab states turned the meeting into an insignificant event.[12]

In May 1981, Saudi Arabia succeeded in bringing about the establishment of the GCC (Gulf Co-operation Council), which included Kuwait, the United Arab Emirates, Oman, Bahrain and Qatar. The GCC enjoyed the support of Iraq, Jordan and Pakistan and was able to draw upon support from Egypt, Sudan, Morocco and also the United States.[13] One of the Council's declared aims was to co-ordinate efforts to thwart both internal subversion and external security threats. There was little doubt, though, that the GCC was created mainly to counter the threat of direct or indirect Iranian aggression. In this context, Syria has played from the beginning a major role in neut-ralising the anti-Iranian tendencies of the Council. The GCC, for its part, has been extremely careful not to alienate the Syrians.[14]

Iranian military victories in April and May 1982, which forced Iraqi troops to leave most of the territories they had initially conquered, increased pressure in the Arab world to unite against Iran. Algeria, the PDRY and the PLO, each for reasons of its own, ceased their formerly friendly relations with Teheran. Nevertheless, Syria remained loyal to its ally. In May 1982, the Syrians succeeded in preventing the conven-ing of an Arab summit conference against Iran.[15] Going even further, Syria arranged a high-level pro-Iranian meeting in Damascus in January 1983 that was attended by its own foreign minister as well as those of Iran and Libya.[16] There can be no doubt that all these Syrian moves were well appreciated in Teheran.

Securing Iranian Presence and Influence in Lebanon. Obtaining influence and, possibly, control over the Shi'ite community in Lebanon has long been an aim of Khomeini, even before he seized power in Iran in February 1979. The importance of this community for Khomeini's revolutionary Islamic fundamentalism stems from a variety of factors. First, there is the personal attachment of Khomeini to Imam Musa al-Sadr, the late leader of the Lebanese Shi'ites, a community of co-religionists that constitutes almost 40 per cent of Lebanon's population. Second, the fact that this Shi'ite community is politically, socially and economically weak is thought to increase the intervention capability of the Iranian revolutionary Islamic forces, with the collapse of Lebanon's central government easing Iranian intrigue and intervention. Third, that the Shi'ite population lives mainly in southern Lebanon, adjacent to Israel, offers the opportunity to incite, with little means and costs, the 'popular struggle against Zionism', and thus demonstrate Iran's specific contribution to the Arab (and Islamic) struggle against Israel. Despite its importance for Khomeini, however, such a role for Iran among Lebanon's Shi'ite community would be utterly impossible without Syrian consent.

Little documentation is available about Iranian activities among Lebanon's Shi'ites. What is known is that as a result of the Israeli invasion of Lebanon in June 1982, the Iranians at first organised cohorts of volunteers to fight Israel. The Iranians were permitted by the Syrians to establish their headquarters and training centre in Baalbek, in northeastern Lebanon, where they also trained terrorists from both Lebanon and other countries in a combination of suicide techniques and Islamic revolutionary doctrine. The Ba'albek training centre engaged most actively in propaganda activities and indoctrinating suitable cadres.[17] The suicidal sabotage acts against the US Marines and French soldiers of the Multinational Force in Beirut in October 1983, as well as similar attacks later that year against Israeli troops in Tyre, were reportedly carried out by members of the Iranian *Hizb ul-allah* (Party of God).[18] Although the political and ideological value of such acts is paramount for the Iranians, they are aware that these activities can only be performed with at least the tacit co-operation of the Syrians.

Maintaining Another Channel towards Moscow. Iran's alliance with Syria has also worked as an effective instrument for improving relations between Moscow and Teheran. On one hand, Khomeini and his foreign policy aides were determined to eliminate, or at least diminish, any vestiges of Soviet presence and influence in Iran. On the other hand, they wanted to maintain a correct working relationship with Moscow, based on Muhammad Mosaddeq's theory of 'negative equilibrium' (*movazen-e manfi*). Mosaddeq had argued that the United States and the Soviet Union would each tolerate a decrease in their direct influence in Iran as long as the interests of the other superpower were also curbed. It has been a traditional Iranian technique to moderate any deterioration in direct relations with Russia (or, for that matter, with Great Britain) by simultaneously maintaining good relations with a third party friendly to the Russians. Nasr ed-Din Shah in the 1870s and, more successfully, Reza Shah in the mid-and late 1920s each tried to involve Germany as such a third party, to act as a go-between with Russia. This permitted the Iranians to decrease Soviet influence without creating strong opposition from Moscow.[19]

Khomeini has been employing Syria in a similar function, aiming mainly to keep the Soviet Union from backing Iraq in its war with Iran. In the early stages of the war, this technique worked effectively. Although Soviet interests in Iran were hit with a variety of measures (for instance, abrogating unilaterally Articles 5 and 6 of the Soviet-Iranian Treaty of Friendship of February 1921; stopping Iranian supplies of gas to the Soviet Union; halting almost totally Soviet economic and cultural activities in Iran[20]), Soviet-Iranian relations were actually if indirectly improved through Syria. When on 8 October 1980, shortly after the outbreak of the Iran-Iraq war, Moscow signed a friendship treaty with Syria, this step could only be interpreted as an indication that the Soviet Union did not look upon Iraq as its main ally in the region.[21] It became known, moreover, that Syria was supplying Iran with Soviet arms.[22] When Saudi Arabia and other GCC Arab states introduced economic pressures to stop Damascus from continuing its alliance policy with Iran, the Soviet Union intervened by increasing economic assistance to Syria, thereby neutralising the anti-Iranian Arab pressure.[23]

By 1983, however, the Soviet Union put an end to its lenient policy towards Iran, for two main reasons. First, Iranian army victories against Iraq created tangible dangers of destabilisation in the region. Second, Iran's purge of the Tudeh communists, which reached its peak in February 1983, when 8500 Tudeh leaders and activists were imprisoned, convinced the Soviet leaders that any real *rapprochement* between Moscow and Teheran would be impossible. Moscow then ostentatiously provided Baghdad with aid and let it be known that relations with Teheran had markedly deteriorated. Nevertheless, this step had no impact on either Soviet-Syrian or Syrian-Iranian relations. Syria's role as a potential bridge between Teheran and Moscow, in fact, became even more desirable from the Iranian point of view.

The Liabilities of the Alliance

In spite of the prevalence of very substantial arguments in favour of an alliance policy towards Syria, such a policy also posed certain liabilities for the Iranians: economic, political and religious-ideological.

The Economic Liability. The economic disadvantage of Iran's liaison with Syria can be measured in financial terms. The Irano-Syrian trade agreements of 1982, 1983 and 1984 provide for the free delivery of

1,000,000 tons of Iranian oil to Syria. At a price of US $28 per barrel, the direct cost to Iran amounts to about US $196,000,000 annually. Syria, moreover, has reportedly been granted barter conditions and price reductions of US $3 per barrel, thus costing Iran, on average, a further US $150,000,000 to US $200,000,000 annually. Given Iran's economic difficulties as a result of the revolutionary chaos and the war effort, these amounts are not unimportant.[24]

The Political Liability. On the political level, the alliance policy towards Syria has created heavy restraints in three different spheres: first, although both the Iranian and Syrian leaderships are unanimous in their common opposition to Saddam Hussein and his regime, they differ fundamentally on the question of which opposition group in Iraq should be encouraged to take its place. An open struggle broke out between Teheran and Damascus on this issue after the Iranians had announced early in 1982 a four-stage plan for the establishment of a new Islamic regime in Iraq,[25] including a Supreme Islamic Revolutionary Council.[26] The Syrians opposed these plans vigorously. The Jordanian newspaper *Al-Dustur* reported that owing to Syrian pressure, the Iranians replaced its designated chairman of this Council.[27] Although the Iranians have thus restrained their support for Islamic revolutionary groups within Iraq in order to preclude open friction with Syria, the issue represents a major potential source of conflict.

Second, the Iranians would prefer to follow a far more activist and radical policy in Lebanon. Iran's immediate goal of increasing destabilisation and radicalisation among that country's Shi'ite community hardly tallies with Syrian interests. Recognising this, the Iranians have in their actions respected Syrian desires. After Iranian forces in Ba'albek clashed with the Lebanese army in November 1982,[28] and the Iranian press reported Syrian fears of an infiltration of further Iranian units into Lebanon,[29] the regime in Teheran immediately restrained the Ba'albek revolutionaries. Iran's ambassador to Damascus, Hojaatul-Islam Ali Akbar Mohteshami, explained apologeticaly that Iranian soldiers in Lebanon were merely volunteers and not official troops, indicating that Iran could not take full responsibility for their deeds.[30]

A third political disadvantage had to do with Iranian tourists to Syria. When following the signing of the Irano-Syrian trade agreement in March 1982 the first tourist groups arrived in Syria, they caused some serious clashes. Immediately after their arrival in Damascus, the Iranians, who presumably were revolutionary activists being remunerated for their services rather than 'real' tourists, distributed posters with pictures of Khomeini and attached religious Islamic slogans on the walls of the airport and its surroundings. The Syrian army was kept busy for over a week pulling down the posters, cleaning the walls and repainting them. Many of the Iranians then protested violently against their accommodations, which, they thought, were situated in red-light districts. Tranquillity was restored only after the Syrian army moved in and transferred the Iranians to other accommodations outside Damascus.[31.] These disturbances tended to enhance the sense of isolation among the Iranian revolutionary rank and file, while at the same time this kind of propagandistic eagerness may have created second thoughts among the Syrian leadership. In the event, both Iranian and Syrian authorities decreased the number of Iranian tourists visiting Syria.

The Religious-ideological Liability.

The 'tourist' incidents demonstrate the depth of the ideological gap separating Teheran from Damascus. In addition, a historically deeper religious-ideological factor creates further potential liabilities for the Iranians.

A major tactic of the Khomeini regime in appealing to the semi-educated and uneducated massses is to revive the memory of the martyrdom of Imam Hussein. On the 10th of Muharram 680, the Imam and his entourage were cruelly murdered in Kerbela (Iraq) by the Umayyad Caliph Yazid, who ruled his empire from Damascus. Hussein's martyrdom is recalled by special passion plays and processions performed once a year, but the story is kept alive during the year by repeated tellings, often several times a week. The plays, processions and stories effectively preach hatred of Sunni Islam. It has been common usage in the past to accuse certain Iranian as well as Arab leaders of being the successors to Yazid, who is represented as the incarnation of evil.[32] Such historical associations create no immediate danger to the Irano-Syrian alliance; but in times of crisis, the permanent negative image of Damascus fostered by Shi'ite tradition may seriously affect the preservation of the alliance.

The foregoing analysis of the assets and liabilities of Iran's alliance policy towards Syria suggests a number of conclusions. From the Iranian point of view, the advantages derived from this alliance have been substantial, especially in military matters, in matters of economic warfare against Iraq, and in matters related to Iran's regional and global policies. Iranian policy-makers have been clearly aware of these advantages. At the same time, the Iranians have had both to pay a certain financial price for maintaining the alliance and make necessary political and ideological concessions. For all its ideological fervour, Iranian policy *vis-à-vis* Syria suggests that ideological considerations are secondary. Management of the alliance from Teheran has been totally pragmatic. It is true that Iranians did try to ascertain how far they could go in following specific ideological and political goals that they knew would not be shared by the Ba'ath regime in Damascus. When, however, the Syrians wanted to stop such endeavours, the Iranians had no difficulty in restraining themselves for the purpose of promoting friendly relations with Damascus.

The Syrian View of the Alliance

Syria's motives for establishing and maintaining the alliance with Iran are, in many ways, ambiguous. This ambiguity can best be illustrated by the following facts. Economically, Syria has a major stake in the alliance because of the large quantity of free and discounted oil received from Iran. Moreover, the blocking of the Iraqi oil pipeline has both taught the Iraqis a lesson and potentially increased the economic value of the Syrian pipeline system. In April 1976, the Iraqis had arbitrarily stopped the flow of their oil via Syria to the Mediterranean, causing Syria a loss in annual transit fees estimated at US $136,000,000. In February 1979, Iraq resumed oil transit through Syria, but fixed the fee at US $0.35 per barrel, compared to US $0.445 paid before 1976. In addition, the Iraqis pumped only 10,000,000 tons via the Syrian pipeline system during 1979, instead of the average 27,700,000 tons sent annually from 1971-6.[33] Thus Syria's temporary closure of the pipeline at Iran's behest might, in the future, guarantee both higher transit fees and a steady, maximal supply of oil for the pipeline.

The undoubtedly substantial economic interest in favour of Syria's maintaining the alliance with Iran is, however, offset by certain contradictory economic factors. Reportedly, the Saudis offered Syria in January 1983 a one-time payment of US $2 billion to reopen the pipeline for Iraq; yet, the Syrians refused.[34] The longer the Syrians keep their pipeline system closed, though, the less leverage they will have because the Iraqis have been engaged in a search for alternative solutions. Iraq is investing much effort and money in enlarging the pumping capacity of the Iraqi-Turkish pipeline from 650,000 barrels/day to 1,000,000 barrels/day. Together with Saudi Arabia, it is building a pipeline to Yanbu on the Red Sea.[35] Construction, moreover, has also been started on an Iraqi pipeline in Zerqa in Jordan and from there to Aqaba on the Red Sea.[36] In other words, Syria's decision to prevent Iraqi oil supplies from reaching the Mediterranean via its territory may well boomerang and render the Syrian pipeline obsolete.

Finally, the Syrians have to realise that the moment Iraq solves its oil transit problem, or perhaps even earlier, their oil supplies from Iran will be vulnerable. Iranian oil must pass through the Straits of Hormuz and the Suez Canal. President Mubarak of Egypt has threatened to stop Iranian oil from passing through the Canal,[37] and tankers in the Straits are at the mercy of the Iraqi planes. It may be concluded, therefore, that Syria's economic stake in an alliance with Iran is, at best, ambiguous.

Nor is the political dimension of the liaison free of contradiction. The Syrians closed their border with Iraq in April 1982, only several weeks after the serious disturbances in Hama in which government troops clashed fiercely with opposition groups led by the Syrian Muslim Brotherhood.[38] There seems to be little doubt that President Assad was anxious to present himself, and the Ba'ath regime, to his people as a supporter and benefactor of religion. A link with Iran could conceivably legitimise such a posture, enabling Assad to split the religious opposition to his regime.[39]

The Syrian Muslim Brotherhood, on the other hand, has historically enjoyed close links with Iraq and opposed Khomeini's brand of Islamic fundamentalism. Khomeini and his followers have found very little appeal among the leadership of the Brotherhood as well as its rank and file.[40] Other Islamic religious groups with political influence in Syria, moreover, have shown little empathy for Iran. In June 1982, Shaikh Muhammad Umar al-Izzi al-Naqshbandi, a former member of the Syrian parliament and a well-known leader of the popular Naqshbandi Sufi order, publicly denounced both the Iranian and Syrian regimes as 'sectarian'.[41] The shaikh was acting within the framework of Naqshbandi tradition, which for many centuries has adopted a strong anti-Iranian bias, for political and religious reasons alike.[42]

The anti-Iranian bias of Islamic religious sects clearly prevails, too, among non-religious Syrians, for whom the identification with Arab nationalism demands an identification with the Iraqi struggle against Iran. Michel Aflaq, the founder of the Syrian Ba'ath Party, expressed these feelings in a speech delivered in Baghdad in April 1982 on the occasion of the 35th anniversary of the founding of the Ba'ath Party.[43] As a matter of fact, Syria's decision to cut off the flow of Iraqi oil to the

Mediterranean was followed in April 1982 by the setting up of the Iraqi-backed 'National Alliance for the Liberation of Syria', a coalition of different Syrian opposition groups.[44] It may be concluded that Syria's alliance with Iran has actually had a destabilising effect in the sphere of internal politics, and any gains have at best been marginal.

The Iranian Impact on Lebanon

It may be argued that one of Syria's goals in Lebanon was to establish indirect control over the country; for this purpose, Syria employed proxies, such as the PLO, the Druze community, some Sunni factions, the Faranjiyyah faction among the Maronites and the Shi'ite Amal faction. The Iranian presence in Lebanon served the same interest, being particulary useful in that Damascus could use its lever in Teheran to control Iranian activites. There can be little doubt that the tactic of Iranian suicide terrorism has served Syrian interests in Lebanon rather well. As was previously described, it appears that Lebanese-based Iranian terrorists were responsible for the attacks in October 1983 against US Marines, French soldiers[45] and Israeli troops, and against the latter in April and August 1984. The October 1983 incident contributed to the withdrawal of both the US and French from Lebanon, without creating the demand for a Syrian quid pro quo. Syrian strategists may well reason, then, that similar tactics against the Israeli presence in south Lebanon may have a similar effect. In addition, Damascus has reason to be pleased about its ability to discipline the Iranian forces.[46]

Nevertheless, the Iranian presence in Lebanon may turn out to be a mixed blessing from the Syrian point of view. First, although Syria may be able to control the Iranians in Lebanon, it cannot necessarily direct the acts of Lebanese Shi'ites. This community is involved in an existential struggle and, under certain circumstances, may turn against Syria. Indeed, any Islamic fundamentalist revolutionary indoctrination of the Khomeini type may provide the ideological stamina necessary to do so. Second, and not unrelated, is that with the decrease, or possibly elimination, of American, French and Israeli influences over Lebanon, the burden of restoring stability in that country will fall squarely on Syria.[47]

The Iranian Impact on Syria's Position within the Arab World

Syria has long aimed at playing a leading role within the Arab world. Its prestige and influence within the Arab community have always been important factors in Syrian policy-making. The question, therefore, of whether the alliance with Iran has affected Syria's standing within the Arab world is exceedingly pertinent. An answer is not easy.

On one hand, Syrian *amour propre* and Syrian prestige have clearly been elevated. In the early stages of the Iran-Iraq war, mainly shortly after the beginning of hostilities in September 1980, Syria was not alone in providing Iran with support. Algeria, Libya, the PDRY and the PLO publicly expressed a similar stand. Moreover, Saudi Arabia and the Arab shaikhdoms had very little reason to desire an Iraqi victory, even though they publicly identified with Iraq. In this situation, Syria succeeded in undermining the Arab summit conference in Amman that had been hastily called in November 1980.[49] As the war went on, Syria repeatedly demonstrated that it was powerful enough to prevent any public condemnation of its alliance policy towards Iran. This was the case at Arab summit meetings held in Fez, Morocco, in 1981 and 1982.[50]

In three meetings of the Gulf Co-operation Council, Saudi Arabia and the oil shaikhdoms of the Persian Gulf took pains to avoid attacks on Syria, despite its open defiance of mediation efforts by the GCC in a Syrian dispute with Iraq.[51] Furthermore, late in December 1982 and in January 1983, the Syrians publicly rebuffed an attempt by King Fahd of Saudi Arabia to bring about a meeting between Hafez al-Assad, Saddam Hussein and Fahd himself.[52] Syria also rejected Iraqi attempts to improve bilateral relations, demonstrating that Syria had obtained the upper hand in the long-standing Iraq-Syria rivalry. In an interview given to *Al-Majallah*, Saddam Hussein had personally welcomed an improvement of relations with Syria.[53] That was at the beginning of December 1983, and at the end of the month, Hussein's deputy, Tariq Aziz, made similar statements.[54] Syria's response was to organise a meeting in Damascus of the Iranian, Libyan and Syrian foreign ministers, who publicly denounced the Iraqis.[55]

There may be no doubt that by his consistent policy in favour of Iran, President Assad gained respect for Syria's willingness to follow steadfastly a policy of its own. As tangible evidence of this respect he obtained a variety of offers from different Arab states, which tended to boost Syrian prestige. The Saudis offered money. Other Arab states expressed hope that Syria might be the one state capable of mediating between Iraq and Iran.[56] Another plan involved Syria more directly: Syria would reopen its pipelines to Iraq in exchange for Iraq's refraining from using its French Super-Etendards against Iran.[57] Taken all together, these various proposals added to a general Arab recognition of and support for Syria's special standing with Iran.

In contrast, Syria's policy towards Iraq produced negative repercussions. First, its policies were at least partly responsible for a *rapprochement* between Iraq and Egypt. Syria's closure of its pipeline to Iraqi oil necessarily turned Iraq to seek Egyptian good will. Iraq's decision to build pipelines to Yanbu (Saudi Arabia) and Aqaba (Jordan) on the Red Sea tends to create Iraqi dependence on Egypt to permit the flow of Iraqi oil via the Suez Canal to the Mediterranean, and thus in the long term may strengthen Iraq's pro-Egyptian inclinations.[58]

Second, although the establishment of the Gulf Co-operation Council was clearly a result of the common fear of the Gulf states of both Iran and Iraq, it has enhanced the power of the Saudis and left less room for the smaller Gulf states to manoeuvre against one another. To be sure, Syrian support for Iran, though not the prime reason, created an additional motive for the establishment of the GCC. A neutral Syria probably could have manipulated matters differently.

Third, support of Iran has put Syria very much on the defensive in its relationship with all-Arab institutions. The convening in May 1983 of the Third Conference of the Arab Parliamentary Union in Baghdad, the capital of Syria's Arab enemy, constituted a defeat for Syria. Worse was the fact that in August 1983 Syria was called before an OAPEC tribunal to defend itself against the implied accusation of treason to the Arab cause.[59]

If all the gains made by Syria from promoting an alliance policy towards Iran were, and still are, ambiguous, something of which Syria cannot be unaware, what then was its true motive for adopting such a policy?

The answer lies in an idea that has become a cornerstone of political thinking in Syria under Assad: Syria can play a leading role in the Arab world, and the Middle East as a whole, only as long as Egypt and Iraq are neutralised and kept out of the Middle Eastern power game. In the words of a Syrian Ba'athist ideologist: Syria's historical task is to protect the strategic balance in the Middle East (which has been upset by Egypt's 'defection' from the Arab camp and Iraq's preoccupation with Iran), and Syria is the only capable force willing to do so.[60]

Assad adopted this political guideline, not from the outcome of theoretical investigation, but from a cumulative reaction to events and drawing lessons from former Syrian frustrations dating back to the 1973-9 period. During those years, Syria was manoeuvred into a position of secondary or even marginal importance in Middle Eastern affairs as a result of the so-called Teheran-Riyadh-Cairo axis. Saudi Arabia, which strongly opposed Iranian predominance in the Persian

Gulf area, had little choice but to join Cairo and Teheran as long as it depended upon the United States.[61] Practical negative repercussions were soon to follow for Syria: the Iraqis were convinced of the need to recognise Iranian superiority in the Persian Gulf region, thereby leading in March 1975 to the signing of the Algiers agreement, which terminated the Iranian-Iraqi border disputes.[62] Iraq's security in consequence of its renewed working relationship with Iran generated a deep sense of Syrian insecurity. It was against this background that in April 1976 the Iraqis informed Syria, in the dispute over transfer fees, that they would cease pumping oil via the Syrian pipeline. Beyond the material damage, the loss of prestige to Syria was even worse.

Worse still for Syria was that after the Algiers agreement Iraq's relations with Saudi Arabia and Jordan improved, which created a non-winning situation for the Syrians. If Egypt forged ahead with the peace process with Israel, as it in fact proceeded to do with the Egyptian-Israeli interim agreement of September 1975, Sadat's journey to Jerusalem in November 1977 and the Camp David accord in September 1978, Syria would be kept out of related diplomatic activity. Egypt's pledge, first of non-belligerency and later of peace, heavily undermined the credibility of any Syrian threat to go to war against Israel. If one or another Arab state and/or the PLO were to join Egypt in the peace process, Syria's position would deteriorate further. If, on the other hand, the other Arab states were to unite against Egypt's unilateral peace diplomacy — as indeed happened late in 1978, with the convening of an emergency Arab summit conference in Baghdad — the Iraqi-Saudi-Jordanian *rapprochement* left no place for Syria to take a leading role in forming a united Arab opposition against Egypt.

The fall of the Shah and the emergence of an Islamic revolutionary regime in Iran thus presented a timely gift to Syria, for these developments weakened Egypt and threatened Saudi Arabia and other Gulf states. Next, the Iran-Iraq war promised, in case of prolonged fighting, to neutralise Iraq in the inter-Arab power game. Syria would be left in a dominant position. A quick Iraqi victory, on the other hand, would turn Baghdad and Saddam Hussein into the unchallenged leader of the Arab world, and thus undermine Syria's and Assad's ambitions.

The alliance with Iran, then, was a perfect device from the Syrian point of view, particularly as Iraq's power steadily weakened. The Irano-Syrian political and military pincer was effective enough to contain Saudi Arabia, the other Arab littoral states and Jordan. As a consequence, Egypt remained totally isolated in promoting the peace process with Israel. The alliance policy towards Iran created a geopolitical situation in which Syria was seemingly the only Arab state capable of taking the lead, one way or another. It is this idea, and this experience, which has motivated Syria to hold on to this policy, despite the extensive degree of incompatibility with a variety of Syrian interests that the alliance with Iran has entailed.

Conclusion

In analysing Iranian and Syrian motives for maintaining their present alliance, the following conclusions may be drawn:

1. As long as the Iran-Iraq war goes on, the Iranian motivation to continue its alliance with Damascus will most likely persist.
2. As long as Iran assists Damascus in keeping both Iraq and Egypt from playing a leading role in inter-Arab affairs, Syria will most probably continue its alliance with Iran, at least so long as Assad remains at the helm.
3. The Irano-Syrian alliance has been asymmetrical. The incentives for the Iranians to maintain the alliance were far more powerful than were the incentives for Syria. This state of affairs has eased the management of the alliance, as it has induced Teheran to assume somewhat atypically a policy of self-restraint, thus encouraging Syrian interest in continuing its co-operation with Iran.
4. Both partners to the alliance have so far been successful in keeping ideological discrepancies — which are very apparent — from causing any serious friction. As long as the conditions which have brought about this alliance prevail, it will endure.
5. It appears that Syria has little reason to fear an Iranian victory in the war against Iraq. Such a development would turn Syria into the only feasible mediator between Iran and the Arab world. It would, furthermore, weaken Saudi Arabia, the oil shaikdoms and Jordan; and it might well encourage radicalisation, thus putting an end to the peace process with Israel and further isolating Egypt.
6. As long as Iran does not achieve a decisive victory over Iraq, time and the flow of oil are working against the Irano-Syrian alliance. The formation of an Egyptian-Jordanian alliance in support of Iraq may prevent Iranian oil supplies to Syria; but more important, it may create an effective counterbalance against the Irano-

Syrian alliance and thus neutralise the benefits of the alliance policy for the Syrians. In the long run, the Irano-Syrian alliance depends on Hafez al-Assad's ability to continue an ingenious balancing act, which at one and the same time has kept Iraq busy along its eastern frontier, blocked Egypt from inter-Arab affairs and neutralised Saudi Arabia, Jordan and the smaller Gulf states, if not paralysed them out of fear of the Irano-Syrian pincer. Assad may be capable for some time of such Bismarckian diplomacy. It remains doubtful, though, whether any other Syrian leader would be as successful in playing the same game under such severe constraints.

Notes

The author is grateful to the Dayan Centre, Tel-Aviv University, which provided substantial assistance in the search for sources.

1. 'Crude Repayment', *The Economist*, (17 April 1982); Mark A. Heller, *The Iran-Iraq War: Implications for Third Parties,* Jaffee Center for Strategic Studies, Tel-Aviv University and the Center for International Affairs, Harvard University, Paper no. 23, January 1984, p. 25.

2. 'Iraq Internal Troubles Escalating as Syria-Backed Front Begins Work', *Arab Press Service,* (18 December 1980); see also: *The Economist,* (19 June 1982).

3. 'Iraqi Kurds and Foreign Backers', *Foreign Report,* (18 June 1981).

4. *Al-Dustur,* 11 January 1982; less specific but in a similar vein was Saddam Hussein's speech to the Jordanian Yarmuk Forces, Radio Baghdad, 3 March 1982 (BBC Summary of World Broadcasts: The Middle East and North Africa, March 1982).

5. 'Secrets of the Syrian-Iranian Alliance', *Al-Majallah,* (27 March 1982).

6. 'Damascus Strikes Blow Against Iraqi Oil Exports', *An-Nahar Arab Report and Memo,* (April 1982); also, 'Deteriorating Relations Between Iraq and Syria Discussed', *Arab World Weekly,* (17 April 1982).

7. Economist Intelligence Unit (EIU), *Quarterly Economic Review,* Annual Supplement of Syria and Jordan , (1982), p. 15.

8. EIU, *Quarterly Energy Review,* 'Middle East', no. 3, (1983).

9. 'Iraq's Costly War with Iran', *Mideast Report,* vol. 16, no. 17 (1 September 1983).

10. R. Khomeini, *Islam and Revolution* (University of California, Berkeley 1981)

11. 'Iraq Wins Arab Cover for its War with Iran', *Monday Morning,* (1 December 1980).

12. See Heller, *The Iran-Iraq War;* see also: Patrick Seale, 'Iraq-Iran Conflict Split Arab World', *Jerusalem Post,* 26 October 1980.

13. Hassan Askari Rizvi, 'Gulf Cooperation Council', *Pakistan Horizon,* (1982).

14. See, for instance, Muhammad Gharib, 'The GCC Foreign Ministers' Conference', *Al-Majallah,* (20 March 1982).

15. 'The Gulf War's Wider Ramifications', *An-Nahar Arab Report and Memo,* (2 May 1982).

16. 'Excerpts from a Joint Communiqué issued by the Foreign Ministers of Libya, Syria and Iran after their meeting in Damascus on 23 January 1983', *Middle East International,* (4 February 1983) (in Arabic).

17. 'An interview with Mr. Kanani, the Commander of the Revolutionary Guards Forces in Syria and Lebanon', *Iran Press Digest*, 3 May 1983.

18. Official Iranian sources, however, denied any connection with these acts of terror; see 'Bloody Sunday', *Monday Morning*, (31 October 1983); 'A Flash of Gunpowder Politics', *Newsweek*, (2 January 1984); Radio Beirut, 24 October 1983 (BBC Summary of World Broadcasts: The Middle East and North Africa, 25 October 1983); and *The Economist*, (29 October 1983).

19. Y.P. Hirschfeld, *Deutschland und Iran im Spielfeld der Mächte* (Droste, Dusseldorf, 1981), ch. 2.

20. Y.P. Hirschfeld, 'Moscow and Khomeini: Soviet-Iranian Relations in Historical Perspective', *ORBIS*, vol. 24, no. 2 (Summer 1980).

21. 'Soviet Tests Dexterity in Middle East Juggling Act', *The New York Times*, 7 December 1980.

22. 'Secret of the "Syrian-Iranian Alliance" ', *Al-Majallah*, (27 March 1982); see *Al-Ba'ath* (Damascus), 13 October 1982.

23. 'Soviets Use Political Links with Syria to Strengthen their Trade', *An-Nahar Report and Memo*, (30 May 1983).

24. For an indication of the Irano-Syrian economic agreements, see: 'Iran Continues Oil Supplies to Syria in 1984', *Middle East Economic Survey*, (7 May 1984); 'Syria: Import Co-ordination with Iran Planned', *Middle East Economic Digest*, (6 May 1983); 'Minister Outlines Oil Purchase Policy', *Mideast Markets*, (3 May 1982).

25. 'Interview with Hashemi Rafsanjani', *Ettela'at*, 15 December 1981.

26. Ibid.

27. *Al-Dustur*, 14 February 1982.

28. *Monday Morning*, (29 November 1982).

29. 'Islamic Revolutionary Movements', *Iran Press Digest*, 7 December 1982.

30. 'Interview with Hojaatul-Islam Ali Akbar Mohteshami, the Iranian Ambassador to Syria', *Iran Press Digest*, 19 April 1983.

31. *Sharq al-Awsat* (London), 21 May 1982.

32. Hamid Enayat, *Modern Islamic Political Thought - The Response of the Shi'i and Sunni Muslim to the Twentieth Century* (MacMillan, London, 1982), pp. 181-94.

33. EIU, *Quarterly Economic Review of Syria, Jordan*, Annual Supplement, 1982.

34. On the circumstances, see: *The Economist*, (29 January 1983); on the offer itself, see: 'Syria Could Alter the Strategic Balance in the Gulf War', *An-Nahar Arab Report and Memo*; also EIU, *Quarterly Economic Review of Syria and Jordan*, (1 January 1983) and (4 April 1983).

35. *Quarterly Energy Review, Middle East*, no. 3 (1983).

36. *Mideast Markets*, (20 February 1984).

37. 'Mubarak Threatens: We Shall Close the Suez Canal for the Iranians', *Ma'ariv* (Tel-Aviv), 10 August 1984, (in Hebrew).

38. On Assad's version of his struggle against the Muslim Brotherhood, see 'Assad Interview by the Italian T.V.', Radio Damascus, 25 February 1982; and 'Assad's Speech on the 19th Anniversary of the March Revolution', Radio Damascus, 7 March 1982.

39. Heller, *The Iran-Iraq War*.

40. See, e.g. 'Ikhwan and the West', *Arabia*, (April 1982).

41. *Alef Beit*, vol. 15, (16 June 1982).

42. Indeed in the early nineteenth century, Shaikh Diya' al-Din Khalid al-Sharazuri, the founder of the Khalidiyya, the most influential section of the Naqshbandi order in Syria, ordered his followers to pray 'for victory over the enemies of religion, the cursed Christians and the despicable Persians'. Quoted from Butrus Abu-Manneh, 'The Naqshbandiyya-Mujaddidiyya in the Ottoman Lands in the Early 19th Century' in: *Die Welt des Islams*, vol. XXII, no. 1-4, p. 15.

43. Iraqi News Agency (INA), 7 April 1982.

44. *Al-Majallah,* (24 April 1982); and *Al-Dustur,* 13 September 1982 and 24 January 1983.

45. 'Bloody Sunday', *Monday Morning,* (31 October 1983); *Newsweek,* (2 January 1984).

46. 'Islamic Revolutionary Movements', *Iran Press Digest,* 7 December 1982.

47. See section on Syrian involvement in Lebanon in Part 1.

48. Patrick Seale, *Iraq-Iran Conflict;* see also 'The Gulf War and the Arab World', *Middle East International,* (24 October 1980).

49. Heller, *The Iran-Iraq War.*

50. *An-Nahar Report and Memo,* (24 May 1982).

51. 'GCC Cannot Exert Decisive Influence on Syria or Iran,' *An-Nahar Report and Memo,* (14 November 1983); *Al-Majallah,* (20 November 1982) and (20 March 1982).

52. *The Economist,* (29 January 1983).

53. *Al-Majallah,* (4 December 1982).

54. *Al-Musawwar,* (31 December 1983).

55. *Al-Hawadith,* (February 1983).

56. Another attempt at Syrian mediation efforts was made at the end of 1983, by the UAE President Shaikh Sayyid ibn Sultan; see *Monday Morning,* (17 October 1983).

57. *The Economist,* (22 October 1983).

58. For other fields of Iraqi-Egyptian co-operation, see Heller, *The Iran-Iraq War.*

59. *Al-Ahram,* 1 August 1983.

60. 'After Andropov's Departure', *Tishrin,* 12 February 1984.

61. Y.P. Hirshfeld, 'Iran's Policy toward Israel and the Arab-Israeli Conflict, 1947-1979' (unpublished).

62. On the Algiers Declaration, see Ali E. Hillal Dessouki, *The Iraq-Iran War-Issues of Conflict and Prospects for Settlement* (Princeton University, Princeton, NJ, 1981), pp. 91-105.

7 IDEOLOGY AND POWER POLITICS IN SYRIAN-IRAQI RELATIONS, 1968-1984*

Amazia Baram

Introduction

Relations between Iraq and Syria are among the most perplexing in the Middle East. Both countries came into existence as a result of the same circumstances; and although Iraq became a British Mandate and Syria a French Mandate, at least in so far as the capitals Baghdad or Damascus are involved, and the largely Arab-Sunni population north and west of the former and north and east of the latter, their individual distinctiveness was for decades more a matter of differences between their respective patrons than of real distinction between societies. Hence, once the British and the French each departed from the scene, it could have been expected that Iraq and Syria would rapidly draw together again and ultimately become what they had previously been: namely, two provinces of the same political entity. This, however, never occurred. In fact, with the passage of time, their differentiation both from each other and from the rest of their regional environment rapidly sharpened, often resulting in dissension that bordered on hostility.

In theory, the ascendancy in the 1960s of Ba'athist regimes in both Baghdad and Damascus should have arrested any process of progressive estrangement. In practice, the ideological similarity not only failed to generate *rapprochement,* but indeed added yet another source of friction.

Syrian-Iraqi relations were not always characterised by dissension and friction. If anything, the hallmark of these relations was a sharp fluctuation between co-operation and conflict. Between July 1968, when the Ba'athist regime gained ascendancy in Baghdad, and the early 1970s, relations between Ba'athist Baghdad and Ba'athist Damascus oscillated, sometimes from month to month, between bitter hostility and close co-operation on the political and military levels. On the economic level, on the other hand, co-operation continued throughout this period. The political-military fluctuations resulted from a deep conflict between both countries' Ba'athist ideological commitment to Arab unity and to the liberation of Palestine, which called for close

125

military co-operation, and the hostility and mistrust that often develop between competing offshoots of the same movement. Since 1973, and more in evidence since 1975, the rift between these neighbouring Ba'athist regimes progressively widened, until it became almost unbridgeable. Anwar Sadat's peace initiative brought the two rivals together for a brief period; but their uncompromising rivalry soon threw them apart again. The rift was so intense that even their economic relations increasingly deteriorated, although it involved a substantial loss for both sides.

What were the most prominent causes and the most significant consequences of the fluctuating relationship? Briefly the answer seems to be as follows: there were many reasons for the growing estrangement of the two countries. One factor was the development of conflicting interests regarding major economic issues like oil and water. Another was Iraq's growing involvement in its dispute with Iran over the Shatt al-Arab and other border areas, which necessitated a growing military concentration in the east and a consequent withdrawing of Iraqi troops from Jordan and Syria; in other words, a certain detachment from Syrian-Iraqi co-operation over the Palestinian issue. The new harsh reality of Iraq's eastern border seems to have helped in bringing about a change of heart by the Iraqi elite regarding Iraq's priorities that took place at the same time as, and possibly as a result of, the rise to power of a new, young Ba'ath leadership, led by Saddam Hussein. Remaining faithful, at least in the long run, to the Ba'athist pledge to Arab unity, the new leaders believed that party rule (or more specifically, the rule of their own branch of the party) in Baghdad should take priority. Intimate relations with Damascus were regarded as too risky because of the danger that they would lead to a pro-Syrian change of regime. *Rapprochement* and eventually unity with Syria would have to wait until the Assad administration was replaced by a true Ba'athist regime; that is, one which was a mirror image of the ruling Ba'ath in Baghdad.

The Ba'ath Party Prior to 1968

The 'Arab Ba'ath Party' was officially born in Syria on 7 April 1947, the day its first congress was convened. The most prominent among the founders of the new party, which adopted a 'constitution' at this gathering, were Michel Aflaq, a Syrian-born Greek Orthodox, and Salah al-Din al-Bitar, a Syrian Sunni. A few years later, the fledgling Ba'ath Party united with a party led by the Hama-born Akram Haurani, and from then on it was called 'the Arab Ba'ath Socialist Party'. Its three most important ideals were, in order of importance, total Arab unity, liberation (from colonialist rule as well as internal democratic liberty) and socialism. By the early 1950s, the party had branches in Lebanon, Jordan and Iraq. In 1958, it was one of the major moving forces behind the Syrian-Egyptian unity that culminated in the UAR. Disillusionment, however, soon set in. Gamal Abd al-Nasser ignored the party and tried to push Ba'athist leaders to the fringe of political life in the united state. Thus the party did not actively oppose Syria's secession from the two-state union in September 1961. Thereafter, a split developed inside the party when a young generation, consisting mostly of army officers, challenged the old guard. In February 1963, the Ba'ath Party came to power in Baghdad, and in March that year it took over in Damascus.

In both countries, the rift between the two factions became more and more evident. In Iraq, where the generation gap was not as evident as the ideological one, a left wing, led by the regime's strong man, Ali al-Sadi, competed with a more right-wing (or as some would define it, centrist,) group revolving around a group of army officers led by Ahmad Hassan al-Bakr. In November 1963, the Iraqi Ba'ath were ousted from power by General Abd al-Salam Arif, who had served until then as the country's figurehead president. During the first months of the new regime, Bakr's faction was prepared to co-operate with Arif in the hopes of eliminating the Sadi leftists. Eventually, however, both Ba'ath groups found themselves out of power altogether, with Arif remaining as sole leader.

The Ba'athist split in Syria involved leftist army officers and civilian intellectuals, on one side, and Aflaq's and Bitar's veterans, on the other side. The rift widened between 1963 and 1966. During this period, Bakr's centrist group, now out of power in Iraq, aligned itself with the ruling Aflaq group in Syria. At the same time, there was growing estrangement between Bakr and the Syrian 'left', led by two colonels, Salah Jedid and Hafez al-Assad. On 23 February 1966, the Syrian leftist officers ousted Aflaq's faction from power, and with it the president, General Amin al-Hafiz, who had aligned himself with Aflaq. The Aflaq-led Ba'ath Party thus found itself out of power in both Syria and Iraq and from time to time even suffered persecutions at the hands of the respective regimes in each country.

In July 1968, Bakr's faction of the Ba'ath took over in Iraq. At its inception, the new government was mainly in the hands of army or ex-army officers. Ideologically, however, it was committed to the paramountcy of the civilian party, mainly as a reaction to what was seen as the evils of military rule in Ba'athist Syria, from which the Iraqis wanted to disassociate themselves. (In the course of time, power did indeed shift into the hands of the civilian leadership, under the present president, Saddam Hussein.) Iraq and Syria now found themselves ruled by two mutually antagonistic elites, each claiming to be the sole representative of the true Ba'ath Party.

Oil Royalties and Pipeline Policy

The upheavals described above, which resulted ultimately in the rise of Assad in Syria and Bakr in Iraq, inevitably led to a great deal of friction between the two Ba'athist regimes. The Iraqis rebuked the February 1966 *coup* in Syria[1] and offered assistance to leaders and supporters of the Aflaq faction in Syria[2] and subsequently (during 1968-70) seemed more supportive of Assad than of his Alawi rival Salah Jedid.[3] The Syrians, for their part, responded fiercely, denouncing Iraq's position on a variety of issues.[4]

None the less, from 1968-70 the two regimes also acknowledged their great amount of interdependence and, their criticism of each other notwithstanding, collaborated in a number of important areas. Co-operation was particularly marked in three spheres of activity: the transit of Iraqi oil exports through Syria to Mediterranean ports, the commitment to the radicalisation and unification of the Arab world and the war against Israel.[5] The consequence was a marked ambivalence in their relations with signs of co-operation and of conflict alternating in rapid succession.

With the passage of time, however, the elements of conflict gradually assumed greater importance. The first fundamental issue to deepen the friction centred on the sensitive issue of oil. On 1 June 1972, Iraq nationalised the property of the Iraqi Petroleum Company, which, in the main, had previously belonged to British, Dutch, French and American companies. Developments that occurred in the wake of this act brought about, for the first time since 1968, a dispute that spread from the economic to the political sphere. Moreover, the economic controversy was solved in a way that was regarded by Iraq as extremely unsatisfactory.

As a result of its act of nationalisation, Iraq ran into economic difficulties stemming from an inability to market all its oil. Syria, meanwhile, which had also nationalised IPC property on its own soil, then dealt a severe blow by demanding that Iraq pay nearly double the fee for the transit of oil through Syrian territory. (The pipeline ran from Kirkuk to Banias in Syria and to Tripoli in Lebanon.) Discussions on the matter lasted until January 1973, when an agreement was reached that met almost all of the Syrian demands. Iraq, with no other outlet for its Kirkuk oil and faced with a Syrian threat to shut down the pipeline, had little choice but to yield to Syrian pressure.

Iraqi frustration over this agreement became the second critical event in altering Iraq's attitude towards co-operation with Syria, the first one being its gradual disengagement from the Palestinian front after September 1970. The first sign of this change was a visit by the Iraqi economic minister to Ankara in late January and early February 1973, in which the question of a crude-oil pipeline from Kirkuk through Turkey to the Mediterranean was seriously discussed. On 1 May 1973, Iraq and Turkey signed a protocol for the construction of a 40-inch pipeline, having an initial capacity of 25 million tons a year, from Kirkuk to Dortyol. In September 1973, the full scope of Iraq's new pipeline strategy was revealed. A leader in *Al-Thawra,* the Iraqi Ba'ath Party daily, praised the 'far-sightedness' of the Iraqi leadership for its 'innovative methods' that were designed 'to safeguard a number of alternative outlets to get the nationalised Iraqi oil . . . to world markets'.[6] In more specific terms, the newspaper publicised the fact that in addition to the proposed Iraqi-Turkish pipeline, Iraq had also started building a 'strategic pipeline' from Haditha to the Gulf as well as a deep-water harbour there that would serve as a major oil terminal. This meant that Iraq was planning sufficient pipeline capacity to export all its oil production without any dependence on Syria. It was hardly surprising that Syria reacted with ferocious accusations that Iraq was betraying the Arab cause by relying on a non-Arab neighbour.

Iraqi resolve was not shaken. On 27 December 1975, the strategic line was opened. It could deliver 48 million tons yearly from Kirkuk through Haditha to the Gulf. In April 1976, Iraq stopped the flow of oil through Syria altogether and diverted oil from Kirkuk through the strategic line to the Gulf. The diversion meant a certain but temporary reduction in oil sales because the new line did not suffice to transport all the Kirkuk oil. In January 1977, the Iraqi-Turkish pipeline was officially opened in the district of Tamim in an impressive ceremony in the presence of Prime Minister Sulayman Demirel of Turkey.

Iraq's new strategy created an unprecedented situation. The country was now more and more dependent on close co-operation with Turkey, as well as with Iran, with whom Iraq had signed an agreement in March

1975 that ended the dispute over the Shatt al-Arab. Both countries were non-Arab, both were close allies of the United States and both had overt diplomatic relations with Israel.

From January 1977, relations between Iraq and Syria reached a nadir. Syria closed its borders to Iraq stopping through-transit commerce, in retaliation for Iraq's suspending the flow of its oil through the Syrian pipeline — which action caused the two trajectories, that of political and that of economic relations, to converge. The transfer of goods and oil through Syria was resumed during the short thaw, from October 1978 to July 1979, that followed the Camp David accord. Thereafter, the pumping of oil was stopped and renewed a few times. However, on 10 April 1982, Syria shut down the pipeline as part of the Irano-Syrian agreement that, among others, compensated Syria for its oil-transit revenue losses. This time, Iraq was in the midst of a bitter war with Iran, and Iraqi outlets on the Gulf were inoperative. Iraq was left with only one pipeline, which went through Turkey and had a capacity of fewer than one million barrels a day, that is less than one-third of its pre-war marketing capacity.

The new situation dictated to Iraq, as it had in 1973, the choice of new long-term allies. This time, in addition to Turkey, these were Jordan and Saudi Arabia, through whose territories Iraq planned pipelines for its oil. This time, however, there may also be a hidden ally, whose co-operation will have to be secured in order for Iraqi oil to reach world markets: the state of Israel.

The October 1973 War and its Aftermath

On 6 October 1973, Syria and Egypt attacked Israel. Apparently in response to a Syrian request, Iraq started preparations on 7 October to send an expeditionary force. The political aspects of these preparations involved the resumption of diplomatic relations with Iran[7] and approaching Barazani in the hope of improving relations and thus securing Iraq's two main fronts, for a brief period at least.

On 8 October, Iraqi units started moving on trucks, tank carriers, trains and planes. On the 12th the first units arrived, and on the 13th an armoured brigade engaged Israeli troops in battle on the Golan Heights. In all, Iraq sent, according to its own reports, two (of its three) armoured divisions and various infantry units amounting to the size of a division[8] — a formidable force, considering the short time that was available (Iraq had been kept completely in the dark in regard to

Egyptian-Syrian preparations.[9]) Despite shortcomings in military co-ordination with Syria and in general performance, the 'Saladin' expeditionary force caught the advancing Israeli armour at a critical moment and forced it to arrest its advance — an act that gives some credibility to the Iraqi claim that they were the ones who saved Damascus.[10] Iraq, though, paid a heavy price[11] for helping out a brotherly country with whom relations were going from bad to worse.

The Iraqi action in the October 1973 war seemed to have pointed in the direction of renewed military, and even political, co-operation with Syria on the Palestinian issue. Political practice immediately following the cease-fire, however, proved that this was not the case, as Iraq was adamant in wanting to avoid not only a long-term involvement on the Golan but also close co-operation with Syria. Alternatively, it may be assumed that were Syria ready to pay the very high price Iraq demanded for such co-operation, the latter would have accepted *rapprochement*. The price was so high, though, that this was hardly a practical prospect: it was the continuation of the war.

When Syria signed the cease-fire agreement on 24 October 1973, Iraq saw this as a defeatist approach that lost the Golan for the Arabs and, more importantly, caused them to miss an historic opportunity to inflict heavy losses on Israel. Worse still, when it signed the agreement, Syria also accepted UN Security Council Resolution 338, which in turn included Resolution 242. Despite Syria's being on record as having certain reservations about the latter resolution, Iraq viewed Syria's actions as complete acceptance of a resolution against which it had fought since the Ba'ath came to power in July 1968. For Iraq, acceptance of the resolution meant the embryo of a recognition of Israel — and the Iraqi army was immediately called back home.

Between the end of 1973 and the Camp David meeting of 1978, the Iraqi condition for co-operation with Syria was that Syria should withdraw its acceptance of UN Resolutions 338 and 242. Even though Iraq did not call for the resumption of an all-out war, its demand that Syria annul a very important international obligation was unacceptable to Syria and, as such, barred the way to any meaningful co-operation.

The Era of Total Alienation, 1975-1978

Between the October war and the Camp David accord, which pushed Iraq and Syria into each other's arms, four major events affected their bilateral relations. The first of these was a confrontation between March and August of 1975 over the allocation of the Euphrates river waters. The second was the disengagement agreement between Egypt and Israel, which forced Iraq, for the first time since the war, to rethink its relations with Syria. The third event was Syrian involvement in Lebanon, which started to draw Iraq's attention from the autumn of 1975. The fourth was Sadat's visit to Jerusalem, which again compelled Iraq to review attitudes towards Syria.

In the spring of 1975, after two years of drought in a row, and the blockage of water by Syria and Turkey, the level of Euphrates water in Southern Iraq decreased sharply. As a result, Iraqi peasants in the lower Euphrates basin suffered greatly, and many crops were lost. This resulted in an unprecedented Iraqi-Syrian confrontation that turned already sour relations into those of coherent hostility.

The escalation of the Syrian-Iraqi rivalry following the Euphrates crisis was reflected in Iraq's attitude towards Damascus in the wake of the second disengagement agreement between Egypt and Israel in September 1975. A communiqué issued by the Pan-Arab Leadership of the Ba'ath Party[12] criticised Sadat in no uncertain terms. The Egyptian leader, however, was given credit for his frankness, having often admitted being in favour of a peaceful settlement with Israel.

Syria's Assad, on the other hand, was accorded no such redeeming feature. As the Leadership saw it, he was following Sadat's footsteps, albeit at some distance: whatever Sadat did today, Assad would do within a few months. Because, however, Assad presented himself as a staunch nationalist and a radical, he was in reality misleading the Arab masses, while betraying the highest ideals of the Arab nation. Assad and the Arab reactionaries, it was charged, were using Sadat as a 'minesweeper': once he had cleared the road for them, they would move along it unharmed.

The Pan-Arab Leadership communiqué heralded a period of constant crisis between Syria and Iraq, on both the political and, for the first time since 1968, the economic level. By contrast, relations with Egypt started to improve again. This was particularly evident in 1976, when Iraq tried to align itself with Egypt (and a few other Arab countries) against Syrian involvement in Lebanon. Iraq was disappointed at the Cairo summit of 25 October 1976, at which Egypt and Saudi Arabia came to an agreement with Syria over Lebanon, according to which the Syrian army could remain there as the bulk of an Arab security or deterrent force. Iraqi-Egyptian relations, though, suffered only a short setback. Moreover, when Sadat announced his intention to go to

Jerusalem in November 1977, the Iraqi attitude was very unusual, considering that this was an act going against everything in which Baghdad believed. For a few days, there were no condemnations but, rather, warnings.[13] Only after Sadat actually arrived in Jerusalem did the Iraqi press start to attack him in a more traditional way.[14]

Soon after Sadat's historic trip, the Iraqi media once again turned on Syria, even more viciously than they did against Sadat, in an almost carbon copy version of their anti-Syrian attacks in September 1975. At the summit meeting of radical states and organisations (Syria, Iraq, Algeria, South Yemen and the PLO) in Tripoli (Libya) on 2 December 1977, Iraq made it clear that only a change in Syria's commitment to the Resolutions 242 and 338 could lead to any Iraqi co-operation with the Syrians. In addition, Iraq demanded that Syria allow the PLO complete freedom of action through the Syrian border into Israel, that the Syrians withdraw from Lebanon, and that Damascus make a clear-cut commitment to the total liberation of Palestine, not just (allegedly) to the Golan alone. Assad flatly refused the Iraqi demands, and Iraq withdrew from the summit, remaining completely aloof from any joint action by the radical Arab states against Sadat's Egypt because of their refusal to boycott Syria. This way, paradoxically, Iraq's staunch nationalistic stances prevented it from taking any meaningful action against Sadat's Egypt, or from getting any closer to that Arab confrontation state whose positions were closest to those of Iraq's, that is to Ba'athist Syria.

To Unity — Steps and Back, 1978-1982

The shift from bitter confrontation to close co-operation was abrupt. Immediately following the Camp David conference, the Iraqi Revolutionary Command Council (RCC) sent out a communiqué in the old style, that, by implication, denounced Syria more than it did Egypt. Yet, on 2 October 1978, the RCC issued a new statement, which appeared in the Iraqi dailies, that opened the gate to Arab co-operation against Sadat without posing any conditions for Iraqi-Syrian co-operation. What had made Baghdad change its mind? The two docu ments that heralded the change of policy, the communiqué of the RCC and, a day later, that of the Pan-Arab Leadership, explained that Iraq was worried about the defeatist atmosphere in the Arab world and had decided to make an effort to halt the spreading sense of desolation. The Iraqi leadership also made sufficiently clear its less altruistic fear that more Arab countries would join Egypt, thus increasing the isolation belt around Iraq. More importantly, Iraqi sources implied that Baghdad now expected to assume the leadership of the Arab world. This meant that Damascus was expected to recognise Baghdad's seniority. These hopes were reflected in the RCC communiqué:

> The eyes of the Arab people everywhere are turned to your great revolution in this region, and to your party.... The principles ... and the ideals of struggle in these critical conditions are laying anew on the party's shoulders the task of entering the difficult terrain like the intrepid knights to defend the ... nation and its historical rights.... The Arab arena is expecting the veteran knight who can confront the challenges.... scatter the pitch-black darkness and melt the frustration and loss of faith....[15]

An important Iraqi party publication put it, in hindsight, even more forthrightly:

> The historical conditions at that moment and the great increase of Iraq's influence in the Arab arena had given Iraq a much better opportunity to influence... the course of Arab events than [ever] before.[16]

As it then appeared to the eye, Iraq's hopes were not frustrated. Following an exchange of messages on 25 and 26 October 1978, it was President Assad, accompanied by a most senior delegation, who came to Baghdad to discuss unity and in November, Baghdad became the scene of an Arab summit meeting that created a united Arab front against Sadat's Egypt.

In terms of Iraqi-Syrian relations, the unity talks produced a Covenant of Joint Pan-Arab Action, which stressed 'determination to endeavour seriously ... to achieve the strongest form of unitary relations'. A supreme political committee under Assad and Bakr was established, along with a host of subcommittees to 'undertake the supervision of all bilateral relations ... and achieve the co-operation and integrity ... towards unionist objectives'.[17]

The two countries seemed, however, to be approaching the issue of unity with the greatest of care. During the next nine months, added steps towards closer co-operation and co-ordination were taken, but these were all of a short-term nature. The most impressive step was in the area of economic relations, which were returned to normal: the borders were reopened, transportation ties were resumed, and oil started flowing once again from the Kirkuk fields to Banias. On the cultural level the Covenant heralded bilateral meetings between various organisations of the two countries: peasants, workers, teachers and others. Some work was done to unify the curricula of schools and universities. There was, on the political level, an attempt to unify foreign ministeries and to co-ordinate economic planning. Most of these activities, however, remained in an embryonic phase; the two sides seemed to be in no hurry to complete them. Nothing was done on the military level, except for a decision to form a United Military Command, which would function as a stop-gap solution until the establishment of the united state. The command never materialised.

There is some evidence that Bakr may have been more inclined towards some kind of federation with Syria than was Saddam Hussein. If so, it was eventually Hussein's views which prevailed, and six months later, in mid-July 1979, Saddam Hussein replaced Bakr as President, Chairman of the RCC and Secretary General of the Regional Leadership of the party in Iraq (RL).

On 30 July 1979 Iraqi media announced the exposure of a would-be *coup d'état* against Hussein that had been planned in connection with a 'foreign country whose name the Leadership sees that Pan-Arab interests require not to mention now'. The leading culprits were five members of the RL and RCC, who, along with 17 others, were sentenced on 7 August to a shooting squad; many more were given various jail sentences. [18] Upon subsequent hints that it was the Damascus regime which had tried to topple the new government in Baghdad, senior Syrian officials went to Baghdad to deny any connection between Syria and the Iraqi plotters, and to try to convince Iraq to refrain from a breach. This effort failed and unity was over.

What made the unity attempt collapse? Iraqi sources give a variety of reasons, some of which are credible: disagreements over the attitude towards the Khomeini regime in Teheran, over the exact form of the future union, and over military co-operation. Most important, however, was the implied admission that appeared in the Resolutions of the Ninth Regional Congress of the party that, if Iraq and Syria united, the Iraqi leadership expected to be recognised as the senior partner in any fully-fledged union. Since Syria turned down this offer, Iraq's enthusiasm for the proposed partnership was greatly reduced. The hint was yet another demonstration of the new line that not only placed local interests very high on the regime's scale of priorities, a policy that was practised by many Arab governments, but also openly admitted and sought to legitimise it, as part of a new emphasis on the Iraqi entity. [19]

The way in which the Baghdad leadership treated the planned *coup d'état* was revealing. A short time after the plot had been exposed, Iraq directly accused Syria of being the moving force behind the attempted take-over. Baghdad then 'reasoned' that a state could not expect to establish unity with a regime that plots behind its back. Whether or not an actual plot existed, the fact was that Baghdad pointed to Syrian infiltration as the principal reason for the failure of the most precious dream of every Ba'athist — unity. The Iraqi accusation may be seen, firstly, as an indication that the fear of infiltration was still very much alive in Iraqi Ba'ath Party circles — and so could be employed as a convincing argument against the unity idea; and secondly, as an implication that the well-being of Ba'athist rule in Baghdad was more important than union with Syria. In view of Baghdad's conviction that theirs was the legitimate party and that Damascus had deviated, the Iraqi attitude was perfectly understandable. It was, however, a very different one from that which prevailed in the late 1960s and early 1970s, or even in October 1978, when the deviationist nature of the Syrian regime and their plots against Baghdad were not regarded as sufficient obstacles to block co-operation or even unity.

For a few months after the Iraqi charges, economic relations between the two countries remained undisturbed. Very quickly, however, the ideological, political and economic trajectories converged again. On 18 August 1980, the heads of Arab diplomatic missions in Baghdad were summoned to witness the removal of 'large amounts of explosives, arms and poisonous materials from Syrian Embassy premises'. Syria was accused of planning 'to carry out massacres, acts of sabotage and killings', and the staff of the Syrian Embassy was told to evacuate the country within 48 hours. Syria, for its part, denied the charges, claiming that the supposed evidence had been planted by Iraqi agents. In retaliation, Damascus expelled the Iraqi ambassador and his 19-man staff. [20]

Relations never recovered — and in fact deteriorated steadily. April 1982 saw the nadir. On 8 April, Syria closed its border with Iraq, allegedly to prevent the infiltration of saboteurs and weapons from Iraq in support of the Muslim Brotherhood's underground and other Iraqi-sponsored movements inside Syria. On 10 April, as already mentioned, the Kirkuk-Banias pipeline was shut down by Damascus.[21] Finally on 18 April, Syria broke off diplomatic relations with Iraq, and Walid Hamdun, a deputy premier, promised to help the Iraqi people in toppling the regime in Baghdad. [22] Syria and Iraq had now completed a 14-year-long process of progressive estrangement.

The complementary elements of this disassociation were not missing. Since the Baghdad summit of November 1978, Iraqi-Jordanian relations had been improving steadily. A few weeks after the onset of the war with Iran, Iraq renewed ties with Egypt. These were, to begin with, military relations; and the worse off Iraq became militarily, the closer these relations became. In May 1982, after Iraq had to retreat from Abadan and Khoramshahr and as Khomeini's army was preparing an assault on Basra, Saddam Hussein 'rehabilitated' Egypt's Mubarak in an interview with a Kuwaiti newspaper. 'Let me be frank with you,' Hussein said in summary, 'if the Egyptian army should come to Baghdad, we would welcome it and would open all the doors to it'.[23]

In late December 1982, Egyptian newspapers were allowed into Baghdad.[24] Iraq's deputy prime minister, Tariq Aziz, said to *Al-Ahram*: 'We are not against restoring ties with Egypt .... As an Arab citizen I say that this step must be taken now.'[25] Full diplomatic relations were not resumed then and Egyptian troops did not come to Iraq, but Iraqi-Egyptian ties were getting closer steadily. Thus, for example, in mid-1982 it was reported that Egypt was selling Iraq large quantities of arms and ammunition, that Egyptians living in Iraq were free to join the Iraqi army and that Egyptian ex-servicemen could enlist on a private basis.[26] In late 1982 there were reports that the Egyptian labour force in Iraq amounted to more than one million. Such reports indicate close ties, and also interdependence.

This Egyptian connection represented, as it did with Jordan and Saudi Arabia, the near-completion of the process of Iraq's estrangement from Syria. This, in its own turn, was a part of a wider change in national priorities, introduced by Saddam Hussein and his associates gradually since the mid-1970s. It involved, among other aspects, a reduced commitment to immediate and, even more so, amalgamative Arab unity; a new balance in relations with East and West; and, at least on the face of it, a somewhat less hostile attitude towards peaceful negotiations between Israel and the Palestinians. It is still left to be seen whether some, or all, of these changes would outlast the war and whether they would be carried any further.

As for the future of Iraqi-Syrian relations, there is reason to believe that under their present leaderships, the two countries will continue to bear the hallmark of mistrust. This does not necessarily mean, however, complete paralysis. Iraq is extremely anxious to return to the pattern of bilateral relations that prevailed between the two between 1973 and 1976; that is, to political hostility accompanied, notwithstanding, by almost undisturbed economic co-operation, at least in so far as Iraqi oil exports were concerned. Syria, for its part, insists on a thorough *rapprochement* and even demands to establish federal unity, possibly with Assad at its head. In view of its obvious inferiority under the present war circumstances, Iraq cannot accept such a proposition, which seems to the Baghdad-based Ba'ath to be a prescription for Syrian infiltration and domination. Until either side changes its position, *rapprochement* is not feasible.

Because of the fact that, in Baghdad, federation is seen as tantamount to annihilation, any change in the present deadlock depends mainly on greater Syrian flexibility. In view of the growing discord between Syria and Iran, such a possibility cannot be counted out.

Notes

(*) Parts of this article are based on a PhD thesis in progress, written under the supervision of Professor Moshe Ma'oz and (the late) Professor Gabriel Baer. Mr. Stanley M. Bogen of New York and the Harry Truman Institute in Jerusalem sponsored the research.

1. See, for example, a report in *Al-Anwar* (Beirut), 23 February 1968.

2. These were Shibli al-Aysami, an ex-minister, and General Fahad al-Sha'ir. See *Al-Ahram,* 13 August 1968; see also *Al-Nahar,* 20 August 1968, and the special praise given by the Iraqi Foreign Minister to General Amin al-Hafiz in *Al-Jarida,* 18 September 1968.

3. See *Al-Jarida* (Beirut), 6 March 1969, and *Al-Anwar,* 9 March 1969.

4. See, for example, *Al-Ba'ath* (Damascus), 5 February 1969; *Al-Hayat* (Beirut), 5 February 1969.

5. See, for example, an interview with President Bakr, *Masirat al-thawra fi khutab wa tasrihat al-Sayyid al rais* (Baghdad, 1971), pp.42-4; for details, see Amazia Baram, 'Qawmiyya and Wataniyya ...,' *Middle Eastern Studies,* vol. 19, no. 2 (April 1983), pp.188-200.

6. *Al-Thawra,* 30 September 1973.

7. *Al-Thawra,* 11,12 October 1973. For the text of the RCC communiqué explaining the reasons for resuming relations with Iran, see The Arab Centre for Strategic Studies, *Dawr al-jaysh al-iraqi fi harb tishrin.* (Beirut, 1973), pp. 237-8.

8. *Dawr al-jaysh,* p.52. The report mentioned 700 tanks, 'hundreds' of armoured troop carriers, 12 artillery batteries and some 60,000 men. It seems that the Iraqi report was somewhat inflated, though not substantially so. (The Iraqi account may have included maintenance and auxiliary units left inside Iraq but belonging to the units that entered Syria.)

9. Communiqué of Pan-Arab and regional leaderships and RCC, *Al-Jumhuriyya,* 30 October 1973; *Al-Thawra,* 11,12,25 October 1973.

10. See, for example, Arab Ba'ath Socialist Party, *About the 1973 October War* (Firenze,1977), p.22.

11. According to the report of its Chief-of-Staff, Iraq lost 835 men, 11 of whom were officers, 73 missing, 271 wounded, 26 jet fighters and 111 tanks and troop carriers. *Dawr al-jaysh,* p.219. In fact the Iraqis lost 130 tanks and 50 troop carriers; the other figures, though, are roughly correct.

12. The Pan-Arab Leadership of the Ba'ath Party, *al-Tahlil al-siyasi lil-awda al-arabiyya al-rahina ... al-qiyada al-qawmiyya* (Baghdad, 3 September 1975).

13. Communiqué of the Pan-Arab Leadership, *Al-Jumhuriyya*, 16 November 1977.

14. *Al-Iraq,* (19 November 1977) *Al-Jumhuriyya,* 18,21,22 November 1977.

15. *Al-Jumhuriyya,* October 1978. See also the communiqué of the Pan-Arab Leadership, *Al-Jumhuriyya,* 3 October 1978.

16. The Resolutions of the 9th Regional Congress of the Ba'ath Party in Iraq, *al-Taqrir al-markazi lil mutamar al-qutri al-tasi* (Baghdad, January 1983), p.313.

17. *Al-Jumhuriyya,* 27 October 1978. See also the full text of the Joint National Action Charter between Iraq and Syria in *The Weekly Gazette,* the official government gazette no. 52 (27 December 1978), pp. 2-5.

18. *Al-Thawra, Al-Jumhuriyya, Baghdad Observer,* 30 July, 1 August 1979; *Baghdad Observer,* 8 August 1979.

19. *Al-Taqrir al-markazi,* pp.323-5. For details regarding the shift in Iraqi national priorities, see A. Baram 'Qawmiyya and Wataniyya' and 'Mesopotamian Identity in Ba'thi Iraq', *Middle Eastern Studies,* vol. 19, no. 2 (April 1983) and no.4, (October 1983).

20. Iraqi News Agency (INA), 18 August 1980; Damascus Radio, 19,22 August 1980. For a detailed report of the Syrian embassy staff's return to Damascus, see *Tishrin,* 22 August 1980, p.4; and INA, 21 August 1980.

21. *Al-Jumhuriyya,* 11 April 1982, p.1; 11 May 1982, p.6.

22. *Keesings Contemporary Archives,* (Keesings Publications, Longman Group Ltd, Bath, UK, 4 June 1982), p.31524a.

23. *Al-Siyasa,* 24 May 1982. See also Foreign Minister Hammadi to *Al-Thawra,* 26 September 1982, p.3.

24. *Al-Musawwar* (Cairo), 21 December 1982.

25. *Al-Ahram,* 29 December 1982, as quoted by *Facts on File,* World News Digest, NY, (December 1982).

26. The Economist Intelligence Unit, *Quarterly Economic Review,* 'Iraq', Fourth Quarter, 1982, p. 8; Third Quarter, 1982, p. 10.

8 SYRIA AND JORDAN: THE POLITICS OF SUBVERSION

Joseph Nevo

Introduction

Till the end of the Ottoman period, the territories that later comprised Syria and Jordan shared much in common, from geography to economics and linguistics. The historical and administrative concept of Syria, furthermore, usually included most of Transjordan. At the same time, however, these two areas also differed from each other in certain social aspects and in levels of local cohesion.

The establishment of Transjordan as a political entity separated from Syria stemmed from considerations that were irrelevant both to historical developments and the desires of the indigenous inhabitants. That separation, together with the differences between the two forms of foreign rule that both countries experienced, somewhat blurred the common denominators, sharpened existing differences and created new ones.

With independence, and the passage of time, the respective regimes of the two countries have taken utterly different directions. Syria, an authoritarian republic, built up an impressive military force with the ambition, as well as the potential capability, of becoming a leading Middle Eastern power. The pattern of its global and regional alliances has shown a tendency to prefer the Soviet bloc and the radical Arab regimes. Jordan, a traditional yet fairly enlightened monarchy, also developed an efficient professional army, but one designated (in the last 30 odd years, at least) to preserve the regime and defend the country rather than to back an aggressive regional and foreign policy. In contrast to Syria, Jordan has persisted in its preferences for a pro-Western orientation and alignment with moderate Middle Eastern states.

Syria has championed the cause of the Palestinians, while often ruthlessly suppressing the PLO. For Jordan, the attitude towards the Palestinian was not only a question of expediency — as it was for Syria — but also a matter of survival. Jordan, too, sometimes followed a repressive policy towards the PLO, but constantly adhered to a policy that considered the Palestinians and the Transjordanians as two segments of the same people and country.

These differences between Syria and Jordan, which have become increasingly more pronounced, have given rise to frequent fluctuations in their mutual relations. On several occasions, the two states attempted to merge into one political entity. On the other hand, diplomatic relations between them have been severed at least as frequently, and in four instances the two countries seemed headed towards large-scale armed conflict. Such extreme ups and downs are uncommon even within the inter-Arab system, which has in general been characterised by rapid shifts from violent animosity to declarations of eternal friendship. Tracing the precise causes of these fluctuations cannot possibly be done within the confines of a brief chapter; however, an overview of the history of Syrian-Jordanian bilateral relations as well as a brief analysis of some of the most conspicuous determinants of Jordanian policy are feasible.

Jordan's Policy under Abdallah

Jordanian interest in Syria dates from the very beginning of Hashemite rule in Amman. Abdallah ibn Hussein, founder of the Emirate of Transjordan, and its ruler for 30 years, arrived in that area in 1921. He had come from the Hijaz with the declared intention of advancing into Syria; at the time, he contemplated taking revenge upon the French for their usurpation of the throne of Damascus from his brother Faysal. Eventually he settled for much less: Colonial Secretary Winston Churchill's offer of the remote desert emirate provided Abdallah with a good enough excuse to change his mind. Nevertheless, during the 1920s and 1930s, Abdallah's name was mentioned more than once as a candidate for the kingship of Syria.[1]

After the outbreak of World War II, Abdallah initiated and publicised the 'Greater Syria' scheme that called for the unification of Syria, Lebanon, Transjordan and Palestine under his throne. Henceforth, that scheme became the cornerstone of all his diplomatic efforts.[2] In spite of strong opposition on the part of almost all the parties concerned, he adhered to his territorial goals until his assassination in July 1951. His only achievement in this respect — the annexation of Arab Palestine in 1948 — was described as the fulfillment of the first stage of the Greater Syria scheme.[3] In 1946, when both Syria and Transjordan (henceforth Jordan) gained their independence, Abdallah's tactics became nothing short of intervention in Syria's domestic affairs. Syria reciprocated by filing a complaint to the Arab

League, launching a propaganda campaign and granting political asylum to opposition activists from Amman. Abdallah retaliated by closing his consulate in Damascus.

The three *coups d'état* that took place in Syria in 1949 and the subsequent changes in its political orientation affected ties with Jordan. There was tension and hostility between the two nations under Za'im,[4] rapid improvement in relations after Hinnawi took over and occasional ups and downs under Shishaqli. One has to bear in mind, however, that at that time (the early 1950s), Iraq — the sister Hashemite country dominated the scene — it was attempting to control Syria by conquest or through a union — while Jordan played a secondary role in Syrian-Hashemite relations. Moreover, relations between Jordan and Syria were influenced by developments not directly associated with bilateral issues. In early 1950, for example, tension between the two countries mounted because of rumours (not unfounded) about Israeli-Jordanian peace negotiations and their reaching of an agreement.[5]

The assassination of King Abdallah in July 1951 not only marked the end of a chapter in Jordan's history, but also heralded a new era in its relations with Syria. Up to that point, Abdallah had dominated the scene, his policy towards Syria having been mainly based on his personal and dynastic considerations.[6] Though he was not the first Arab statesman to push for union with Syria,[7] he was the only one to insist that Jordan, under his own leadership, be the core of that unified entity. Thus, it would not be unreasonable to assume that Abdallah aspired to a Greater Jordan rather than to a Greater Syria.

The Impact of Hussein

Hussein's ascendancy to the throne channelled relations between the two countries into an 'ordinary' bilateral pattern. The conduct of the young monarch within the inter-Arab system indicated the return of Jordan to its true political size: Hussein neither introduced grandiose unity schemes nor contemplated shaping other Arab regimes in his own image. As a result, Syria gradually became the dominant factor in their bilateral relations. Jordan's position as the 'junior partner' was maintained because it was (and still is) ruled by the same man. In contrast, Syria underwent frequent internal political changes, with each ruler seeking to demonstrate that he was not a lesser patriot or Arab activist than his predecessor. True, violent or subversive measures directed against Jordan were duly reciprocated. But Jordan did not initiate crises; it merely responded to Syrian challenges.

Hussein's first years on the throne were years of grace. They were characterised by gradually improved ties with Syria, leading, in 1955, to the resumption of full diplomatic relations. From 1955-7, correctly referred to as 'Hussein's Arab-nationalistic era', Jordan was closer than ever to its militant Arab neighbours. Its non-admittance to the Baghdad Pact, together with the dismissal of John B. Glubb and the rest of the British officers from its army, accelerated cordial relations with Syria. Within less than six months, the heads of state, ministers and senior army officers of the two countries exchanged frequent visits, and concluded several military and civil agreements.

The period that followed showed a deterioration in these friendly relations that was even more rapid. The turning point came in April 1957, when a *coup d'état* by some Jordanian army officers was nipped in the bud and Jordan's provocative national-socialist prime minister was dismissed. Although Syria was not behind the plot, it was sympathetic to the conspirators and granted political asylum to the scores of army officers and civilian politicians who escaped from Jordan. In the second half of 1957, their common border was closed, diplomatic relations were broken off and propaganda warfare was commenced.

The tension between the two countries stepped up early in 1958, when Egypt and Syria merged into the United Arab Republic (UAR),[8] and gave way to violence. Armed groups trained in Syria for subversive activities infiltrated into Jordan. Relations undoubtedly reached their lowest ebb in November 1958, when Syrian Migs intercepted Hussein's private jet (flown by the king himself) *en route* to Europe and forced him to return to Amman.

Jordan's rejection of the idea of a Palestinian entity (promoted by Egypt and Iraq in 1959) only made matters worse. Terrorist attacks from Syria against Jordanian targets continued, reaching a peak in August 1960 with the assassination of the prime minister, Haza' al-Majali. The murderers escaped to Syria and Jordan attributed the crime to the UAR intelligence services. The constant deterioration in relations was curbed only in March 1961, thanks to Hussein's initiative. Though mutual suspicions remained high, political dialogue between Hussein and Nasser replaced the attacks against Jordan.

Despite the merger of Egypt and Syria and nothwithstanding their common foreign policy, a distinct pattern of Jordanian-Syrian relations between 1958 and 1961 can still be traced. During this period, Jordan disregarded Syrian violence, to which it had been subjected before and after the foundation of the UAR, and took pains to demonstrate hostility *vis-à-vis* Egypt in order to cultivate Syrian goodwill. Jordanian propaganda indirectly attributed to the Egyptians the violent attacks on its territory and citizens that originated from Syria in 1960. It frequently accused Egypt of using the UAR framework to oppress Syria and to destroy 'anything that is Syrian'.[9] Insinuating that Egypt was working against both Syrian and Jordanian interests and diverting the relations between the two from their 'natural' course, Jordanian broadcasts urged the Syrians to liberate themselves from the Egyptian yoke.

Upon the dissolution of the UAR in 1961, Jordan was the first country to recognise Syria and to offer it support against political attacks by Egypt and other Arab states for breaking an 'historical' union and becoming an isolationist. These improved relations lasted for a brief interlude, as the Ba'athist revolution in 1963 widened the ideological gap between the two countries. Syria's subsequent renewal of amiable relations with Egypt (and Iraq) not only isolated Jordan but also made it the prime target of Syrian propaganda.

A slight improvement in Syrian-Jordanian bilateral relations in 1964-5 was soon checked by the establishment of the PLO — with the blessing of the inter-Arab system — and the revival of Palestinian nationalism. These events introduced a new dimension into the relations of the two countries. Syria developed the idea of a 'popular war of liberation' (against Israel) and made the Fatah organisation its protégé. Jordan, less than happy about the concept of a Palestinian renaissance, was forced to choose between acquiescence or confrontation within the inter-Arab system. The split between Jordan and the PLO in 1966 placed further strain on already tense Syrian-Jordanian relations, and several other developments accelerated their deterioration.[10] By the end of May 1967, the two countries were on the brink of open conflict; and it may be plausibly assumed that the outbreak of the Six Day war prevented escalation into all-out hostilities.

After a year in isolation, Jordan was provided by the 1967 war and its outcome with renewed legitimacy among the Arab states, Syria included. Conflicts over the Palestinian issue, however, were to crop up again. Syria unequivocally supported the Palestinian organisations whenever they were involved in battles with Jordanian authorities. In September 1970, Syria went so far as to send an armoured division into Jordanian territory to reinforce the Palestinians during the Black September showdown with Hussein's army. When Jordan once again operated against the Palestinians in July 1971, Syria severed diplomatic relations and closed the border.

The outbreak of the Yom Kippur war found both countries in the midst of a gradual and cautious *rapprochement*. Jordan's contribution to the Syrian military effort, albeit token, accelerated the improvement of relations. In 1975 and 1976, the two countries were on the verge of a union. A common supreme leadership was established, and practical measures for merging several systems (civil as well as military) were taken. Both parties benefited: Jordan became the only Arab state to back the Syrian invasion of Lebanon, while Syria recognised Jordan's special status regarding the Palestine question. President Assad publicly supported Hussein's federation scheme as a solution to that problem.[11]

Nothwithstanding the continuous political co-operation, disagreements on matters of principle between Syria and Jordan cast a shadow on the *rapprochement* in 1977. The visit that year of Egypt's President Sadat to Jerusalem led in its wake to a clear cleavage between Syria and Jordan, the gap widened by Syria's not unfounded suspicions that members of the Muslim Brotherhood, its most dangerous internal opposition, had escaped to Jordan.[12] In reaction to Syria's mounting hostility, Jordan was quick to improve relations with Iraq, Syria's ideological and political arch-enemy. Taking advantage of the Gulf war to prove its loyalty to its new ally, Jordan became the first Arab state explicitly to side with Iraq and placed resources and facilities at its disposal. In doing so, Jordan secured Iraqi amity, which it intended to use as a counterweight to Syria's demanding influence.

The unavoidable outcome was a new crisis; and in December 1980, Jordan and Syria came very close to violent confrontation[13] as massive military concentrations were deployed along the common border. It took several weeks of Saudi mediation to defuse the tension, which only mounted again in early 1981, following the kidnapping of the Jordanian military attaché in Beirut[14] and the uncovering of a plot to assassinate the prime minister. Jordan accused Rif'at Assad, brother of the Syrian president, of initiating and organising the murder attempt; and Syria retaliated by sending a few Palestinian groups to operate against Israel through Jordanian territory, thereby embarrassing Hussein.

The war in Lebanon in 1982 only increased the tension; the unclear future of the PLO, after having lost its territorial base in Beirut, sharply exposed the divergence of opinions between Jordan and Syria regarding that organisation and the Palestinian question in general. Syria was apprehensive lest Arafat's weakened position produce a *rapprochement* between him and Hussein and Jordan be granted the desirable mandate to negotiate a political settlement. Such possibilities placed Syria's vital interests and ideological tenets in jeopardy. The first round of Hussein-Arafat talks in March-April 1983 were followed by extreme Syrian pressure on both sides in order to thwart the dialogue. Aside from a series of attempts (some of them successful) on the lives of Jordanian diplomats all over the world, Syria encouraged the split within the PLO and the challenge to Arafat's leadership. In fact, respective reactions to the internal struggles of the PLO somewhat reflected Syrian-Jordanian relations in general: Syria made considerable efforts to replace or at least constrain Arafat, and thereby guarantee an obedient, pro-Syrian organisation; Jordan remained ostensibly passive,[15] expecting Arafat to make the next move. In fact, most of the events that either fostered advancement or caused regression in their bilateral relations originated from Syria. Jordan was usually the respondent, though at times its reactions were sometimes as decisive as were Syria's provocations.

The brief historical overview suggests a pattern of mild-to-tense inter-relations, which at certain points improve — rather quickly and for relatively short periods — only to deteriorate once again to mildness or even hostility. From the Jordanian perspective the history of these relations can be divided roughly into five periods as follows:

1. The era of King Abdallah (till 1951),
2. King Hussein's early years (till 1961),
3. Up to the Six Day war (1967),
4. Till the October 1973 war and its aftermath,
5. Since 1974.

The determinants of the content and texture of Jordanian-Syrian relations in each of these periods call for a focused discussion at some length.

The Determinants of Jordanian-Syrian Relations

Broadly speaking Jordanian-Syrian relations were determined by seven factors: the dynastic ambitions of the Hashemites, the Greater Syria scheme, domestic social processes and historical processes, the changing military balance, economic dependence, inter-Arab pressures and ideological and structural differences.

Hashemite Ideology and the 'Greater Syria' Scheme

King Abdallah ascribed the utmost importance to Syria in both dynastic and pan-Arab terms, considering that country a family realm, as his brother Faysal was its first ruler after the disintegration of the Ottoman empire. He himself departed his native Hijaz 'for the sake of Syria and Palestine',[16] following the French usurpation of the Syrian throne. Even his eventual agreement to settle for rule over Transjordan stemmed from the prospect of regaining Syria for his family. Winston Churchill, when offering him the emirate in 1921, had pointed out that successful prevention of anti-French activity from Transjordan might lead to the return of Syria to the Hashemites within six months.[17] In other words, the French might accept Abdallah as emir in Damascus under their auspices.[18]

Aside from his dynastic aspirations, Abdallah considered Syria the historical and territorial centre of the Arab nation. He saw the re-establishment of the historical *bilad al-Sham* (Syria's ancient Arabic name) as the most important territorial objective of the Arab revolt in World War I.[19] He referred to Greater Syria (*Surriya al-kubra*) not only as an historical entity, but also as a natural (*Surriya al-tab'iyya*) and geographical (*Surriya al-Jughrafiyya*) entity.[20] Abdallah, moreover, developed a series of arguments to substantiate his claim to rule over Greater Syria. These arguments provided him with an ideological justification for interfering in Syria's internal affairs and, in fact, defined the scope and nature of the relations between Jordan and Syria.

King Hussein has also made extensive use of the Hashemite heritage and the memory of the Arab revolt. His deep emotional commitment to the legacy of Abdallah is evident. Nevertheless, he has made no efforts to fulfill his grandfather's ambitions or to utilise his ideas politically or ideologically.

Upon the accession to power of Hafez al-Assad, the tables turned. Assad exploited the concept of Greater Syria for his own ends, to justify controversial actions like the invasion of Lebanon (and later, the refusal to withdraw) and to threaten recalcitrant Arab colleagues. Yassir Arafat's somewhat critical reference in 1974 to Syria's patronisation of the PLO was immediately followed by Assad's statement that Palestine had no independent standing and was actually southern Syria.[21] The *rapprochement* that brought Jordan and Syria to the brink of union in 1975-6 was considered by foreign observers as a Syrian attempt at Syrian-Jordan 'integration'. The Greater Syria objective was not ignored by King Hussein, who eventually rejected all proposed measures that would have made the 'integration' irreversible.[22] The idea of Greater Syria, so aggressively promoted by King Abdallah, now made contemporary Jordan a potential victim of Syrian ambitions of geographical expansion. Jordan's Crown Prince Hassan once complained that 'the Syrians say there are no Palestinians, Jordanians, Lebanese — that they are all Southern Syrians.'[23]

Domestic Social Processes

The territory composing the Emirate of Transjordan in the 1920s (and later, the Hashemite Kingdom of Jordan) had never been an integrated administrative or political unit before Abdallah assumed the throne. Throughout history, considerable portions of that area had been administered from Damascus for rather long periods, beginning with the rule of the Umayyad dynasty (7th-8th centuries AD). Under the Ottoman empire, northern and central Transjordan were part of the vilayet of Sham (the provinces of Syria); and during the Faysal regime in Damascus (1918-20), his realm also included most of Transjordan, which was within the eastern section of the post-war Occupied Enemy Territory Administration/East (OETA/E). When Abdallah established himself in Transjordan, his administration was largely based on Syrian personnel. Moreover, all his prime ministers until 1931 were Syrians.[24] Consequently, many inhabitants of the northern part of Transjordan, especially the Ajlun area, remained Damascus-oriented for years after the establishment of a central administration in Amman.

The north was inhabited by a sedentary population (as opposed to the nomadic character of the south), more economically and socially developed, albeit more critical and resentful of the Hashemite regime. Indeed, most of the opposition in Jordan after 1948 (excluding Palestinians) originated from the north, mainly the Ajlun and Balqaa districts. The most conspicuous of these activists were army officers involved in plots to topple the regime, such as Abdallah al-Tall, Mahmud al-Rusan and Sadiq al-Shara' from Ajlun, and Ali Khiyari and Ali Abu Nuwar from Balqaa.[25] Many conspirators and opposition leaders escaped to Syria, which granted them political asylum.

Some of the Bedouin tribes in the north settled; others, though, wandered along both sides of the border. The Jordanian sections of these tribes were inclined to threaten to cross the border and join their brothers in Syria in order to extract various concessions or benefits from the authorities.

The Changing Military Balance

The unitary territorial ambitions of the Hashemites (and of Abdallah, in particular) during the late 1940s and the early 1950s constituted a viable threat for Syria because of its military strength *vis-à-vis* Jordan (and Iraq). Jordan's British-equipped, trained and commanded Arab Legion, a professional standing army, was considered by many as the best Arab force. Its success in the 1948 war with Israel, which enabled Abdallah to annex the West Bank, contributed to its reputation. The Legion outnumbered the young, ill-trained and poorly equipped Syrian army, the core of which were the '*Troupes spéciales du Levant*' of the mandatory period that had been trained and commanded by the French. Inferior to the Legion in its scope, quality and military experience, the Syrian army in 1948 also had rather meagre achievements in comparison.[26]

The military gap was gradually narrowed during the 1950s, and the balance began changing in favour of Syria. The turning point came in 1958, when, on the one hand, the Hashemite regime in Iraq was eliminated and, on the other hand, Syria entered into a union with Egypt. Even after the dissolution of the United Arab Republic, Syria constantly increased its military edge over Jordan. The order of priorities of the various Ba'athist regimes, Syria's relations with the Soviet Union and the less selective opening of the Soviet arsenal augmented the size and equipment of the Syrian army and ameliorated its quality.[27]

The fear of Syrian military power and apprehension that it might use it have become, since the late 1960s, a dominant factor influencing Jordan's attitude towards its neighbour. As already indicated, Jordan has been compelled on several occasions to respond to a military challenge when the Syrians did not hesitate to back their political claims with military pressure.

Jordan's Dependence on Syria

Because of political and geographical constraints and particularly the absence of an outlet to the Mediterranean, most of Jordan's links to Europe have passed through Syrian territory or air space, consequently making Jordan considerably economically dependent on Syria. This dependence has been augmented in recent years, since most of Jordan's revenue comes from hundreds of small factories engaged in production for the Syrian market and for the Gulf.[28] The need to utilise Syrian air space to Europe has also had political repercussions, as in the case of the Syrian interception of King Hussein's plane in November 1958.

This dependence has both affected bilateral relations, reinforcing Syrian dominance, and has been influenced by them. Whenever a deterioration in relations led to conflict, Syria did not hesitate to take advantage of Jordanian dependency by closing the border, an action that proved to be an effective weapon more than once. Jordan endeavoured to minimise the negative consequences of such situations by providing special inducement for the use of the port of Aqaba and increasing its maritime communications with Europe via the Suez Canal. Upon the closure of the Canal in 1967, Jordan returned to square one, its dependence upon Syria now even stronger. The Syrians did not fail to exploit the situation when they closed their border with Jordan between July 1971 and December 1972.[29]

The political implications of this dependence sometimes exceeded certain limits for Jordan. It forced Jordan to solicit Israel's good will, which was not only humiliating but also hazardous, owing to the Arab reaction that such a move could evoke. In July 1958, following the *coup d'état* in Iraq that terminated that country's union with Jordan, British troops were hastened to Amman to protect Hussein and his regime from any potential aggression. Because of Syria's hostile attitude, the only possible flight course from British bases in Europe and Cyprus was via Israel's air space. The Israelis consented and Hussein was forced to acquiesce. Several months later he found himself in a similar situation, when Jordan's oil supply, which had come by truck from Lebanon, was cut off by the Syrians. Neither the Iraqis nor the Saudis would allow shipments from the Gulf to be flown over their territories. Eventually the Americans obtained permission to fly oil to Jordan through Israel's air space.[30]

Economic dependence was not entirely unilateral, however; Jordan also had something to offer. When the Suez Canal was blocked and even afterwards, goods destined for Syria (especially from the Far East) often arrived in Aqaba. That dependence, however, was not a decisive factor whenever tension prevailed between the two countries.

Mutual economic interests sometimes produced two levels of relations: ideological conflicts had political repercussions bringing relations to a low ebb, but economic connections were maintained.[31] The Syrians, nevertheless, did impose an economic blockade in 1958, when Jordan was geographically and politically isolated, and it apparently was effective. A second blockade was imposed in 1971, immediately after Assad assumed power. He was eager to demonstrate his decisiveness and commitment to the Palestinian cause; however, he also wanted to take revenge on the Jordanians for their successful resistance of the Syrian invasion less than a year before.

The Inter-Arab System: The fear of the Hashemites and of Abdallah's initiatives had originally pushed Syria into a bloc with Egypt and Saudi Arabia with the founding of the Arab League. In spite of the political and ideological regroupings of the 1950s and the changing alliances and coalitions, Syria and Jordan remained in different camps. Against the Saudi-Jordanian *rapprochement*, on the one side, stood the 'progressive' sector of the Arab world, Syria together with Egypt and (republican) Iraq.

The location of Syria and Jordan on the Arab chess board is rather important, since as from the late 1950s the inter-Arab system has played an active role in the politics of the Middle East. Its members have been unable to ignore the decisions or the recommendations of their common framework as they had been able to do a decade before.[32]

Syria has generally enjoyed a more senior status in the Arab world than has Jordan because of the former's size, location and political importance. Concomitant with the growing prominence of the inter-Arab system — mainly during the 1960s and the 1970s — Syria's influence increased and Jordan became obliged, even more than before, to take Syria's views into account. This development fostered gradual Syrian dominance in their bilateral relations. Since the early 1980s, however, the influence of the inter-Arab system on these bilateral relations has weakened. First, the importance of that system has diminished because of sharp polarisations in the Arab world and basic divisions over such crucial issues as the Arab-Israeli conflict and the Gulf war. Second, Jordan's status within the inter-Arab system has undergone amelioration (particularly in 1984, when its relations with Egypt and the PLO were renewed) — and it could counterweight Syrian influence.

Different Ideologies, Different Levels of Stability: The frequent fluctuations in Syrian-Jordanian relations should also be attributed to the different nature of the respective regimes and, in particular, to the differences in their internal strength. Whereas Jordan has been ruled for more than 30 years by the same monarch, and for the 30 years before that by his predecessor (if we consider Talal's reign as a mere intermezzo), rule in Syria has frequently been challenged, usually by force. In 1949 alone, Syria experienced three take-overs, each ushering in a new regime that possessed different views, *inter alia,* towards Jordan. Internal instability was one of the hallmarks of Syrian regimes during the 1950s and 1960s, and bilateral relations with Jordan often reflected political agitation in Damascus. Although it is true that Syria has now been ruled by the same man for the past fourteen years and that his regime has been amazingly stable and durable, basic ideological disagreements that existed before Assad came to power continue among Syria's different political-religious groupings and must also be taken into consideration.

Jordan, a monarchy that has been consistently pro-Western, possesses both a form of government and a political orientation that are not too popular in the contemporary Middle East. The history of Jordan, the nature of its regime and the structure of its economy indicate that its relations with the West are deeper than are those of any other country in the region. Syria, on the other hand, is a republic, having very close ties with the Eastern bloc. In the last 20 or so years, it has been ruled by various sections of the Ba'ath Party; but even before then, its regime was ideologically associated with 'Nasserism' and 'progressive' Arab nationalism. As a result of this basic ideological gap between the two countries, cordial relations arising from pragmatic considerations (such as the *rapprochements* of 1956, 1961 and 1975/6) usually did not last. Political realism may sometimes override ideological differences, but the sort of co-operation that can then be obtained is vulnerable and exposed to agitation.

Ideological differences provide an explanation, too, for the relatively frequent Syrian-sponsored attempts to topple the Jordanian regime. From the Syrian point of view, abolition of the Jordanian monarchy might also narrow the ideological gap and pave the way for closer links. It might eventually lead to Syrian hegemony.

Finally, ideological diversities have provided an excuse (mainly to the Syrians) for further tension, even when the real underlying cause was inter-Arab rivalries or the need to distract local public opinion from internal difficulties. In that respect, the Syrians attributed the tension with Jordan in early 1981 to Hussein's attitude to the Palestinian problem and to his alleged attempts to overthrow the Syrian regime. At the time, however, there were no signs that Amman was either planning to abandon its frequently reiterated position on Palestinian rights or conspiring against Assad. Moreover, neither of these options would have served Jordanian interests.[33]

Major Issues Dominating the Bilateral Relations

A study of the central issues confronting Jordan and Syria and the measure of their agreement or disagreement on these matters contribute to a better understanding of certain aspects of the bilateral relations of these two countries. The following summarises the three key issues discussed in this chapter.

1. *Unity Plans.* Plans for the creation of a new political unit that would be comprised, *inter alia*, of Jordan and Syria was the main bilateral issue at the time of King Abdallah. Diversity of opinion over this subject dominated relations in the late 1940s and has been the prime source of the prevailing tension.
2. *The Question of Palestine.* The attitude towards Palestine became a controversial issue from the early 1960s. Syria's ideas regarding the means and methods of 'liberating' Palestine and Syrian views on the future of that country have constituted a threat to Jordan's integrity and stability. All-out Syrian support of the Palestinian organisations — especially since 1967 — stands in opposition to Jordan's interests and aspirations and has undermined the latter's political position.
3. *The Ideological Gap Per Se.* Conceptual differences have had an effect on bilateral relations from the outset. Ever since 1946, when both countries gained their independence, the Syrians have claimed that if Abdallah had genuinely desired unity, he merely had to give up the monarchy and attach his country to a republican Syria.[34] The different orientations and constitutions of the respective regimes have been the cause of most of the verbal and active confrontations between Syria and Jordan.

Conclusion

An attempt (in the first months of 1984), to map Syrian-Jordanian bilateral relations between their highest and lowest points would place these relations below the middle mark. This position may be described as a 'stable depression', with the relatively few fluctuations, being mainly expressed in political terms. Their more violent aspect has been manifested in the series of attempts, attributed to Syrian agents, on the lives of Jordanian diplomats at the end of 1983 and in early 1984. Conflicting attitudes regarding the leadership of the PLO, Jordan's support of Iraq and the ideological gap contribute to the low placement of these relations.

The most conspicuous process of Jordanian-Syrian bilateral relations has been the latter's becoming the dominant element, starting in the early 1950s. Simultaneously the military balance between the two countries also shifted; and since the late 1950s, there has taken place an increasing gap in favour of Syria. This latter process is particularly important, as Syrian regimes have had no constraints on using their armed forces to promote their regional foreign policy. Thus the possibility of the current situation deteriorating into open hostilities should not be ruled out. On at least four occasions, a 'stable depression' escalated into a mass concentration of forces along both sides of the border. On one such occasion (i.e. in September 1970), the Syrian military deployment turned into an armed invasion of northern Jordan.[35]

The sharp fluctuations in Syrian-Jordanian relations have had, as has been seen, several causes, some of them influencing these relations constantly, others having only temporary importance or occurring during special situations. Most of these factors are still valid and, therefore, may have an effect on future events. In view of both recent and earlier developments, one can assume that as long as ideological differences between the two countries prevail, any *rapprochement* will be based merely on *ad hoc* interests and, therefore, will be limited in scope and duration. In the long run, a substantial improvement is feasible only in the case of a basic change in the ideological character of one of the two regimes or in the case of conspicuous political changes within the inter-Arab system. Nevertheless, judging from an historical perspective, even these developments would not guarantee durable and lasting amity between the two countries.

Notes

1. Ahmed M. Gomaa, *The Foundation of the League of Arab States: Wartime Diplomacy and Inter-Arab Politics, 1941 to 1945* (Longman, London, 1977), p. 81; Itamar Rabinovich, 'The Question of the Syrian Monarchy', *Zmanim*, vol. 1, no. 3 (April 1980), pp. 92-9 (in Hebrew); Werner E. Goldner, *The Role of Abdallah Ibn Hussain, King of Jordan in Arab Politics 1914-1951* (University Microfilm, Ann Arbor, 1954), pp. 272-6. The rumours were usually meant to serve the interests of the French authorities, certain political parties in Syria or members of the Hashemite family.

2. On the origin and details of that scheme and attempts to implement it, see *Al-Kitab al-urduni al-abiyad: Al-wathaiq al-qawmiyya fi-al-wahda al-suriyya al-tab'iyya*, The Jordanian White Paper: The National Documents on the Natural Unity of Syria, The Government of Transjordan, Amman, 1947; Majid Khadduri, 'The Scheme of Fertile Crescent Unity: A Study in Inter-Arab Relations', in R.N. Frye (ed.), *The Near East and the Great Powers* (Harvard University Press, Boston, 1951), pp. 137-77.

3. A motion in that respect was made in December 1948, at the congress of Jericho, which called upon Abdallah to annex Arab Palestine. See Joseph Nevo, *Abdallah and the Arabs of Palestine* (Tel-Aviv University, 1975), p. 113 (in Hebrew).

4. Za'im was quoted as having said: 'Jordan is merely a Syrian province. When Abdallah dies I shall take over his domain.' He later denied ever having made such a statement. *Hamizrah Hehadash* (Quarterly of the Israel Oriental Society), vol. 1, no. 1 (October 1949), p. 51.

5. *Hamizrah Hehadash,* vol. 1, no. 4 (July 1950), p. 317.

6. Mohammad Ibrahim Faddah, *The Middle East in Transition: A Study of Jordan's Foreign Policy* (Asia Publishing House, London, 1974), p. 160.

7. On his predecessors' attempts, see, for example, Barry Rubin, *The Arab States and the Palestine Conflict* (Syracuse University Press, Syracuse, NY, 1981), p. 102.

8. This merger was immediately followed by the 'Arab Union' between Jordan and Iraq that lasted only a few months and was violently terminated by the Iraqi *coup d'état* in July 1958.

9. Asher Susser, 'A Political Biography of Wasfi al-Tall', unpublished MA thesis, Tel-Aviv University, March 1980, pp. 13-14.

10. In September 1966, Jordan granted political asylum to the Syrian Druze major Salim Hatum, a leader of an abortive *coup d'état,* as well as to hundreds of his followers. Syria insinuated that Jordan had backed the foiled plot. The outcome of these accusations was mutual and extremely violent propaganda warfare. Sabotage activities and even military movement ensued. In late May 1967, a car bomb arriving from Syria exploded at the Jordanian border check-point at Ramtha, killing 16 people; see, *Middle East Record,* vol. 3, (1967), pp. 126-7.

11. *Middle East Contemporary Survey* (MECS), vol. 1, (1976/7), p. 154.

12. On Jordanian support of Brotherhood activities, see *Al-Safir,* 29 December 1979, and 14 June 1980; *Boston Globe,* 16 July 1980.

13. Syria again accused Jordan of supporting the Muslim Brotherhood and betraying the Palestinian cause. *MECS,* vol. V, (1980/1), p. 236.

14. Ibid. Syria's involvement was obvious although the actual kidnappers were Palestinians. The ransom they demanded was the extradition of two Syrian pilots who had deserted to Jordan several months before.

15. Actually Jordan had taken some indirect steps, such as the reconvening of the National Assembly in Amman in early 1984.

16. *Al-Takmila min mudhakirat al-malik abdallah* (The Completion of the Memoirs of King Abdallah) (Amman, 1951), p. 39.

17. Abdallah ibn Hussain, *Mudhakirati* (My Memoirs), (Matba'at Beit al-Maqdas, Jerusalem, 1945); reprint, Amman, 1965, p. 168.

18. Churchill's own account is less unequivocal on that point. See PRO/FO, 371-6343, pp. 109-14; also Gomaa, *The Foundation of the League of Arab States,* p. 79.

19. Israel Gershoni, 'The Arab Nation, the Hashemite Dynasty and Greater Syria in the writings of Abdallah' (Part II), *Hamizrah Hehadash,* vol. 25, no. 3 (1975), p. 166.

20. Israel Gershoni, 'King Abdallah's concept of a "Greater Syria",' in Anne Sinai and Allen Pollack (eds.), *The Hashemite Kingdom of Jordan and the West Bank. A Handbook* (American Academic Association for Peace in the Middle East, New York, 1977), p. 140.

21. *Oriente Moderno,* vol. 54, 1974, p. 73.

22. Daniel Dishon, 'Old Rivals: New Quarrels', *Jerusalem Post Magazine,* (6 March 1981), p. 4.

23. *Los Angeles Times,* 7 August 1983.

24. They were Rashid Tali'a, Madhar Raslan, Ali Rida al-Rikabi and Hassan Khalid Abu al-Huda.

25. For more details, see Uriel Dann, 'Regime and Opposition in Jordan Since 1949', in Menachem Milson (ed.), *Society and Political Structure in the Arab World,* (Humanities Press, New York, 1973), pp. 153, 163-71. See also P.J. Vatikiotis, *Politics and the Military in Jordan,* (Frank Cass, London, 1967), pp. 97-136.

26. There are different estimates regarding the size of the two armies. Most data, however, indicate that the Jordanian army was larger. Not a single source questions the qualitative preference of the Arab Legion. John B. Glubb, *A Soldier with the Arabs* (Hodder and Stoughton, London, 1957), p. 94; Jon and David Kimche, *Both Sides of the Hill* (Secker and Warburg, London, 1960), p. 162; David Ben Gurion, *The Restored State of Israel* (Am Oved, Tel-Aviv, 1969), vol. 1, p. 71 (in Hebrew). Iraq, too, has to be put in the Hashemite side of the equation. One has to bear in mind that in that period, it was even a greater menace to Syria than was Jordan (see p. 252). The combination of the Jordanian and Iraqi armies considerably increased the gap between the Syrians and the Hashemites.

27. For details on the military power of Syria and Jordan, consult the various issues of the annual of the Institute for Strategic Studies (London), *The Military Balance.* See also Nadav Safran, *From War to War: The Arab-Israeli Confrontation, 1948-1967* (Pegasus, New York, 1969), pp. 227-35, 439-41, 445-7, 449-52.

28. Nancy Good, 'Hussein's Priorities', *Jerusalem Post,* 12 August 1979, p. 10.

29. *Middle East Economic Digest,* (12 May 1972).

30. Peter Snow, *Hussein* (Barrie and Jenkins, London, 1972), pp. 124-5.

31. *Hawadith,* 11 May 1981; *The Middle East,* (April 1981), pp. 64-5.

32. The measures taken by the Arab League in 1948-50 against Jordan's annexation of the West Bank were indecisive and ineffective. In 1964, however, Jordan could not disregard the Arab summit conference resolution to establish the Palestine Liberation Organisation, even though it challenged Jordan's national interests.

33. Adid Dawisha, 'Much Smoke, Little Fire', *Middle East International,* (27 February 1981), pp. 10-11.

34. Khadduri, 'The Scheme of Fertile Crescent Unity', p. 150.

35. In the second half of 1984, there were indications that the recession in Syrian-Jordanian bilateral relations was continuing, particularly after the elections in Israel and the USA, Jordan's resumption of relations with Eygpt and improvement of ties with the PLO mainstream.

9 SYRIA AND ISRAEL: THE POLITICS OF ESCALATION

Avner Yaniv

Introduction

The Israeli-Egyptian peace and the Israeli invasion of Lebanon have, in their ensemble, brought the encounter between the Jewish state and Syria to a new level of mutual risk. The Egyptians' concept of peace may differ from Israel's, but though this is occasionally a source of some tension between Egypt and Israel, the former's abdication from the Arab war coalition against the latter seems complete. Having challenged Egypt's decision to follow this course as vehemently as Syria has, she was left with no alternative but to continue to carry the anti-Israel banner practically alone. During 1976-81 there was a brief moment in which a rare convergence of interests between Syria and Israel over Lebanon and the PLO seemed to point the way towards something amounting to a détente. Yet the nature of the tacit understanding was such that it also contained the germs of a large-scale collision. When this occurred in June 1982, tensions between these adversaries peaked. Moreover, Syria's partial yet quite spectacular defeat led to a frantic Syrian effort to offset Israel's visible superiority through a combination of assiduous diplomacy and a much accelerated process of force construction. The upshot was a new level of tension and danger, not only to Syria and Israel, but increasingly to the entire Middle East and, quite conceivably, to the whole world.

Superficially it could be argued that Israel's actions under Begin and Sharon or, alternatively, that Hafez al-Assad's 'irrational' militancy were the main causes of these developments. A far more sophisticated evaluation would lead, however, to the conclusion that the Israeli confrontation with Syria at the present cannot be fully comprehended unless it is firmly anchored in an analysis which goes back all the way to the aftermath of the 1948 war. Such an approach, it will be argued here, shifts the emphasis from the idiosyncratic traits of individuals such as Begin, Sharon or Arens on the Israeli side and Hafez al-Assad, Rif'at al-Assad, Mustafa Tlas and Abd al-Halim Khaddam on the Syrian side to broader impersonal processes. Consequently it also offers a far sounder basis for an evaluation of future trends in this lethal powder keg.[1]

The North of the Militarised Zone

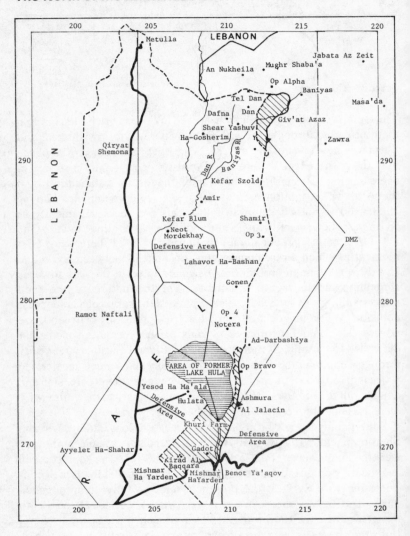

The South of the Militarised Zone

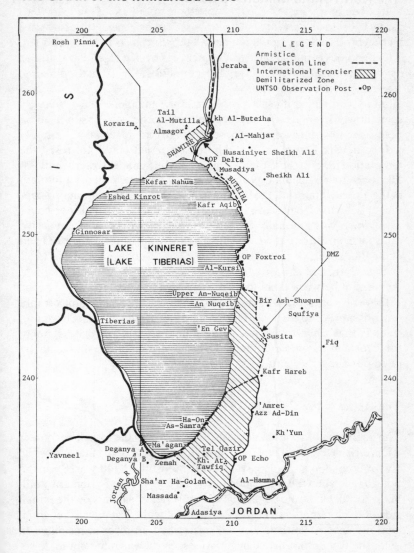

More specifically the argument here is that the seeds of the present state of danger were sown in the immediate aftermath of the 1948 war. Israel insisted on carrying out a number of development projects on the Syrian border. Syria would not permit those projects to be carried out. This deadlock eventually led to a sequence of ever-worsening hostilities in which both sides were, it is argued, perfectly rational but the outcome was nevertheless escalation.

Israel completed all these projects in the middle of the 1960s. By then, however, images of implacable hostility had so consolidated on both sides that the escalatory process continued apace and eventually led to the Six Day war. For this reason Israel could not resist the temptation to seize the Golan Heights, and thus made it utterly imposs-ible for Syria not to join Egypt in the Yom Kippur war. In the aftermath of the Yom Kippur war, the interim agreements and the simmering con-flict in Lebanon facilitated a tacit understanding between the two coun-tries which was gradually eroded, however, as a result of a massive arms race, on the one hand, and the disruptive activities of the PLO and of the Phalanges, on the other hand. Against this background, the 1982 war led Syria and Israel to yet another collision, which in turn brought the tension between them to its present level.

Does all this imply that the two protagonists are heading inexorably towards an Armageddon? The conclusion to which this discussion leads is that while this is not entirely unlikely, the opposite, namely some form of accommodation in the not so distant future should not be ruled out altogether either.

The Roots of the Conflict: 1948-1956

The beginning of wisdom in trying to understand the Israeli encounter with Syria is to appreciate the critical importance of the fact that while Egypt, Lebanon and to an extent Jordan, lost the 1948 war, Syria did not. In fact when the war ended in January 1949, the Syrian army still held a small but strategically significant series of salients on the Israeli side of the international border. As a result while Egypt and Lebanon, anxious to retrieve their lost territories, had a powerful incentive to enter the Rhodes armistice negotiations, Syria was reluctant to do so. Indeed, as the debate on the issue in the Syrian legislature was approaching, there was a vociferous outcry in the Syrian press against joining the negotiations in which, it was argued, the politicians could lose the Syrian army's gains. Ultimately Syrian Premier Khalid al-

Azam succeeded in prevailing upon his opponents. A debate was held and a majority of the deputies gave their approval to negotiate a limited military agreement with the Zionist enemy. But Azam did not demand, and neither he nor any of his numerous successors ever received, a mandate for a Syrian withdrawal.

From the Israeli point of view this Syrian position was totally unacceptable. If Israel were to accept the continued presence of Syrian forces west of the international border she would be unable to reclaim the Hula swamps, she would lose exclusive control over the Sea of Galilee and she would be hardly capable of defending the Galilee 'finger' formed by the narrow elongated valley which lies between the Lebanese and Syrian borders. Israel therefore insisted on the evacuation of the Syrian army. The upshot was a deadlock in the armistice negotiations. But since neither Israel nor Syria wished to engage in renewed hostilities, both accepted ultimately a compromise solution suggested by UN mediator Ralph Bunche.

According to the agreement, which was signed on 23 August 1949, Syrian forces would be evacuated but the areas held by them at the cessation of hostilities would remain demilitarised. Since the sovereign rights over these areas (see map on pp. 158-9) were not determined and since neither side would give up hope ultimately to establish full sovereignty in the demilitarised zones (DMZs), the latter became a festering wound, a constant source of contention, during the following years.[2] Israel hoped to contain the growing friction by gradually moving towards a *de facto* partition of the DMZs. Syria would have the southern DMZ and Israel the other two zones. Syria, however, was unwilling to endorse such a solution.

High-ranking Israeli officers met with their Syrian counterparts several times during 1949-53 and attempted to pursuade them to accept the idea of *de facto* partition. Their efforts were, however, to no avail. Hence Israel decided to act unilaterally. Paramilitary kibbutzim were established in several parts of the DMZ and Israeli earth-moving equipment moved to the Hula Lake and swamp area in order to reclaim it.[3] At first Syria reacted calmly and merely complained to the Mixed Armistice Commission (MSC). But as of February 1951 Syria decided to resort to force in order to thwart the Israeli activities. The upshot was escalation sometimes leading to pitched battle involving large ground forces and even air power.[4]

Having been beaten and unwilling to face a general war, the Syrians eventually yielded and order was restored. During 1951-5, however, the focus gradually shifted to the Sea of Galilee, where Syria demanded fishing rights despite the fact that the Armistice Agreement had given Israel full sovereign rights over the entire lake. Israel insisted on adhering to the letter of the Armistice Agreement. Syria reacted by force and sought to prevent Israeli vessels from moving in the north-east corner of the lake. Again the result was escalation which climaxed on 11 December 1955 in an Israeli raid on Syrian forces in which 50 Syrian soldiers lost their lives.[5]

By this time Syrian-Israeli relations had already frozen into rigid hostility. The direct negotiations between high-level military personnel were not resumed. Communication was maintained only indirectly, through UN machinery, or, worse still, through vicious media coverage. The die was cast and when Syria fell into the Nasserist (and Soviet) orbit the stage was set for an almost deterministic process of escalation in the years ahead.

Deterioration Gathers Momentum: The 1956-1967 Period

The 1956 Suez campaign deterred Syria — in the face of a clear demonstration of Israeli superiority — from taking on Israel single-handedly. At the same time, the swift Israeli victory added weight to Syria's determination to do her utmost to confront the 'Zionist threat'. Moreover, the Syrian-Egyptian union of 1958-61 must have convinced Israel that Syria was turned into little more than Egypt in disguise. But since the Sinai confrontation line was *defused* by the restrictions on the Egyptian armed forces in the Sinai following Israel's withdrawal in 1957, the Syrian-Israeli front was inevitably turned into the single most important line of confrontation between Israel, on the one hand, and *both* Egypt and Syria, on the other hand. The upshot was that local incidents along this line were inevitably perceived in a wider context which could only precipitate further escalation.

The Tawfiq raid of February 1960 was a good case in point. The immediate cause of this clash was Israel's insistence on her right to cultivate parts of the southern DMZ. Again, as in the past, there was a certain logic to this insistence. Not to cultivate these lands would mean yielding to Syrian pressure and allowing Syria gradually to take effective control. Cultivating could either bring Syrian shooting — in which case Syria would be the culprit — or a tacit Syrian acquiescence — in which case it would be a clear Israeli gain. At the same time if the Syrians were to shoot, Israel would have no alternative but to escalate.

An alternative interpretation is that faced with frequent Syrian fire on a small scale, Israel looked for an excuse to deal Syria a major blow for deterrence purposes. But in order to have adequate pretext *vis-à-vis* the UN, Israel decided to begin agricultural work in the southern DMZ. Syria — it could be reasoned in advance — would have no option but to open fire and Israel would then be able to engage in an action which could be presented for international consumption as a legitimate act of retaliation.[6]

In the event, Syria chose the latter course of action. Israel therefore escalated further and the incident led eventually to an Israeli raid on Syrian positions in the high ground above the disputed plot and even to the employment of the Israeli air force. The upshot was general alarm in the Northern District of the United Arab Republic (Syria) and requests for help from the Southern District of the union (Egypt). The latter could not resist such a challenge to her leadership position in the Arab world and moved large forces into the Sinai. Not having foreseen such an escalation Israel was caught, as (then) Deputy Chief-of-Staff Rabin told the (then) Commander of the IAF, Ezer Weizman, with her 'pants down'. A secret mobilisation of reserves was ordered in Israel. The Egyptians were quietly threatened that if their forces were not withdrawn forthwith Israel would view it as a *casus belli*. The Egyptians — whose credibility had not been challenged in public — concurred, and the crisis was alleviated virtually at the brink.[7]

There was, it seems, an uncanny resemblance between this crisis and the events which lead seven years later to the Six Day war. In 1960, however, Egypt was deterred. Not so, however, with Syria. The small-scale incidents of the 1955-60 period continued and intensified. Israel was therefore forced (by her own deterrence-oriented perception) to resort again to reprisal action — as was done, for example, in the Nuqeib raid of mid-March 1962. Meanwhile the pending completion of the Israeli National Carrier irrigation project, which was resumed after the collapse of the Johnston plan, had prompted the Arab League to take further action. In August 1961 the Arab Defence Council approved an Arab League plan for diverting the sources of the Jordan river in order to thwart Israel's National Carrier project. In addition there was an agreement in principle among the Arab defence ministers to establish a joint Arab command for the purpose of military operations to support the diversion scheme. The fact that these military designs led to naught was mainly due to Nasser's procrastination. For, with the bulk of the Egyptian army bogged down in the Yemen, he did not want to be dragged into a premature war with Israel. Nasser did agree, however, to the diversion scheme and in order to capitalise on this he called for a summit conference in Cairo on 13-16 January 1964. Syria attempted to challenge Nasser on this issue but ultimately settled for what the conference agreed upon, namely, in the first place, a joint scheme for the diversion of the sources of the Jordan.[8]

As soon as the Syrian diversion work began, Israel was faced by a new dilemma. The Syrian action as such posed no challenge to the credibility of Israel's deterrent nor did it pose a threat to day-to-day life in the Galilee. At the same time it amounted to a grave threat to the Jewish state's very lifeline. The choice was therefore between massive punishment with a view to dissuading Syria in one major blow or, alternatively, limited and specific operations which would simply stop the Syrians from carrying on their project. A massive blow might stop the Syrians at once. But if it did not, escalation into a major confrontation would be a foregone conclusion. Limited action might demand a long series of small-scale confrontations in which the Israeli population along Syria's border was bound to suffer, but the risk of major escalation might be smaller.

Ben Gurion and Dayan might have opted at once for the massive action alternative, but Levi Eshkol — who succeeded Ben Gurion as Premier and Minister of Defence in 1963 — as well as the Chief-of-Staff of the day Yitzhak Rabin, opted, perhaps typically, for the limited, disruptive alternative. But if the control of escalation was their purpose they clearly failed. Having demanded an Arab League backing for a full-scale war, Syria could not back down after a series of small-scale skirmishes without a grave loss of prestige. Indeed backing down would play straight into the hands of Nasser (and of the Syrian regime's domestic rivals). The Syrians therefore had no choice but to play for once Israel's own game of escalation for the purpose of de-escalation. They responded to Israel's fire against their earth-moving equipment with fire against both Israeli military and civilian targets. Israel's choice was either to yield or to further escalate in the hope that de-escalation would result. The upshot was the introduction of armour, of heavy artillery and eventually of the Israeli air force.[9]

Frustrated, the Syrians now changed their tactics. The Jordan diversion project was halted. But artillery attacks on the Hula valley's civilian population intensified and *al-fath* (Fatah) — at the time still a Syrian surrogate designed to offer a Syrian reply to Nasser's PLO — was increasingly employed for disruptive actions inside Israel. Not by chance the Fatah's initial targets were all connected to Israel's National Carrier installations.

What could Israel do to stop this new instrument of harassment? Theoretically it could dismiss it as insignificant and ignore it. But the tendency to perceive practically every interaction with the adversaries in terms of deterrence clearly ruled out such a response from the very start.[10] The upshot was a further intensification of the encounter with large-scale exchanges of artillery practically every day and an occasional — and increasingly more frequent — resort to air power.

The growing frequency of air strikes could be attributed to six factors. First, as the conflict intensified Israel's geostrategic inferiority owing to the vulnerability of her population in the Hula valley was underlined. Indeed, this population gradually became hostage to the Syrians who could assume a certain Israeli reticence to engage Syria for fear of the consequences for the population. Hence, increasingly Israel's only effective means of stopping Syrian fire became the IAF. Second, the experience up to the Nuqeib raid of March 1962 prompted Syria to fortify her positions on the Golan. Consequently, night raids by Israeli infantry of the Sea of Galilee, Tawfiq and Nuqeib type, had become non-cost-effective. Third, in April 1966 the former commander of the IAF, Ezer Weizman, became Chief of IDF Operations Division and as soon as he assumed his new office he began to press for a more extensive employment of air power which, he argued, would be incomparably more cost-effective an instrument of reprisal.[11] Fourth, during this veritably critical period the Officer-in-Command of the northern command in Israel was General David Elazar, earlier the Officer-in-Command of Israel's armoured corps, who, in his own words,

> always thought that in .... [Israel's] relations with Syria ... [Israel] must perpetually escalate, in order to deny ... [Syria] the game of false peace, while they carry on a permanent guerrilla war. The Syrians had to learn that even if they knew when and how an incident would start — they would never be able to tell how it would end — Israel should be able to dictate the end of such incidents ... For the quicker the escalation the earlier the moment in which ... [Israel] brings her advantage in the use of heavy and sophisticated weapons such as tanks and planes to bear.[12]

Fifth, Israel's ruling party at the time was outflanked by two offshoots of the same political movement which, for all their differences, always advocated a forceful, massive retaliation-oriented, *activist* approach to the Arabs. Prime Minister Levi Eshkol was subject to a relentless campaign from his right flank by Israel's grand old man,

David Ben Gurion, who at first supported his nomination but later declared him unfit to govern. Eshkol, Meir, Aranne, Sapir and others also felt beleaguered by Ben Gurion's protégés Dayan, Peres, Yaakobi, Offer and others. At the same time Eshkol's foreign and defence policies were also nudged into greater activism by *Ahdut HaAvoda*, represented by personalities such as Yigal Allon and Israel Galili, who on other matters would be on Eshkol's left flank. Eshkol's old guard Mapai fought both wings tooth and nail. But while doing so they showed a great deal of susceptibility to some of the (converging) policy advocacies of both groups. Thus although by inclination Eshkol was the epitome of moderation, his policies in their ensemble proved to be at least as *activist* as Ben Gurion's in the 1950s and, to an extent, even more so.

The sixth factor involved changes in the Syrian perspective. Whether or not the internal Israeli scene was fully comprehensible to the Syrians is impossible to tell. Yet there is ample evidence to suggest that Syria was embarking on a similarly escalatory course. In February 1966 power in Syria was seized by the most militant wing of the Ba'ath Party under the leadership of two prominent Alawis: Salah Jedid and Hafez al-Assad. The former was ideologically an ultra militant. The latter was commander of the Syrian air force. By August 1966 this led to a decision to embark upon a strategy which would mirror image Israel's own strategy. Instead of merely reacting to Israeli action or attempting to stop one or another Israeli project, Syria would henceforth initiate military action on a large scale, including an extensive use of air power. The purpose of such a strategy would be either to score a victory against Israel or to accelerate the deterioration in Israeli-Arab relations and ultimately bring about a large-scale war in which the rest of the Arab world would have to participate. By 15 August 1966 the new strategy was carried into effect. The Syrian air force launched two air strikes on Israeli boats in the Sea of Galilee. The incident ended with one Syrian Mig 17 shot down by Israeli ground fire and one Mig 21 shot down by an Israeli Mirage. Nevertheless an official communiqué on Radio Damascus stated the same day that Syria

would not confine herself to defensive action but would attack defined targets and bases of aggression within the occupied area (alias Israel). Syria has waited for a suitable opportunity to carry out this new policy. That opportunity was presented today ... Syria decided that the attack should be carried out by means of her air force in order to prove to the Arab people and the whole world the untruth of the Israeli claim of air superiority.[13]

Syria's fiery rhetoric notwithstanding, the logic of the Syrian decision to escalate *vertically* by employing air power was strategically
irreproachable. Having attempted to thwart the Israeli National Carrier project, having failed in this move and having suffered a series of
humiliating punishments from Israel in which Israeli air power loomed
very large, Syria was faced by a clear choice. If she were to refrain from
escalation Israel's superiority and in particular the IAF's ability to fly
freely over Syrian territory would be underlined. In the event Syria's
own ability to employ other means for stopping Israeli development
projects in the Hula valley would also be seriously hampered. Sooner or
later Syria would thus be — in fact — disarmed and a wide gap would
develop between her official rhetoric and her real actions. This could
not only damage Syria's place in the Arab world, but it could also be
used by the regime's numerous and still powerful domestic opponents.
If, on the other hand, Syria were to escalate she would be embarking on
a collision course with Israel. In the short run this could lead to fresh
Syrian defeats. But Syria would at least be able to claim that she —
unlike Egypt and Jordan — was doing *something* to advance the common cause. In the long run such a policy could lead to a full-scale war
with Israel in which — backed by the Soviets — Syria could not suffer a
total defeat and which could conceivably drag other elements in the
Arab world, and especially Egypt, into active participation as well.
And if the latter possibility materialised, the danger of an unacceptable
defeat would be correspondingly diminished. Cast in these terms, then,
the Syrian choice of escalation entailed a reasonably calculated risk.

Against this background the outbreak of the Six Day war appears to
have been virtually inevitable. For if Israel escalated because she was
more concerned to sustain the credibility of her deterrence than to control the escalation, and if Syria acted concurrently in a similar fashion,
everything which happened between the summer of 1966 and the
summer of 1967 was little more than a countdown towards a full-scale
collision. The triggering event was the great air battle on 7 April 1967 in
which Syria lost 6 Migs. At this juncture the Syrian calculus must have
been roughly as follows. After such a major defeat she could not simply
bury the hatchet without an unacceptable damage to her position in the
Arab world and to her regime internally. Having already employed the
most formidable weapons in her arsenal, Syria could only engage the
Israeli air force on a larger scale, launch a combined operation which
was bound to lead to an even more formidable Israeli response, or call

on Egypt to make a move which would pose a restraining threat *vis-à-vis* Israel.

Nasser, Syria knew, was not at all in a position to attack Israel. But he was desperately in need of an excuse for disengaging from the Yemen quagmire and, in any event, he was in no position to deny Syria a helping hand without a serious loss to his waning prestige. If Nasser were to turn down the Syrian request for help, Syria would have an excellent excuse for de-escalation on the Israel front on the grounds that Syria alone was not a match for Israel. If Nasser were to rise to the challenge, Syria's plight *vis-à-vis* Israel would be ameliorated too as it had been in the February 1960 incident. Thus, calling on Nasser for help must have appeared to the Syrians as a 'heads I win, tails I win' solution.

The Six Day War and its Aftermath

In the event, Nasser overplayed his hand. The upshot was that Israeli attention switched entirely to the Egyptian front. At this juncture the Israeli predisposition was to avoid a two — not to speak of a three — front war. Hence Israel pre-empted against Egypt on 5 June 1967 without any intention to take on either Jordan or Syria. The latter, however, was impaled on the horns of a difficult dilemma. Having dragged Egypt into war should Syria come to Egypt's rescue? Had Egypt started the war or at least succeeded in checking Israel's initial strike, Syria would have been likely to enter the war in order to be able to claim her fair share in the political spoils. But the Syrians were informed by the Soviets on the first day of the war of the full scope of Egypt's disastrous defeat.[14] Hence, while joining the conflict made no sense, Syria could not afford the risk of being blamed by Egypt, Jordan and the others for causing the war but shrinking from actively participating in it. The Syrian decision to put in merely a token military effort and, at the same time, make vastly exaggerated claims of great victories must be seen in this light.

From the Israeli perspective, the fact that Syria did not participate in the war in a meaningful way implied one thing: in the final analysis the choice whether or not to escalate the conflict lay with Israel. If Israel decided to ignore the essentially symbolic Syrian attack during the first four days of the war, the territorial *status quo* of the previous 19 years would be preserved and the single most escalatory step in the entire confrontation might never have taken place. In the event the process of escalation which has been charted above would have undoubtedly continued apace. The magnitude of the Egyptian and Jordanian defeat constituted a form of indirect escalation. For by being a sufficient cause for alarm from the Syrian point of view it prompted them to step up their efforts to build a formidable military machine. But, having speculated that this was bound to be the case there is no escape from the conclusion that if Israel had shrunk from capturing the Golan, Syria's incentives for challenging Israel in the years to come would have been incomparably smaller.

Haunted by the possibility of a confrontation with the Soviets, Israel's Defence Minister during the Six Day war, Moshe Dayan, offered precisely this argument in order to convince his colleagues that Syria should not be attacked.[15] But Dayan was overruled by a powerful combination of forces which were determined not to let this golden opportunity to get even with Syria slip by. General Elazar, OC northern command, was hardly enamoured by the idea that while his peers in all other commands had their share of the action, he alone would have to settle for a marginal contribution to the victory in the West Bank. The leadership of the population in the Eastern Galilee, which had suffered greatly at the hands of the Syrians during the previous 19 years, was clamouring for the ejection of the Syrian forces from their Golan positions above the Hula and Kineret valleys. Yigal Allon, Dayan's rival who had just missed rather narrowly an opportunity to become minister of defence himself, was still bemoaning Ben Gurion's decision in 1948 to stop the war without taking the Golan (and the West Bank). Hence he argued for a bold thrust across southern Syria with a view to reaching Jabal Druze. If Israel were to do so, Allon presumably believed, the Druzes could be detached from Syria and induced to form their own state which would be in alliance with Israel. Syria would thus be reduced in size and in stature. The Galilee would be redeemed of a constant nightmare. And a new order based on an Israeli alliance with the Christians in Lebanon, the Druzes in Syria, the Kurds in Iraq (and Syria) and ultimately a reduced Jordan could be created. In turn Egypt would have no choice — or so Allon led himself to believe — but to come to terms with the Jewish state too.

Moved by such a combination of personal motives, political incentives and grandiloquent dreams, Allon sidestepped Dayan, brought the Galilee lobby's leadership practically into the cabinet room, cornered Premier Eshkol, whose poor performance during the pre-1967 war crisis made him highly susceptible to such pressures, and succeeded in prevailing upon Dayan to authorise the hasty conquest of the Golan Heights in the last two days of the Six Day war.[16]

Within the Israeli perception a conventional deterrence based on a combination of proven military prowess with what was termed 'defensible borders' the occupation of the Golan was an inestimable gain.[17] The other side of the same coin was, however, that Syrian dependence on the Soviets (a critical dimension of escalation in itself), and Syrian commitment to another war which would retrieve the lost territories would grow too. This could not have been seen as clearly in advance as it appears in retrospect. But with the benefit of hindsight it can be plausibly argued that while Israel's geostrategic position was enhanced *arithmetically* by the occupation of the Golan, the overall Syrian menace to Israel grew *geometrically*. Differently stated, if in 1948 Syria's participation in the war was limited and if in 1967 Syria could drag Egypt into war but then refrain from actually applying any serious pressure on Israel, in 1973 Syria could not help but do her very utmost to assist Egypt in the war. For if Egypt were to attempt the crossing of the canal without Syria when sovereign Syrian territory was held by the common enemy, the Syrian regime would at once miss an opportunity to retrieve Syrian lands and help along a holy Arab cause more generally. And since the massive Soviet presence in Syria on the eve of the Yom Kippur war was a virtual guarantee that a war could not lead to an unacceptable calamity, Syrian inaction in the 1973 war would be virtually inexcusable.

The corollary to such hypotheses is that the 1973 war was not an act of escalation by Syria but rather an outgrowth of the Israeli decision to occupy the Golan during the 1967 war. At the same time the actual fighting in the 1973 war did entail a number of critical escalatory elements. For one thing, Syria launched SCUD missiles into Israel's rear — a critical element of escalation in both *vertical* (weapon systems) and *horizontal* (geographic) terms as well as in terms of a new emphasis on counter-city targeting. In order to deter Syria and others from further resort to such a practice Israel responded by deep-penetration bombing of Syrian targets which escalated the conflict in these same terms. Second, the sheer size of the military effort on both sides in qualitative and quantitative terms had brought the confrontation to a new level of mutual peril. Third, superpower involvement politically and in the form of unprecedentedly large airlifts was also a critical element of escalation. In short, in the aftermath of the Yom Kippur war the calculus of both Israel and Syria had been altered beyond recognition.

Nor was this deadly deterioration reversible. For one thing, the vicious rate of attrition, resulting in itself from the near saturation of the battlefields, led quite inevitably to a process of recovery on both sides in which greater quantities and a greater variety of weapons of a greater sophistication were hastily introduced. Second, the Yom Kippur war ended with a virtual Egyptian betrayal from the Syrian point of view. For whereas Syria was pushing for a new offensive against an exhausted Israel, Egypt was in fact seeking a way out of the conflict altogether. Syria was therefore put in a position in which she had to take into account the possibility of facing a grimly determined Israel, whose arsenal was rapidly expanding to a colossal size, without Egypt, and quite possibly without Jordan.

Against this background the Syrian decision to follow Egypt in accepting a cease-fire, signing a disengagement agreement and proceeding to accept an interim agreement was double-edged. On the one hand, it gave Syria a respite in which to reorganise for a solitary confrontation with Israel. On the other hand, it could serve as a basis for a gradual search for a *rapprochement* some time in the future.

If at this stage the Syrian-Israeli confrontation could be restricted to the Golan front, the combination of a saturated battlefield in the Golan, which made a head-on collision there increasingly non-cost effective, with the isolation of Syria, as a result of the Israeli-Egyptian peace, could conceivably tip the balance in favour of *rapprochement*. Indeed, the heavy Soviet involvement in Syria, Hafez al-Assad's effective leadership and the sobering effect on Iraq of the latter's defeat in the war against Iran might have also reinforced such a tendency. Unfortunately, at this critical juncture in the latter part of the 1970s further escalation was stimulated once again, as a result of the deterioration in Lebanon.

The Effects of the Lebanese Conflict

One of the most important instruments of Israel's deterrence strategy all along was the enunciation of *casi belli*. Among these the preservation of the *status quo* in Lebanon, Jordan and, indeed, Syria herself always loomed very large. If either Iraq or Syria attempted a direct or even an indirect take-over of Jordan, Israel threatened to intervene. If either Iraq or Jordan (and both had such designs in the early part of the 1950s) were to attempt a direct or even an indirect take-over of Syria, Israel, again, threatened to intervene. Finally, if Syria — or any other power for that matter — were to attempt a direct or an indirect take-over of Lebanon, Israel, once again, would intervene.

Paradoxically this Israeli policy coincided with a maxim of the Arab

League that as long as an all-Arab union remained a distant dream the territorial integrity of member states would have to be strictly observed. When this maxim was not observed — as in the course of the upheavals in Lebanon and in Jordan during the summer of 1958 and the autumn of 1970, respectively, Israel — in tacit agreement with the US and Britain in 1958 and the US in 1970 — signalled clearly that she would intervene and the *status quo* was preserved.

The 1975-6 civil war in Lebanon, however, caused an Israeli reassessment. In the autumn of 1975 the Phalanges attempted to expand the domain under their control. The PLO which had hitherto abstained from direct involvement in the conflict was faced by a distinct possibility of a Christian victory, which would be followed sooner or later by a Christian onslaught against the PLO. The latter's decision to throw its weight behind the beleaguered Lebanese 'left' immediately tipped the balance against the Christians. Thus by December 1975-January 1976, it already appeared that the PLO and the left might ultimately emerge as Lebanon's rulers.

At this point both Syria and Israel were faced by a difficult choice. A PLO - Lebanese left victory could result in the appearance of an assertive Lebanon which might seek alliances with Iraq, Egypt, Libya or all together, in order to offset the weight of both Syria and Israel and thus preserve Lebanon's own independence. Syria could not tolerate such an outcome lest it might spill over into Syria's own internal political scene and reduce her inter-Arab stature. Israel could not tolerate it for fear of an intensified instability along the Israeli-Lebanese border. Both countries therefore moved in a manner which would check the advance of the PLO - Lebanese left coalition. Syria at first attempted mediation between the camps in Lebanon. Having failed, she gradually interfered by force — at first through proxies such as the *Saika,* the Palestine Liberation Army (PLA) Yarmuk Brigade and Gibril's Popular Front/General Command — and subsequently through means of direct intervention of the Syrian army on the side of the beleaguered Phalanges. Israel paralleled Syria's action by building up supportive elements in southern Lebanon.

Paradoxically the caution of both Israel and Syria *vis-à-vis* the Lebanon war was largely due to their fear of collision between themselves. Both countries supported the same party in the Lebanese imbroglio, namely the Phalanges. But the incompatibility of their other interests was such that the risk of collision between them seemed very great.

At this juncture the US offered the good offices of L. Dean Brown as a means of helping along the stabilisation of Lebanon through a mutually agreed Israeli-Syrian intervention. Syria concurred with the Israeli request that her forces would not move roughly south of the Zaharani river and west of the Beqaa valley and that she would not deploy SAM missiles on Lebanon's territory. Israel, in turn, refrained from direct intervention. The PLO-Lebanese left coalition was ruthlessly restrained and the Phalanges were saved.

Apart from the fact that Israel compromised her long-held objection to direct Syrian interference in Lebanon, these new arrangements contained the seeds of a future confrontation, which would not only shatter the precarious and limited Syrian-Israeli accord but would also lead to yet another step up the ladder of escalation between the two countries. One of the results of the tacit 1976 accord was the creation of a vacuum in southern Lebanon between the Israeli border and the 'red' line beyond which the Syrians agreed not to move. Within a short while this virtual no-man's land was filled by the PLO which sought refuge there from the tightening Syrian embrace in the rest of Lebanon. As the PLO for its own reasons could not afford to hold such an autonomous domain right on Israel's border without using it as a launching pad for further attacks against Israel, both Syria and Israel were soon confronted by a new set of problems. From the Israeli point of view, the problem boiled down to the following: how to restrain the PLO without provoking the Syrians into a new confrontation at a time in which the Arafat trail — the most critical life-line of the PLO — ran through Syrian lines. From the Syrian point of view, the problem was the obverse: how to pay its dues to the sacrosanct goal of the Palestinians which Syria had so vociferously espoused all along without inviting Israeli counteraction against Syrian forces in Lebanon which could easily escalate 'horizontally' to the Golan.

Israel could not curb the activities of the PLO in Lebanon without effectively isolating the PLO from Syria. The latter could perhaps observe the ground rules with Israel but seemed reluctant actively to operate against the PLO. Hence a new twist to the Israeli-Syrian escalation process became virtually inevitable as a direct result of the intensification of hostilities between the PLO and Israel between 1976 and 1982. In July 1977 Syria abandoned the Phalanges and resumed her support of the PLO. In March 1978 Israel launched Operation Litani against the PLO. Thereafter the PLO was forced to abandon guerilla operations and rely instead on long-range artillery and multiple rocket launchers which could cause damage inside Israel while flying over the heads of the UNIFIL and Haddad forces which were supposed to maintain a buffer between Israel and the PLO. By July 1981 this exchange reached a deadly climax in a three-week war of attrition. The damage to the Israeli population in the area was so extensive that Begin's government accepted a cease-fire with the PLO. But, — simultaneously, Begin, Minister of Defence Sharon and a number of other members of the cabinet also decided to launch a major operation against the PLO which would drive the latter out of Lebanon altogether. Operation SHELEG (Hebrew acronym for Peace for the Galilee) in July 1982 was the result.

Theoretically Operation SHELEG did not have to lead to fresh hostilities between Israel and Syria. After all, the declared purpose was to deal with the PLO and *not* with Syria. In practice, however, a new confrontation with Syria was — in the Israeli perception — inescapable. For one thing, Syria was — with some justice — perceived as the main force behind the stepping up of the PLO's campaign against Israel. Second, during 1981 the Syrians increasingly encroached on Palestinian positions north of the Beirut-Damascus road. Third, faced by the provocation of the Phalanges and by Israel's decision to back the latter, Syria abrogated her commitment under the tacit agreement which L. Dean Brown negotiated in 1976 not to deploy SAMs inside Lebanon. The upshot was that the freedom to fly over Lebanese territory which the IAF had enjoyed was gradually diminished. Soon, Israel could argue, the Syrians would gain complete control over the air space of northern Lebanon and Israel's ability to deal with PLO bases there and to protect the Phalanges would have been completely eroded. All this took place against the background of the most acrimonious election campaign in Israeli history. And in the heat of the campaign Begin was several times carried away emotionally to such an extent that he issued bellicose statements against Syria. In turn he would have to make good his word or lose credibility both with his domestic constituency and, worse still, with Syria.

Beyond this there was a reasonable strategic argument for taking on the Syrians along with the PLO. The forces of the latter were mainly concentrated along the Lebanese coastline between Tyre and Damour. The Syrians, on the other hand, controlled parts of the Shouf mountains overlooking the coastal plain. If Israel were to drive the PLO to the north but leave the Syrians in the Shouf, she would find herself after the fighting in a most uncomfortable strategic abyss. In this situation, the Syrians could at any time threaten the IDF forces below them on the coast. Moreover, the Syrians could — and did — allow the PLO to use long-range artillery against the Israeli Galilee from behind their lines which, in the Beqaa valley, were far less than 42 kilometres away from the Israeli border. Differently stated, if Begin promised his supporters in Kyriat Shemonah (on the Israeli side) that there would be 'no more Katyushas', he had to make sure that this would be the outcome of the war even if the implication was that Syria too would have to be attacked.

As soon as the invasion of Lebanon was under way Begin called upon President Assad 'who has always kept his agreements' not to fight. On the whole the Syrians complied. But apart from the fact that they did allow the PLO to fire a few artillery rounds from behind their lines, the Syrians also poured massive reinforcements into the Beqaa valley. Using this as a pretext, the IDF attacked them on the fourth day of the war. The Israeli Air Force (IAF) was ordered to knock out the Syrian SAMs in the northern sector of the Beqaa valley. The IDF ground forces simultaneously moved into the Shouf and drove the Syrian forces in the southern sector of the Beqaa valley to the northern shores of the Qar'awn Lake. Finally, the IDF successfully drove a wedge between the Syrian forces on the high ground around the Beirut-Damascus road and the Syrian contingent in Beirut.[18]

Syria suffered a defeat — especially in the air war. As a result of this war her capital became exposed to Israeli artillery while her air defence system was practically shattered. The upshot was, inevitably, a frantic Syrian drive to rearm. The Soviets responded by supplying Syria with SAM 5 missiles and large quantities of T-72 tanks, helicopters and other items. The Soviets also had to commit their personnel or, which probably seemed worse, let the Syrians handle the SAM 5 system.

A process of escalation which began 35 years earlier with small and strictly localised skirmishes involving far more diplomacy than actual fire and not involving the superpowers had thus expanded dramatically. *Geographically* it could lead to war on a long front from central Lebanon all the way to southern Golan. *Functionally,* it could lead to exchanges at practically every 'rung' of the spectrum of conventional violence. Indeed, handled with less than utmost care this confrontation could even involve both the US and the USSR, complete with their awesome nuclear arsenals.

The Future: Armageddon or Conflict Reduction?

Broadly speaking, the escalation of any international conflict can be attributed to one of three factors. It can be attributed to the aggressiveness of one party; it can be attributed to the aggressiveness of the other party or it can be attributed to the existence of a situation in which both parties are on the whole logical but the system of their relations nevertheless goes berserk. Given the polemical atmosphere in which the Arab-Israeli conflict has been conducted, the fact that most writings have tended to blame either Israel or her adversaries is not at all surprising. In fact from a certain perspective it may be argued that the literature on the conflict is part and parcel of it.

The foregoing suggests, however, that the escalation in the Syrian-Israeli sector of the Arab-Israeli conflict has been more the result of the structure of the interaction than of the deliberate malevolence of either party. Syria's decision to take part in the 1948 war was unquestionably an 'original sin' which must have affected its own as well as Israel's conduct for many years to come. Moreover, Syria's harassment of the Israeli population in the Galilee 'Finger', her decision to divert the sources of the Jordan river and her role in the drawing of Egyptian forces into the Sinai in February 1960 and in May 1967, also constituted major escalatory moves. However, it is equally true to say that Israel's Kineret raid of 1955, Tawfiq raid of 1960, and Nuqeib raid of 1962, her decision to capture the Golan in 1967 and her challenge to Syria in Lebanon during April 1981 and June 1982, all constituted major acts of escalation.

The tragedy, however, is that for the most part neither side actually preferred escalation to accommodation. In fact, with the exception of the 1966-70 period in which Syria seems to have been bent on escalation almost for its own sake, both Syria and Israel have apparently invested a great deal of thought in attempts to avoid deterioration. Yet, as in a prisoners' dilemma game, in the final analysis the logical thing for both parties to do in most decisional contexts was to escalate (defect) rather than co-operate. Hence while both would acknowledge that in the long run co-operation would be more beneficial than confrontation, while the fundamental predisposition of both was 'containment' rather than 'role back', the outcome in most of these situations was nevertheless confrontation. Both parties, then, can be accused of a myopic oversight of the long-term consequences of their actions. But with a few exceptions neither can be accused of madness, loss of control or stupid bloody-mindedness.

This gloomy retrospect leads, however, to a not entirely pessimistic view of future prospects. The paradox with escalatory processes is that by increasing the risk to the parties they also increase their caution and prudence. This is not the case if one of the parties, and certainly if both, are irrational. But if the record of both parties in a process of 35 years, *under different regimes,* is that of a great deal of rationality, albeit of the bounded type, the long-term prospects for greater prudence on either side are considerable. This point is underlined by one important feature of the Israeli-Syrian conflict. In the 1950s and 1960s Israeli-Syrian relations were marked by a great number of small skirmishes. By the 1970s and 1980s this pattern had been transformed. In fact ever since 1967, the picture has been that of a small number of large encounters and of increasingly more extensive periods of tacit understandings on a fairly broad horizon of problems. Thus it can be argued that not only the *power* of the US and USSR has been *refracted* into the balance of forces between Syria and Israel but, to an extent, also aspects of the superpowers' behaviour. Détente, or at least a kind of restricted cold war, may therefore be the overriding long-term feature not only of East-West relations but also of conflict relations such as between Syria and Israel.

Notes

1. For another statement of the same general thesis with regard to the Israeli invasion of Lebanon, see A. Yaniv and R.J. Lieber 'Personal Whim or Strategic Imperative: The Israeli Invasion of Lebanon', *International Security,* vol. 8, no. 2 (Fall 1983), pp. 117-42).

2. See Nisan Bar-Yaakov, *The Israeli-Syrian Armistice: Problems of Implementation 1949-1966* (The Magness Press, Jerusalem, 1967).

3. Moshe Dayan, *Avnei Derekh* (Idanim, Tel-Aviv, 1976), p. 106; Yehezkel Hameiri, 'Demilitarization and Conflict Resolution: The DMZs on the Israeli-Syrian Border, 1949-1967', unpublished MA thesis, Haifa University, 1978 (in Hebrew).

4. See *HaAretz,* 5 June 1981, 1 July 1981 and the Israeli *Air Force Journal,* no. 111 (July 1979), p. 21. On one occasion, the IAF intervened without authorisation. Premier Ben Gurion was in the USA and had left strict instructions that the IAF should *not* be employed. One pilot, however, disobeyed the order. He was not punished because his superiors were convinced that his unauthorised intervention literally decided the battle.

5. Dayan's biographer argues that the disastrous results of this operation were due to a failure of communication between Ben Gurion and Dayan, on the one hand, and Dayan and Ariel Sharon, on the other hand. See Shabtai Tevet, *Moshe Dayan: A Biography* (Shocken, Jerusalem, 1975), p. 427. (in Hebrew).

6. The head of UNTSO at the time, General Carl von Horn, was convinced that the Israeli action was a deliberate provocation. That Ben Gurion's thinking was not beyond such schemes can be seen from his remarks to Sharett on an identical issue a few years earlier. See Sharett, *Yoman Ish* (Am Oved, Tel-Aviv, 1978), p. 378; Carl von Horn, *Soldiering for Peace* (Cassell, London, 1966), ch. 21.

7. Yitzhak Rabin, *Pinkas Sherut* (*Maariv,* Tel-Aviv, 1979), vol. 1, pp. 106-8. Rabin's account seems to have confused the dates in which all this occurred. He speaks about the Egyptians having moved to the Sinai in January - probably meaning February. See M. Brecher, *Decisions in Crisis* (University of California Press, Berkeley, 1980), p. 46. M.

178   *Syria and Israel: The Politics of Escalation*

Handel's dates on this event are also off the mark since he speaks of 1962. See M. Handel, *Israel's Political-Military Doctrine,* Harvard University, Center for International Affairs, Occasional Papers in International Affairs, no. 30 (July 1973), p. 47.

8. For a detailed account see A. Sella, *Ahdut Betoch Perud BaMaarechet Habein Arvit: Veidot HaPisga HaAravit* 1964-1982 (Unity Amidst Diversity: Arab Summitry 1964-1982), (The Magness Press, Jerusalem 1983), pp. 26-38 (in Hebrew).

9. Rabin, *Pinkas* pp. 121-2. Also Lieutenant-Colonel Shimon Golan, 'The Struggle for the Jordan Waters' in Avshalom Shmueli, Arnon Soffer, Nurit Kliot (eds.), *The Lands of Galilee* (Haifa University Press, Haifa, 1983), vol. 2, pp. 856-7 (in Hebrew).

10. For a discussion of Israel's concept of deterrence, see A. Yaniv, 'Deterrence and Defense in Israeli Strategy', *State, Government and International Relations,* no. 24 (1985); also Avner Yaniv, 'Israel's Conventional Deterrent: A Reappraisal' in Louis Rene Beres (ed.), *Security or Armaggeddon* (DC Heath & Co., Lexington, Mass., 1985).

11. See Ezer Weizman, *Thine the Sky, Thine the Land (Maariv,* Tel-Aviv, 1975), pp. 253-4 (in Hebrew).

12. Quoted by Y. Ha'Meiri, *On Both Sides of the Heights* (Levin-Epstein, Tel-Aviv, 1970), p. 38 (in Hebrew).

13. Quoted by Bar-Yaakov, *Armistice,* p. 270 from report No. S/7432/Add. 1 of the UN Secretary General.

14. Ha'Meiri, *On Both Sides,* p. 63. Ha'Meiri's book draws heavily on a great number of Syrian documents which were captured by the IDF in Kuneitra during the Six Day war.

15. Dayan, *Avnei Derekh,* pp. 474-5.

16. Brecher, *Decisions in Crisis,* ch. eight; Ha'Meiri, *On Both Sides,* ch. 1; H. Bar Tov, *Daddo - 48 Years and 20 More Days,* vol. 1, pp. 121-49, (in Hebrew).

17. See Dan Horowitz, *Israel's Concept of Defensible Borders,* The Leonard Davis Institute, Jerusalem, Jerusalem Papers on Peace Problems, no. 16, (1975).

18. This section draws heavily on Yaniv and Lieber, 'Personal Whim'.

10 THE CHANGING PRISM: SYRIAN POLICY IN LEBANON AS A MIRROR, AN ISSUE AND AN INSTRUMENT

Itamar Rabinovich

Introduction

For nearly a decade, Syria's involvement in Lebanon has been a focal point of the Ba'athist regime's foreign policies and domestic politics. The course of Syria's policy in Lebanon, originally shrouded in secrecy and controversy, has been traced and reconstructed, at least in its broad lines, in earlier works. Attention can now be shifted to an effort to place Syria's conduct in Lebanon in the larger context of the country's politics. As its title implies, this chapter views Syria's policy in Lebanon as a defined issue: as a reflection of the regime's priorities and capabilities and as an instrument calculated to accomplish additional, far more ambitious, purposes. It also suggests that the relative importance of the country's alternative preferences has changed several times during the past decade.

Syria's military intervention in Lebanon in 1976 is a convenient point of departure. The manner in which this intervention was carried out and the aims it sought to accomplish reflected the transformation that had taken place during Hafez al-Assad's first five years in power.[1]

Syrian Politics and the Challenge of Lebanon

Assad seized full power in Syria in November 1970 after seven and a half years of Ba'athist rule. In Syrian terms, this was a relatively lengthy tenure of power. The Ba'athist regime, though, was torn by factionalism, and it rested on a narrow public base — Syria's urban Sunni population would not accept the legitimacy of a regime it viewed as minoritarian, sectarian, radical and irreligious. Externally Syria was weak and isolated — at odds with practically every Arab state and relying on a close but uncomfortable relationship with the Soviet Union.

Domestically, Assad could not eliminate the fundamental tension between this regime and a large segment of the population, but he was

179

quite successful at attenuating it. He was still more successful at building a regime remarkably free of factionalism and internecine squabbling. Upon this unprecedented state of domestic stability was based a transition to a new era in Syria's foreign policy: first, breaking out of isolation and then, in the aftermath of the October 1973 war, an attempt to become a regional power. Syria's new regional position was to rest on its military strength, on its hegemony over its weaker Arab neighbours (Lebanon, Jordan and the Palestinians) and on its ability to manoeuvre between the two superpowers.[2] A comparison of Syria's position regarding Lebanon during the previous 30 years with the role and place assigned to the latter country within this scheme readily reveals the change that occurred in the goals and capabilities of Syria's foreign policy in the early 1970s. Lebanon had been important to Syria's leaders in those earlier decades, too; but Syria's domestic weakness, instability and lack of external resources had prevented its leaders from translating their interests and ambitions into actual influence.

Underlying the Syrian state's attitude to Lebanon was the view that the whole of Lebanon and, even more so, the territories added to it by the French in 1920 were part of Syria. The explicit Syrian demands to reintegrate Lebanon or parts of it faded during the years, but an implicit claim was maintained through the refusal to establish normal diplomatic relations with Lebanon. Until the mid-1970s this claim was essentially ritualistic, and Syria's conduct towards Lebanon was shaped by a cluster of more mundane interests. Some of these were of an economic nature — the heritage of the partial economic union in the days of the French Mandate, Syria's dependence on Lebanese ports and a large number of Syrian workers employed in Lebanon. Then there were military and security interests — Lebanon's territory was seen by Syrian military planners both as their soft belly *vis-à-vis* Israel and as a potential staging ground within an offensive scheme. Syria's outlook on Lebanon, however, was primarily coloured by political interests and considerations — the existence of an open political society coping with the problems of pluralism alongside a closed polity trying to sweep its confessional problems under an iron carpet. Lebanon was also an important centre of Arab and international political and intellectual activity, a media and communications centre and the reluctant host of the political and military headquarters of the Palestinian organisations. In the early 1970s, Syria's Alawi rulers began to cultivate Lebanon's large and effervescent Shi'ite community. The Shi'ites presented both a potential new constituency in Lebanon and also a potential source of religious and political legitimacy to members of a sect that had branched out of Shi'ite Islam.[3]

Hafez al-Assad was the first Syrian leader to address these interests with a comprehensive and effective policy. By establishing Syria's supreme influence in Lebanon, he could control the impressive array of interests clustered in its territory. Furthermore, hegemony over Lebanon would also bring the PLO under Syria's wings, so that two out of Syria's three prospective Arab clients would be harnessed. Assad's Syria began playing the dual role of benefiting from the decline of Lebanon's traditional political system and expediting that process. Syria soon replaced Egypt as the external centre of loyalty and influence of Lebanon's Muslims, and was far more effective in that role, because of its proximity. Assad also cultivated other groups and factions in Lebanon — the Palestinians, the Druzes and parts of the Lebanese left.

The Civil War, 1975-1976

In 1975, Lebanon's process of decline led to the outbreak of civil war. For some six months, Syria was able to play another dual role — part-time supporter of its friends and clients in the opposition and part-time mediator and peace-maker. That strategy collapsed at the end of 1975, and Assad was forced to choose a more decisive line.

The crisis of December 1975-January 1976 revealed a complexity of considerations hitherto unfamiliar in Syrian foreign policy. In Lebanon itself, the situation threatened to get out of hand, and Assad realised that he could not afford to accept the victory of either party to the civil war. Although the Maronites could not hope to re-establish their supremacy in the whole of Lebanon, some of them seemed determined to fall back upon the notion of a 'smaller Christian Lebanon'. This notion — a 'Maronite Zion' — was anathema to Assad as well as to all Arab nationalists. The alternative, a victory of the leftist-Muslim-Palestinian alliance, was equally repelling. It could result in an Israeli or other external intervention. In any case, Assad did not wish to be sandwiched between a radical Iraq and a radical Lebanon. He explained his views at length, first in closed sessions with Arab visitors and critics and then in an unusually candid and revealing public address, on 20 July 1976. 'Decisive military action in this sense in a country like Lebanon,' Assad argued, is impossible because 'the issue does not depend solely on might ... there are other factors and conditions which must be available but are not present'. By crushing the dominant Maronite political establishment, as Kamal Jumblatt and Yassir Arafat wanted to do, Assad continued, a host of negative consequences would be created — international and Israeli intervention, partition and further division of Arab ranks — 'an ugly picture detrimental to Arab interests and objectives'.[4]

Assad, however, failed to mention another dimension that had been added to his calculations. For a Syria seeking a regional and an international role, the crisis in Lebanon presented an opportunity as well as a challenge. By demonstrating that it and it alone could solve the crisis in Lebanon, Syria would prove to the United States that in that part of the Middle East one had to deal directly with Syria. The humiliating experience of 1973-4, when Syria was perceived and treated as Egypt's subordinate partner, would be written off. Syria would become an autonomous regional power, on a par with Egypt and Iraq, and able to deal confidently with both superpowers.

This line of thinking reinforced the conservative streak already apparent in Assad's view of the Lebanese crisis. He had come to see Lebanon as a complex entity in which the Christian-Maronite element had a crucial role that could not be eradicated by sheer force. He had already been conducting a dialogue with such Maronite groups as the Faranjiyyah clan and the Phalanges. The American factor, which had become paramount in his thinking, and the fear of Israeli intervention confirmed his conviction that Syria's intervention should aim at consolidation and moderate reforms rather than radical transformation.[5]

The degree of co-ordination with the US that preceded Syria's limited military intervention in Lebanon in January 1976 and the indirect ('red line') agreement with Israel were not publicly known at the time. The conservative bent in Syria's new policy in Lebanon first became known with the publication in February 1976 of the 'Reforms Document' that the Syrian leadership had prepared together with President Faranjiyyah. This document resulted in an acrobatic *renversement des alliances.* Syria was now opposed by its former allies, who resented the limited change envisaged by Damascus and refused to accept Syrian domination. It was supported by the conservative, predominantly Maronite Lebanese Front, whose leaders saw the Syrians as (at least temporary) saviours.

There seemed to be an inescapable logic to the new turn of events. Most of the organisations and individuals constituting the National Front, the anti-*status-quo* coalition fighting on the other side of the civil war, were willing to take up arms in order to obstruct Syria's new policy. The same considerations that had motivated Assad's intervention and initial direction now forced him to use his army against the Front. His interests in Lebanon itself and his regional ambitions had become far too important for Assad to tolerate defeat. It was also a classic case of interventionism — once the initial investment had been made, additional investments had to be made in order to justify its cost. In the event, the Syrian army in Lebanon found itself in the improbable position of fighting alongside conservative militias against the PLO and the Druze militia of Kamal Jumblatt.

In the summer of 1976, the Lebanese situation was further confounded by the military setbacks sustained by Syria in June and by its open rift with the Soviet Union. September saw a reversal of this tide, and the Syrian army came close to crushing its rivals, but Saudi Arabia's intercession prevented a military decision. The Riyadh conference in October 1976 formalised the ambiguity with which the fighting ended. The Arab consensus recognised Syria's hegemony in Lebanon, which condition it legitimised by accepting Syria's military presence in the guise of an Arab Deterrent Force and agreeing to subsidise it. Syria, however, was forced to accept the continued presence and role in Lebanon of the PLO and some of its other rivals.

The mixed results of the Riyadh conference were illustrative of Syria's regional and international standing in late 1976 and 1977. Syria achieved an unprecedented degree of prestige and influence that was, to a considerable extent, a consequence of its achievements in Lebanon. In 1977, Assad met with the Soviet and American leaders on his own terms, and he played a cardinal role in obstructing US President Carter's efforts to deal with the Arab-Israeli conflict through an international conference.[6] But this new eminence rested on a very slender base.

In the Arab arena, Assad overplayed his hand *vis-à-vis* Egypt. The veto power he exercised repeatedly over Egyptian policy served to finalise Sadat's decision to deal directly with Israel. It was a move that left Syria without an effective response. In Lebanon, Syrian policy had to navigate through the serious limitations imposed by the vested (and semi-recognised) interests of Israel and Syria's Arab rivals. Equally perplexing was Assad's relationship with the Maronite militias of the Lebanese Front. They were the most powerful local force, but cooperation with them was difficult and ideologically awkward.[7] Assad realised that Lebanon could not be annexed or even taken over in a brief span of time. Syrian supremacy had to be consolidated and formalised over time. But was that time available?

Between 1977 and 1980, the Assad regime confronted its severest crisis,[8] and it appeared that time was running out for Syria in Lebanon. The principal problem was domestic, but Assad's domestic difficulties were to a certain extent a by-product of his intervention in Lebanon. At the core of the crisis was the Muslim fundamentalist offensive against the regime, but it acquired other dimensions such as the appearance of internecine squabbling and economic difficulties.

The principal domestic lesson of Syria's intervention in Lebanon was that it was extremely difficult for one fragmented polity to try to settle the affairs of another fragmented society. Candid and detailed as Assad's explanations of his conduct in Lebanon were, he could not persuade Syria's Sunni public that his Lebanese policy was anything but an Alawi-Maronite conspiracy against Syrian-Lebanese and Palestinian Sunnis. Syria's intervention in Lebanon and the direction it took were clearly the catalysts that triggered the domestic crisis of 1977.[9] In addition to exacerbating confessional tensions in Syria, these policies generated friction within the ranks of the regime, exacted an economic price and invited subversion by the regime's Arab rivals.

From War to War, 1977-1982

As the late 1970s wore on, Syria's position in Lebanon loomed increasingly as a liability. The domestic crisis of these years was accompanied by a decline in Syria's regional standing — the end of the Jordanian alliance, the absence of an effective response to Sadat's new policies, Iraq's increasing pressure. The difficulties in Lebanon were both a symptom of Syria's decline and a contributing factor to its aggravation. By the end of the decade, Syria faced an increasing challenge in Lebanon posed by Israel and the Lebanese Front.

Israel's Menachem Begin, during his first two years in office, continued the Lebanese policy of his predecessor, Yitzhak Rabin. In the summer of 1979, however, Begin authorised greater support of and commitment to Bashir Jumayyil and his militias. One common goal of the Israeli-Maronite alliance was to challenge and weaken Syrian supremacy in Lebanon, which had been accepted, with reservations, as an unavoidable evil in 1976.[10]

There was little that Assad could do against this challenge until the end of 1980. By that time he had defeated his domestic rivals, signed a treaty of friendship and co-operation with the Soviet Union and completed an important part of his military build-up plan. He had not closed the 'strategic gap' with Israel that had been opened by Egypt's departure from the Arab consensus in 1977, but he felt that Syria had the military capability to challenge Israel even if the challenge were likely to trigger an Israeli military reaction.

The series of challenges and counter-challenges posed, respectively, by Israel and the Lebanese (Front) Forces and by Syria finally led to a show-down at Zahle: the so-called 'missile crisis' of the spring and early summer of 1981. Syria did not seek a showdown and was probably not interested in a military clash with Israel, but the prospect of a Lebanese Forces' take-over of Zahle was simply unacceptable to Syria. Zahle is situated in the Beqaa Valley, the part of Lebanon considered most vital to Syria's national security. A Lebanese Forces' outpost in Zahle and a possible link-up with Israel were perceived as a grave threat to Syria's position in Lebanon and, indeed, to Syria proper. They warranted the risks that the 'missile crisis' entailed. In the event, the self-confidence and determination displayed by Syria in the course of the crisis had larger repercussions for the region. The message Assad conveyed was a double one: he had overcome the domestic crisis of 1977-80 and his was the only Arab state actively confronting Israel. It should be emphasised, however, that this confidence was the by-product of a crisis which arose within the well-defined confines of the Lebanese arena. It was not a case in which Lebanon was deliberately chosen by Syria as the most suitable stage for a regional drama.[11]

In retrospect, it is also clear that the 'missile crisis' of 1981 was an important link in the chain of events that led to the June 1982 war. In several respects it can also be seen as a dress rehearsal for that war. This does not mean that Assad wanted to fight in that war. He certainly saw himself the winner in the limited engagement of 1981, and he probably understood that the onus had shifted to the Israeli side of the Lebanese equation. He must have thought, however, that the Israeli government would accept yet another shift in the complex Syrian-Israeli relationship in Lebanon; that the collapse in 1981 of the rules of the game established in 1976 would be seen as a single aberration in this relationship, which despite its awkwardness and peculiarity could go on.[12] Even when it understood in 1982 that Israel was about to launch a large-scale military operation in Lebanon, the Syrian leadership hoped that fighting between Syria and Israel could be avoided or at least minimised. In fact, it sent an open and an explicit message to that effect:

If the Israeli intervention takes the form of strikes against Palestinian positions and camps in Lebanon, Syria's intervention will remain limited ... (But) if it is a matter of occupation, Syria will certainly give the Palestinians and the Lebanese patriotic forces all the means necessary for checking the occupation and turning the occupier's life into an unbearable hell, and this in addition to conducting the battles that will be called for in a time of need. It is no secret that Israel's military force is now larger than Syria's; therefore, the possibility of Syria's turning to a full-scale war at a time and a place determined by Israel should be excluded ... The activity will be limited to resistance to the occupation and to the attrition of the occupying forces ... but might develop into all-out war if circumstances so determined.[13]

A close examination of the military moves of the first days of the June 1982 war indicates, indeed, that the Syrian leadership must have acted on the assumption that Israel had received its signals and would act accordingly. It must also have thought that as long as Syrian troops limited themselves to minor operations, Israel would be happy to limit the scope of the fighting and refrain from attacking the bulk of the Syrian army in Lebanon. When the full scope of Israel's plans had revealed itself, the Syrian army in Lebanon had been outmanoeuvred and was about to lose most of its positions in that country.[14]

Syria and the Israeli Invasion of Lebanon, 1982-1984

The complications into which the Israeli operation ran enabled Syria to save some of its positions in Lebanon towards the end of June. Nevertheless, a few weeks later, when the PLO had left Beirut and Bashir Jumayyil had been elected president of Lebanon, the future of Syria's influence seemed bleak. During this period, two characteristics of Assad's political style became fully evident — his perseverance and his ruthlessness. The assassination of Bashir Jumayyil was but one of the measures initiated by Syria during the late summer and autumn of 1982 in order to salvage its position in Lebanon.

For some time, Syria's efforts were solely concerned with that salvaging operation. Syria's position in Lebanon had to be restored and Syria's enemies and competitors (the United States, Israel and the Lebanese Forces) removed or subdued. With the passage of time and as the success of Syria's efforts in Lebanon became more apparent, additional and more ambitious goals were added. Lebanon became the focal point of regional politics; and since Syria could rely on several advantages in Lebanon, it could realistically aspire to regain the regional and international prominence it had briefly enjoyed in 1976/7.

For one thing, Lebanon was the arena in which Syria's supremacy over the PLO, weakened and dispersed by the 1982 war, could be consolidated. The supremacy could, in turn, be used to obstruct the implementation of the Reagan plan of September 1982. By so doing, Syria would not only thwart an objectionable development but also demonstrate, once again, that the US could not afford to ignore, let alone snub, Damascus. It was, in addition, an excellent way of offering a service to the Soviet Union that was fully congruent with Syria's own interests. The Soviet Union, by rehabilitating Syria's ground-to-air missile system at the end of 1982, had played a crucial role in rebuilding Syria's position in Lebanon. It was rewarded a few months later when Syria thwarted an American diplomatic initiative.

The campaign against the 17 May 1983 agreement between Israel and Lebanon was conducted on a number of levels simultaneously. Syria objected to the agreement as such. It also vehemently opposed President Amin Jumayyil and his policies and saw the accord as a suitable object against which a broad coalition could be put together. From yet another vantage point, Syria viewed the 17 May agreement as a leaf from the tree planted at Camp David — a political agreement between Israel and an Arab state negotiated under American auspices. If this agreement could be destroyed, then damage could possibly be done to the approach that Camp David came to symbolise.

Syria's perception of the 17 May agreement, the American-Jordanian-Palestinian negotiations of 1982-3 and the Camp David framework as distinct manifestations of the same underlying evil is clearly illustrated in a commentary published by the Damascus daily *Tishrin* in July 1983:

> When Arafat sheds tears about independent decision-making, he certainly wants to lend legitimacy to the independent decision of others. Sadat's treasonous decision was also an independent decision and an expression of sovereignty. Hussein's decision to sell out the cause is also an independent decision and an expression of sovereignty. Consequently, the Lebanese Phalangists' decision to conclude an agreement with Israel is an independent decision and an expression of sovereignty according to the Arafatist concept of independent decision-making. Wasn't the Lebanese regime's main excuse for concluding the submission agreement that it was an independent Lebanese decision emanating from Lebanese sovereignty?[15]

Later in 1983 and in 1984, as Amin Jumayyil's government encountered ever greater difficulties and required American military assistance, the US and Syria clashed directly. Syria was now at the centre of international politics and in a position to affect the outcome of the 1984 American presidential elections. The hasty American withdrawal removed Lebanon from the domestic American political agenda, but provided Syria with an exploit in both Lebanese and larger terms.

Syria's achievement was marred by two sets of problems. It was, in the first place, difficult to translate its 1984 victory in Lebanon into concrete political facts. Amin Jumayyil capitulated and the 17 May agreement was abrogated, but Syria's effort to exert influence and force the Lebanese president and his rivals to make concessions and agree on a reasonable reform plan were to no avail. Assad was determined — a lesson drawn from the sad experience of his original intervention — not to become enmeshed in the minute details of Lebanese politics. The Syrians had discovered what the Israelis, who followed in their footsteps, would learn: that an external force seeking to reshape Lebanese politics tended, through the pressures of its partners and their rivals, to become merely an actor among actors — perhaps more powerful, but not more effective than the Lebanese contenders. Assad wanted to avoid this pitfall and to remain above the fray; but he soon realised that without intimate involvement, Syria's achievement in Lebanon would be wasted. Thus far (at the time of writing) the gamble has paid off. Syria's cause has been advanced without additional, costly investment. But the Syrian leadership must know, as its own trepidation has shown, on what a slender basis its current position in Lebanon rests.

It was an ironic twist of fate that at the height of his political achievement at the end of 1983, Hafez al-Assad became seriously ill. His illness resulted in the first significant internecine struggle in the regime's upper echelons. At the time, the winter and early spring of 1984, it also added to Syria's difficulties in Lebanon. Syria's rivals and clients there were evidently reluctant to make concessions when the future of the Assad regime appeared uncertain. Assad's physical recovery in the spring of 1984 suspended, but did not entirely eliminate, such doubts and speculations.

The Syrian outlook on the Lebanese crisis at the end of 1984 was, thus, remarkably similar to that of late 1976. Having re-established its hegemony in Lebanon, the Syrian leadership was fully aware of the complexity of the Lebanese arena and of the constraints on its freedom of action. It knows that, given time, it can overcome these constraints and consolidate and formalise its supremacy. Nor does it conceal its intentions. Louis Fares, the Damascus correspondent for Radio Monte Carlo, has expounded the Syrian outlook on Lebanon, placing it in its larger context. Quoting an anonymous senior Syrian source who commented on the renewal of diplomatic relations between Egypt and Jordan, Fares wrote:

During the next phase, the Lebanese portfolio, in all its aspects, will continue to be the central issue focusing Syrian attention in view of the continued Israeli presence in Lebanon. The daily contacts on various levels and between Syria and Lebanon will continue regarding national reconciliation, security and the implementation of Lebanon's sovereignty over its entire territory. Syria will continue to look after the Lebanese issue, despite the numerous obstacles, for as long as it takes. Execution should be in phases even if these are slow, but it should be meticulous, solid and under no time pressure. All are aware of the successes that have been accomplished thus far, but additional successes are needed ... Uppermost on Syria's mind is the need to get rid of the Israeli presence in Lebanon in a fashion forcing no conditions or limitations on the Lebanese state and it should be accomplished without a direct contact. The role of the Americans should not be ignored. The Americans recognized Syria's political and military victories and *Syria's success in forcing the fact* that it is the decisive factor regarding the Lebanese crisis and the Middle East crisis ... But the Syrians ... will not agree to the US acting alone in the region or in Lebanon.[16] [Emphasis added.]

Notes

1. See Adeed I. Dawisha, *Syria and the Lebanese Crisis,* (MacMillan, London, 1980); and I. Rabinovich, 'The Limits of Military Power: Syria's Role', in P. Edward Haley and Lene's W. Snider, (eds.), *Lebanon in Crisis,* (Syracuse University Press, Syracuse, NY, 1979), pp. 55-73.

2. See I. Rabinovich, 'The Foreign Policy of Syria: Goals, Capabilities and Restraints', *Survival,* (July 1982).

3. I. Rabinovich, *The War for Lebanon, 1970-1983,* (Cornell University Press, Ithaca, NY, 1984), pp. 36-8. See also the contribution by Yair Hirschfeld above.

4. Ibid., pp. 201-2.

5. No one was more effective in depicting (and criticising) the conservative trends in Assad's regime than his Lebanese opponent, Kamal Jumblatt, in his memoirs-cum-political testament, *I Speak for Lebanon,* (Zed Press, London, 1982).

6. See Jimmy Carter's memoirs, *Keeping Faith* (Bantam Books, New York, 1982), pp. 286-95.

7. The best guide to Syria's relations with the Maronites as well as many other aspects of Syria's policy in Lebanon is Karim Pakardouni's *La Paix Manquée* (Beirut, 1984). Pakardouni, a leader in the Phalanges, served for several years as the party's liaison with Syria.

8. See A. Drysdale, 'The Assad Regime and its Troubles', *MERIP Reports,* (November-December 1982), pp. 3-11.

9. For comprehensive treatments of the confessional factor in Syrian politics, see N. Van Dam, *The Struggle for Power in Syria,* (Croom Helm, London, 1979); E. Picard, 'Y-a-t-il un Problème Communautaire en Syrie?', *Maghreb-Machrek,* (January 1980), pp. 7-21; and A. Drysdale, 'Ethnicity in the Syrian Officers Corps: A Conceptualization', *Civilizations* (1979), pp. 359-76.

10. Z. Schiff and E. Ya'ari, *A War of Deception* (Shocken, Tel-Aviv, 1984), pp. 40-76 (in Hebrew).

11. Ibid., pp. 21-7.

12. See Z. Lanir, *Israel's Involvement in Lebanon: A Precedent for an Open Game with Syria?* (Jaffee Center for Strategic Studies, Tel-Aviv University, Tel-Aviv, April 1981).

13. The message was sent through Louis Fares, Radio Monte Carlo's Damascus correspondent, on 13 February 1982. Fares has often been used by the Assad regime as a vehicle for transmitting its 'real' views in an informal fashion.

14. For an assessment of the Israeli-Syrian fighting in Lebanon, see M. Heller, D. Tamari and Z. Eytan, *The Middle East Military Balance, 1983,* (Jaffee Center for Strategic Studies, Tel-Aviv University, Tel-Aviv 1983), particularly pp. 260-2. The Syrian Ba'athist regime's version of the war in Lebanon was recently published as *The Israeli Invasion of Lebanon,* written by a group of researchers supervised by the Syrian Minister of Defence.

15. *Tishrin* (Damascus), 9 July 1983.

16. Radio Monte Carlo.

11 ON A SHORT LEASH: SYRIA AND THE PLO

Moshe Ma'oz and Avner Yaniv

Introduction

Syria's policy towards the PLO, especially with regard to Fatah, the organisation's mainstay since 1968, has fluctuated with bewildering intensity from support and collaboration to suppression and persecution. Having virtually baptised *al-Fatah* as a guerrilla organisation in 1964, thereafter championing its cause, training its personnel and providing its equipment, the Syrians proceeded to turn against it within less than half a decade. Not long after having arrested the entire Fatah leadership, Syria again changed course, embraced the PLO and even went as far as invading Jordan with a view to rescuing Fatah from the fury of Hussein's troops. Fully supportive of the PLO/Fatah for the next half-decade, Syria once again turned against it in the course of the 1975-6 civil war in Lebanon. Less than two years later, a Syrian-PLO *rapprochement* took place, co-operation between the two entities developed and lasted until the autumn of 1982. Following the PLO's massive defeat at the hands of the Israelis, Syria turned against it yet again, instigated a violent rebellion within its ranks and then proceeded to conduct a war of nerves against the Palestinian organisation.

How can one account for these radical fluctuations in the Syrian attitude to Fatah? Were Syria's actions a reflection of whimsical changes in the preferences of individual Syrian leaders? Or were they inspired by ideological considerations? Was its conduct motivated by a cynical pursuit of self-interest? Or was it, perhaps, a combination of all these factors? Given the impenetrability of the Syrian 'black box' where policies are determined, options canvassed and critical decisions formulated, a definitive answer to such questions seems impossible. Nevertheless, an overview of Syrian policy towards the PLO in general and Fatah in particular since the early 1960s does offer a number of plausible clues.

In the first place, Syria's support of the PLO hinges on the latter's conforming to Syria's ideological objectives. A PLO that drifts too far afield from the prevailing ideological orthodoxy in Damascus is likely to be subject to extreme pressures. An ideologically quiescent PLO, on the other hand, is likely to enjoy Syria's unswerving support. This applies both to the Ba'athist blend of socialism-cum-nationalism and to Syria's declared goals in the Arab-Israel conflict.

Second, and perhaps of greater importance during the reign of Hafez al-Assad than previously, Syria's attitude towards the PLO/Fatah is determined by the degree to which that organisation has been inclined to subordinate its own practical and immediate priorities to Syria's. If the Syrian national interest dictates militancy (for instance, against Israel), the PLO should toe the line. If, conversely, Syrian interests call for pragmatism and accommodation (for instance, in the Lebanese context), the PLO is expected to follow suit.

To be sure, this distinction between the *operational* (i.e. practical) and *aspirational* (i.e. ideological) levels of the Syrian approach is fuzzy and perhaps difficult to apply to Syria's political praxis. Ultimately, the two domains may well be inseparably intertwined. Ideology is defined according to perceived practical needs, and practical politics is pursued within broadly defined ideological parameters.[1] Indeed, from the PLO's point of view, it all boils down to one and the same thing: if the organisation wishes to survive, it cannot afford to defy Syria too abrasively. Yet, if its own policies are restricted to the narrow confines of the Syrian national interest, the PLO's ability to advance its own goals is severely, perhaps fatally, limited. This predicament has not always been painful in the same degree; but after two decades of PLO-Syrian relations, it seems to have become a conspicuous and even an enduring pattern.

The Formative Years, 1964-1975

Syria's relations with the PLO or, more precisely, with the organisation's backbone, Fatah, were born of the challenge to Nasserism. As early as 1958, Syria had pressed Nasser to resume fedayeen action against Israel. Unwilling to face a war with Israel, the Egyptian president refused. The issue became a major bone of contention between Egypt and Syria throughout the 1958-65 period, and especially after the dissolution of the Egyptian-Syrian union in September 1967. Late in 1964, the Syrian regime was ready to translate this challenge to Nasser from diplomacy into military action against the Jewish state. The logic of this departure was simple enough. Both domestically and in the wider Arab context, the Syrian regime could not criticise Nasser incessantly while declining to take any risks itself. If, on the other hand,

Syria were to initiate small-scale hostilities with Israel and face Israeli retributions, it could always employ this sacrifice as a means of further challenging Nasser's lead in the Arab world.

The chief architect of this policy was the head of Syria's military intelligence, Colonel Ahmad Suwydani. By 1964, Suwydani succeeded in obtaining the blessing of his superiors as well as the consent of Yassir Arafat and the nascent Fatah organisation. Arafat was fully aware, of course, of the fact that the Syrians meant to use Fatah for their own ends. But since he and his colleagues shared, for their own reasons, Syria's criticism of Nasser, they were quite prepared to collaborate with Suwydani's design. On 1 January 1965, Syria permitted the Assifa (Fatah's operational arm) to undertake its first raid against Israel. The troubled partnership between Syria and Fatah was thus baptised in military action.[2]

Fatah raids in Israel during the winter and spring of 1965 were of little military significance. With Syrian and Lebanese help, however, they drew a great deal of attention in the Arab world and presented a severe challenge to the Egyptian-sponsored PLO under Ahmad Shukairi. This latter organisation was seemingly far larger and better endowed than Fatah. In practice, however, it was strictly prohibited by Egypt from engaging in military activities. Nasser's response to the Arafat-Syrian challenge was double-edged. He pressed most Arab governments to deny Fatah any help, especially through publicity, finance and permission to operate against Israel. At the same time, though, he attempted to persuade Fatah to toe the line. Solidly backed by Syria and, owing to this, beyond Nasser's reach, Fatah could ignore Nasser and carry on its operations.[3] Nevertheless, Nasser's campaign against Fatah had one important effect: Egypt, Jordan and Lebanon would not permit the organisation to operate from their territories. Fatah, therefore, became entirely dependent on Syria's good will.

During the latter part of 1965, the Syrians were divided on whether or not to permit Fatah members to cross into Israel from Syrian territory, and the organisation suffered a certain loss of freedom. Following the Jedid *coup* on 23 February 1966, it seemed for a moment that this militant Syrian regime would at last allow Fatah all the freedom to operate which the organisation demanded. In fact, the opposite took place. Within two months of the *coup*, it became clear that the new regime was, if anything, even less inclined than the previous regime to allow Fatah real freedom of action. Friction between Syria and Fatah could be discerned on two critical issues. The first was ideological: the Jedid regime sought to impose its militant brand of

Ba'athism on Arafat's pragmatically oriented organisation. The second bone of contention was practical: namely, the degree to which Fatah raiding parties should be subject to Syrian army control. Faced with stiff Fatah resistance, the Jedid regime attempted to oust Arafat and replace him with its own man, Captain Yousef Ourabi. Failing this, the Syrian authorities in May 1966 suddenly jailed the entire Fatah leadership.[4]

Arafat and his associates were released after 40 days. What apparently saved the Fatah leadership from a long imprisonment was a shift in Egyptian policy. For reasons that cannot be clearly established, Nasser decided at about this time to authorise Shukairi's PLO to adopt the Fatah method of armed struggle, provided that operations would be carried out from Lebanese and Jordanian territories. Thus Syria's claim of being the only Arab government to allow the Palestinians to pursue the armed struggle was suddenly challenged. In response, the Syrians freed Arafat and his colleagues and stepped up support for their cause. Fatah was now allowed to engage in more actions, to increase its recruitment and propaganda campaign and to expand its training programmes on Syrian soil. Syria, however, also set up a rival Palestinian organisation — the Palestine Liberation Front, under the command of Ahmad Gibril, a Palestinian officer in the Syrian army. This rival to Fatah capitalised on the Palestinian cause without claiming as much autonomy as Arafat's Fatah. Indirectly, the move to set up the PLF also reflected rivalries among the ruling Ba'ath elite. Whereas Suwydani and, increasingly, Hafez al-Assad sponsored the Fatah, their rival, Colonel Abdal-Karim Jundi, acted as patron to the PLF.[5]

The intensification of the activities of Fatah, of the PLF and of the PLO against the background of fierce rivalry between Nasser, Jedid and King Hussein of Jordan ultimately hastened the escalation in the conflict with Israel which led to the 1967 war. Following this catastrophe Syria and the PLO did not change course but, if anything, increased the emphasis on revolutionary warfare. Nasser's conventional warfare strategy seemed doomed. A popular liberation struggle based on the population of the West Bank and Gaza could therefore be presented as the only viable alternative. This was Fatah's view. It also served well the Syrian challenge to Nasser's declining leadership.[6]

As part of Fatah's effort to establish bases of operation in the Israeli-occupied West Bank, Syria provided the organisation with three to four training centres in the vicinity of Damascus. All bases were supervised by the Operations Division of the Syrian General Staff. In addition, the

Syrians set up a command post in Dera (on the Jordanian border), whose task was to guide Fatah squads *en route* to the West Bank through Jordan. Finally, Radio Damascus expanded the activities of its Palestine section.

The transfer of the centre of Fatah activity to the West Bank and, subsequently, to Jordan gave the organisation an unprecedented degree of freedom from Syrian control. After the 1967 war, moreover, Egypt rejected Shukairi and endorsed Arafat's leadership, not only of Fatah, but also (as of August 1968) of the entire PLO. Syria attempted to buttress its flagging influence on the Palestinian movement — and its decline as a patron — by further consolidating its own Palestinian organisations. Thus, during the spring of 1968, Syria unified three separate Palestinian Ba'athist organisations — the Popular Palestine Liberation Front, the Pioneers of the Popular Liberation War and the Upper Galilee Liberation Organisation — into one entity under the title al-Saika. Within a short time, the Saika organisation took Fatah's place as Syria's main Palestinian client. Formally it became a constituent organisation within the new PLO under Yassir Arafat's chairmanship. In practice, Saika remained largely subordinate to the Syrian Ba'ath Party.[7]

These important changes in Syria's relations with Fatah did not, however, result in a new crisis. For his part, Arafat was careful to avoid friction with the Syrians while seeking to reduce their influence over the PLO. The Syrians reciprocated Arafat's prudent policy. Consequently, relations between Syria and the PLO remained close enough to withstand their first major test, the 1970 civil war in Jordan.

What turned the Jordanian-Palestinian showdown in September 1970 into an important landmark was the coincidence of two processes: first, the challenge of Syria's declared commitment to the Palestinian cause as a result of King Hussein's action; second, the fact that the decision whether or not to rise to this challenge became intertwined with the struggle for mastery in Syria between the two Alawi leaders, Hafez al-Assad and Salah Jedid. Neither process was totally unexpected; yet, their convergence turned the occasion into an important juncture.

Syria's decision to invade Jordan in order to rescue the PLO from the wrath of Hussein's troops, a momentous decision in terms of the inter-Arab rules of the game, was apparently taken by Jedid. Whether or not the cautious and much more astute Assad raised any objections is a moot point. What matters is that once the invasion was under way the Syrian air force, which was under Assad's command, declined to give the invading armoured column critically needed air cover. Strategically

Assad was of course, right, since Syrian air force participation in the fighting would have tilted the balance against Hussein. In that event, Israel and the United States, both of which were determined to save the Hashemite king, would have intervened. Thus by denying air support to the armoured column, Assad saved Syria a possible débâcle of major proportions.[8]

At the same time, however, this non-move by Assad turned Jedid's decision to invade Jordan into a fiasco, which could not but sharpen the already great differences between them. Jedid tried to defend himself by calling on the 10th Extraordinary National Congress of the Ba'ath Party a month later in order to remove Assad from office. Assad had no alternative but to resist the move, which he did with a *coup d'état* on 13 November 1970. A chain of events triggered by Palestinian actions thus caused still another transfer of power in Syria.[9]

During the next five years, Syrian policy towards the PLO seemingly did not change. The PLO was permitted to recoup from its disaster in Jordan by operating from Lebanon, largely with Syrian blessing. Indeed, it is inconceivable that the PLO would have been able to renew and even intensify the fighting against Israel from Lebanese soil as it did from 1970-3 without Syrian support. In the final analysis, however, the deterioration of Lebanon as a consequence of PLO actions and Israeli reprisals was bound to expose Syrian-PLO relations to new, and far greater, tests.

Civil War in Lebanon, 1975-1976

The civil war in Lebanon impaled both Syria and the PLO on the horns of excruciating dilemmas. From the Syrian point of view, it was essential to restore stability in Lebanon under conditions that would ensure the Ba'athist regime's ability to steer, shape and direct the course of Lebanese politics. Domestically the Assad regime could be severely shaken by a failure to contain the crisis in Lebanon. Syria could not tolerate an assertive, independent Lebanon that was capable of playing balance-of-power politics in the arena of inter-Arab relations in a manner which would be detrimental to the Syrian regional position. On the other hand, Syria did not want to countenance the complete disintegration of Lebanon and its partition into separate entities, each of which would turn either to Israel and/or to Syria itself for protection. Nor did Syria wish to become so deeply involved in the Lebanese imbroglio that it would have to maintain a large garrison in Lebanon on a permanent basis. Such an outcome would sap Syria's military strength and demoralise its troops, and it might even send ethnic/religious shock-waves through the Syrian body politic. Syria's ultimate aim in the civil war, therefore, was a restoration of the *status quo ante bellum.*

The PLO's dilemma was quite different. The organisation's position in Lebanon had been fairly convenient. The city of Beirut, with its vast infrastructure, extensive media and attractive comforts, offered an ideal locus for the PLO's headquarters. Lebanon's hilly and populated south gave the PLO an ideal terrain for operations against Israel. Last, but certainly far from least, the weakness of the Lebanese polity enabled the PLO to possess a freedom of action the likes of which it had never enjoyed anywhere in the Arab world. If, however, Lebanon were to come under the domination of the Phalangists, who had extensive links with Israel, the PLO's freedom would be severely curtailed. Indeed, this scenario could well lead to a vigorous attempt by the Phalangists to deal with the PLO as Hussein had done in Jordan five years earlier. If that were to happen, the PLO would have no other safe haven in which to train, recruit and carry out both military and political operations.

In order to prevent a Phalangist victory a PLO alignment with the Lebanese left was essential, and indeed some of the more radical elements in the PLO were eager to embrace such an alliance. Somewhat superficially, they assumed that it could overcome the Phalangists, effect a complete reshuffle of Lebanon's domestic constitution and, thereafter, turn Lebanon into a radical state, free of the ambiguities towards the Palestinian cause with which traditional Lebanon had been saddled. The Fatah leadership, though, seems to have been far less eager to take part in such a radical experiment. It was fully aware of Syria's opposition to a major change in Lebanon's internal complexion. In any case, Fatah leaders had for years been committed to the principle of non-intervention in the internal affairs of host Arab states. They feared that a victory for Lebanon's anti-*status quo* coalition might face the PLO with greater difficulties than the prevailing order had ever posed.

Thus, in a paradoxical way, both the Syrians and the leadership of Fatah initially saw eye to eye on the issue of the Lebanese civil war. Both entertained a hidden temptation to exploit the deterioration to their advantage. But in the end, both preferred the pre-civil war *status quo.* The course of the civil war in Lebanon was from the outset beyond the control of either the Syrians or Fatah. The sources of the conflict were ingrained in the complexity of the Lebanese system *per se.* The forces which launched the civil war and kept it going during the first ten months were mainly Lebanese. At first, both Syria and the PLO were confined to the role of keen, but essentially passive, spectators. When this changed, it was not due to either a Palestinian or a Syrian initiative. Rather, a new twist in the war — specifically, the growing prospect of a Christian victory — prompted the PLO to intervene. Once it did, so the Syrian calculus was altered, and Syria, too, was impelled to become directly involved.

The PLO's intervention was inspired by a desire to prevent the elimination of a favourable *status quo.* So was Syria's intervention. But by so doing, Syria and Fatah suddenly found themselves in conflict. What made this new twist in their complex relations even more confusing was the fact that, for a variety of reasons having little to do with the PLO itself, Syria made extensive use of the PLO's own cause while actually suppressing Fatah, the PLO's most important constituent organisation.[10]

By a strange paradox, Syria's conflict with the PLO in the Lebanese civil war had its origins in an act of co-operation between them. From 4-18 January 1976, Christian forces succeeded in laying siege on a number of Palestinian and Muslim areas in and around Beirut. The PLO and the (leftist) Lebanese National Movement retaliated by attacking the Christian cities of Damour and Jiyeh. In turn, the Lebanese air force was ordered to strike the leftists. The Palestinians and their Lebanese allies turned to Syria for help. Concerned with avoiding Israeli intervention, but determined to halt the deterioration, Syria deployed in the Beqaa valley the Yarmuk Brigade of the Palestine Liberation Army, formally a constituent part of the PLO but in practice a Syrian army unit.[11]

Syria then proceeded to mediate among Lebanon's warring parties with a view to restoring order on the basis of a number of moderate changes in the Lebanese National Pact. The Muslims, and especially Kamal Jumblatt's Druzes, were not satisfied with Syria's proposals and sought to force Syria to press for more extensive changes. To achieve their aims they renewed hostilities and even attacked the presidential palace in Baabdeh, the residence of Sulayman Faranjiyyah, the Syrian-supported president of Lebanon.

This challenge to Syria faced the PLO with a difficult choice. Should it join the National Movement and risk a breach with Syria or should it side with Syria and risk its alliance with Lebanon's National Movement? Sensing the PLO's dilemma, Assad summoned Yassir Arafat to Damascus on 15 April 1976, in an attempt to prevail upon him to side with Syria. An agreement was reached, but it proved to be short-lived. On 8 May 1976, Syria succeeded in ensuring the election of Ilyas Sarkis to the presidency of Lebanon. The move was openly defied by the National Movement. For its part, the PLO could no longer defer a choice between going along with Syria and throwing in its lot with Kamal Jumblatt and the National Movement. Under pressure from the PFLP and the PDFLP, and probably assuming that even a 'friendly' Syria would undercut his organisation's independence and freedom of action in Lebanon, Arafat drifted towards an alliance with Jumblatt.

Arafat's move was a virtual act of rebellion and exposed Assad to a great deal of criticism at home. Deciding to increase Syria's involvement in Lebanon, Assad first ordered Zuheir Mohsen's al-Saika, ostensibly a part of the PLO, to join PLA units in a campaign against the Lebanese National Movement, Fatah, the PFLP and the PDFLP. When this action failed to quell the resistance, Assad, with tacit Israeli acquiescence, finally ordered (on 1 June 1976) regular Syrian army units to intervene in the fighting. The die was cast: Syria was determined to force the PLO and its Lebanese allies to accept a *Pax Syriana* in Lebanon.

The Syrian offensive proved surprisingly sluggish. Nevertheless by 30 September 1976, the PLO seemed to the Syrians to have been sufficiently bruised to be amenable to fruitful negotiations. Assad ordered a halt to the Syrian attacks and attempted once again to talk the PLO into a more acquiescent position. His reasoning contained a typical blend of pragmatic and ideological arguments. The Palestinian resistance, he argued:

> Does not have any right to interfere in internal affairs of the host country. For the resistance to get involved in Lebanese affairs is, in fact, a conspiracy against the Palestinian cause. Firstly, it dissipates Arab potential and diverts it from its dedicated cause, the cause of Palestine. Secondly, it transforms the Arab-Israeli conflict into a conflict between Arabs. Thirdly, Palestinian intervention in Lebanon's internal affairs is a reactionary move, even by Marxist standards. The struggle against Zionism is the yardstick of how reactionary or progressive people are. Any Palestinian or Arab potential diverted from the battle against Zionism and directed against national forces is a reactionary move, even if these national forces happen to be right wing.[12]

Arafat and his colleagues were, however, slow in responding to the

Syrian call for a cease-fire. Syria, therefore, launched another offensive on 12 October. It was so devastating that this time the PLO had no alternative but to yield. On 16 October 1976, Presidents Assad of Syria and Sadat of Egypt (the latter in fact representing Fatah) met in Riyadh. A formula for a settlement in Lebanon was worked out and subsequently confirmed in an Arab summit in Cairo on 25 October. It basically conferred on the Syrian force in Lebanon a peace-keeping mission. The PLO's (and the Lebanese) challenge to Syria thus came to a brutal end.

Reconciliation, War and a Renewed Rift, 1977-1984

Following the Riyadh and Cairo conferences, Syria and the PLO gradually moved towards a *rapprochement.* The reasons for seeking accommodation were, from the points of view of both parties, rather compelling. In the first place, Syria had not abandoned its self-ordained role as guardian of the Palestinian revolution. If anything, the open conflict with the PLO had damaged Syria's position in this regard, and Syria felt impelled to redress its tarnished image.

Second, both Syria and the PLO had to seek ways and means of offsetting the potential effects of the visibly growing co-operation between Israel and the Phalangists. The PLO needed Syrian support in its renewed struggle with Israel in the south of Lebanon. Syria, for its part, was deterred by Israel from a direct role in the south and, therefore, needed the PLO as a proxy in that area.

Third, and perhaps most important, Sadat's peace initiative of November 1977 inevitably drew the PLO and Syria together again. For both, that initiative was a momentous challenge, militarily, ideologically and politically. It called for a vigorous attempt to unite all forces in the Arab world to oppose Sadat's move. It implied that Israel would be far more capable of affecting the situation *vis-à-vis* Syria in the Golan Heights and *vis-à-vis* the PLO in Lebanon. The implication was that militarily, too, Syria and the PLO should again close ranks.

Even before Sadat went to Jerusalem, Syria and the PLO had by July 1977 reached a modicum of understanding (itself impressive, considering the scope of their rift the previous year). After the initiative, they moved fast towards a degree of co-operation that superseded anything achieved in this respect previously. This trend was reinforced under the impact of the Israeli invasion of south Lebanon in March 1978 (Operation Litani). Following that Israeli operation, the PLO hastened to overhaul its entire deployment in the south of Lebanon. It was in urgent need of training facilities, of far heavier equipment and of Soviet assistance. Syria was both able and willing to satisfy all three needs; indeed, like the PLO, the Syrians increasingly anticipated a far greater Israeli military incursion in the (then) foreseeable future. Thus they had an added incentive for helping the PLO in its own attempts to prepare for the apparently inevitable showdown.

The renewed alliance had clear limits, of which both parties were fully aware. For one thing, the PLO had been engaged since 1974 in internal debate concerning its fundamental disposition. Arafat and some of his associates in Fatah apparently favoured a gradual, and cautious, opening to the West, which while avoiding a clear-cut recognition of Israel would nevertheless qualify the PLO as a legitimate participant in an American-sponsored peace process. Syria was not at all enamoured of this idea. Having gained substantially in stature despite (or perhaps because of) its militant positions *vis-à-vis* Israel, it was not ready for a grand compromise with Israel. Hence, Arafat's viewed campaign was essentially unacceptable to the Syrians. If he was successful in changing the PLO's position in the peace process, he would thereby add impetus to the Egyptian campaign for peace, indirectly legitimise a change in the position on this issue of others in the Arab world and thus leave Syria out in the cold, together with Libya and the PDRY (South Yemen). Beyond this short-term utilitarian consideration, Syria might have been motivated by a longer-term ideological objective: a commitment to a Ba'athist Syrian hegemony in an area consisting of Lebanon, Jordan, Syria proper and Israel. If Arafat accepted the notion of a mini-state in the West Bank, this modern version of the Greater Syria ideal would be dealt a severe, indeed fatal, blow.[13]

It was, therefore, essential from the Syrian point of view to make sure that Arafat's campaign inside the PLO for a reorientation of the organisation's posture would fail. Since Arafat acted ambiguously, stressing simultaneously the old-standing rejectionist maxims of the PLO charter and the need for tactical adaptation (through a series of perennial Palestine National Council [PNC] decisions), Syria did not have to confront him head on. Instead, it could use equivocal public statements by government officials and back-stage diplomacy based on Syrian supporters inside the PLO framework to slow down the shift in the organisation's position. Assad's policy proved fairly successful. President Carter's attempts to bring the PLO to accept indirectly the essence of UN Resolution 242 were aborted. Sadat's subsequent attempt to martial support on the West Bank for the autonomy scheme born at Camp David was foiled, too. And lastly, despite much effort by Arafat and some of his more pragmatic lieutenants, the PLO's position remained sufficiently unyielding to ensure that the organisation would remain unacceptable to Israel as a partner in the peace process.

The second major limit to the Syrian-PLO *rapprochement* from 1977-82 was far more strategic than political or ideological. During Operation Litani (March 1978), Syrian forces in Lebanon had remained totally inactive. Israel was determined to avoid war with Syria and the latter, for reasons which were explained elsewhere in this volume, was also determined to avoid such a conflict.[14] As it happened, the Israeli attack was launched in a cumbersome and unimaginative manner, which enabled the PLO combatants in the south of Lebanon to retreat to Syrian and Lebanese-controlled areas without suffering heavy casualties. Syria's inaction in support of the PLO was, nevertheless, conspicuous. The PLO, therefore, had to assume that Syrian devotion to the Palestinian cause notwithstanding, the Ba'athist republic would not risk its national interest for the sake of the PLO.

Such a lesson might have added impetus to the frantic effort to strenghten its military capabilities in which the PLO thereafter engaged. And when Israel invaded Lebanon on 5 June 1982, this PLO perception of the Syrian position was doubly reinforced. Syrian forces left the PLO to their own devices. Even when they came under heavy Israeli attack, the Syrian contingents in Beirut and in the Beqaa valley reacted rather passively.

If this attitude dismayed the PLO, it was still far less painful than Syria's position towards the PLO in the wake of the Israeli invasion. One of the most striking outcomes of this invasion was the destruction of the PLO infrastructure south of Beirut, the occupation by various Lebanese forces (Phalangists, Druzes, Shi'ites) of areas which were previously under PLO control and, above all, the pushing of the PLO either out of Lebanon altogether or into Syrian-held areas of the country. Given Syria's declared attitude to the Palestinian cause, this might not have seemed such a disaster. In reality, it amounted to the greatest calamity in the annals of the PLO. For the implication was cruelly simple: If henceforth the PLO wished to remain close to Israel's border, it would have to pay the price of complete Syrian control over its affairs. Conversely, if the PLO wished to escape this fate (which would reduce its stature to what it had been in the mid-1960s), it would have to disperse to various Arab countries that have no common border with Israel. In either case, the PLO would suffer a drastic eclipse.

Arafat and Fatah attempted to hedge their bets. Some 50 per cent of their troops departed from Beirut late in August 1982 to Tunisia, Algeria and the PDRY. The rest retreated to the Syrian-held areas of east and north Lebanon and attempted to re-establish themselves there *as an autonomous force*. The obvious consequence of this latter act was a head-on collision with Syria. The Syrians instigated the so-called Abu Mussa rebellion, a challenge to Arafat's leadership led by Syrian loyalists in the PLO. The Abu Mussa following was, of course, negligible. But it posed a major threat to Fatah because wherever it could not force itself on the latter, it could still count on solid backing by al-Saika, by PLA units and, above all, by regular Syrian forces. By 1983, Fatah was cornered in Tripoli, from which it was eventually evacuated by sea. Thus, the combined effect of the Israeli invasion of Lebanon and Syria's later actions against Fatah ejected the PLO from its last remaining foothold in the vicinity of Israel.

At this juncture, Arafat could either have capitulated to Syria or continued to challenge the Syrians by adopting a political stance that would bring Fatah back into the forefront of Middle Eastern diplomacy. Oddly enough, the opportunity for the latter alternative was offered by President Reagan's peace initiative of 1 September 1982, in which the PLO is not even mentioned. The Reagan plan called for a settlement based on a Jordanian-Israeli agreement. Jordan, however, is bound by the Rabat summit decision of 1974, which declares the PLO to be the 'sole legitimate spokesman of the Palestinian People'. Syria, which led the Rabat summit (against Egyptian and Jordanian objections) to this decision, would not allow Jordan, or anybody else, to ignore it. From the Jordanian and PLO points of view, this position amounts to a subterfuge guaranteeing deadlock on the Palestinian/West Bank issue unless and until the PLO makes itself acceptable to Israel as a negotiating partner. Nevertheless, King Hussein would not by-pass the Rabat decision without PLO consent. Thus, despite the fact that the Reagan plan ignores the PLO altogether, Hussein's decision of whether or not to respond to the American initiative hinges on the PLO's consent. In turn, the PLO faces a hideous choice. The Reagan initiative and Jordan's position have created a badly-needed opportunity for the PLO to remain in the centre stage of Middle Eastern diplomacy. But it was also impaled on the horns of the dilemma whether or not to challenge Syria and allow Hussein to enter into negotiations with Israel.

To be sure, even if Arafat overcomes his fear of Syria and allows Hussein to proceed, Jordan and the PLO will still find it difficult to agree on the terms of such a deal. The question is, who will ultimately inherit the West Bank? Will it be Jordan as the senior partner and the PLO as a subordinate entity, or should Jordan merely offer its good offices to the PLO? From the PLO's point of view, this question was early in 1983, and has so remained when this book went to print, secondary to the more pressing problem of whether or not to challenge Syria openly. Overtly Arafat has attempted to placate the Syrians by continuing to adhere to a rigid line that upholds the sacrosanct maxims of the Palestinian charter. Covertly, however, Arafat seems to have been heading since the beginning of 1983 towards a joint approach with King Hussein. Such an approach has also been a useful means of keeping together PLO diehards and their moderate counterparts, whose differences have been greatly sharpened by the events since the Israeli invasion of Lebanon.[15]

Syria, however, apparently has refused to permit Arafat such a game. This was manifested by a barrage of Syrian statements warning Arafat against any ideological heresy. In addition, Syria seems to have been behind the assassination of leading PLO moderates, such as Issam Sartawi and Fahed Qawasmeh. After two decades of turbulant relations, Syria and the PLO seem to be facing a critical moment of truth. If Arafat yields and accepts the limits imposed by the Syrian position, the entire edifice he has laboured to build will crumble into little more than a Syrian front. If, on the other hand, he maintains the challenge to Syria's hegemony on the Palestine issue, in itself one aspect of Syria's struggle for regional preponderance, he and his followers may face a mortal risk.

Notes

1. For a similar interpretation of Syrian foreign policy in general, and not only with respect to the PLO, see Raymond A. Hinnebusch, 'Revisionist Dreams, Realist Strategies: The Foreign Policy of Syria', in Bahgat Korany and Ali E. Hillal Dessuki (eds.), *The Foreign Policies of Arab States* (Westview Press, Boulder, 1984), pp. 283-322.

2. See Ehud Ya'ari, *Fatah,* (Levin-Epstein, Tel-Aviv, 1970), pp. 39-54.

3. For Syria's and Fatah's attitudes to Nasser's approach and to Shukairi's PLO, see Moshe Shemesh, 'The Representation of the Palestinians', unpublished PhD thesis, The London School of Economics and Political Science, 1982, pp. 138-44.

4. Ya'ari, *Fatah,* pp. 55-70.

5. Ibid.

6. Ya'ari, *Fatah,* pp. 82-102.

7. Aryeh Yodfat and Yuval Arnon-Ohana, *PLO Strategy and Policy* (Croom Helm, London, 1980), pp. 20-30.

8. For the background, with an emphasis on the US approach, see Alan Dowty, *Middle East Crisis* (University of California Press, Berkeley, 1984), pp. 175-81. See also the contribution in this volume by Joseph Nevo.

9. N. Van Dam, *The Struggle for Power in Syria* (Croom Helm, London, 1979), p. 88.

10. Itamar Rabinovich's contention in the previous chapter that for Syria the war in Lebanon was an opportunity appears to the authors to be debatable. This analysis of the Syrian-PLO encounter in the course of the Lebanese civil war draws heavily on five principal sources: Helen Cobban, *The Palestine Liberation Organization* (Cambridge University Press, Cambridge, 1984), esp. pp. 58-80; Walid Khalidi, *Conflict and Violence in Lebanon,* Harvard Studies in International Affairs No. 38, (Center for International Affairs, Harvard University, Cambridge, MA, 1979); Adeed I. Dawisha, *Syria and the Lebanese Crisis* (MacMillan, London, 1980); Itamar Rabinovich, *The War for Lebanon* (Cornell University Press, Ithaca, 1984), pp. 34-60; P. Edward Haley and Lewis W. Snider, *Lebanon in Crisis* (Syracuse University Press, Syracuse, 1979), pp. 21-90.

11. For an informative analysis of the PLA, see Sara Bar-Haim, 'The Palestine Liberation Army: Stooge or Actor?', in G. Ben-Dor (ed.), *The Palestinians and the Middle East Conflict* (Turtledove, Ramat Gan, 1976), pp. 173-94.

12. *Events,* (London) (1 October 1976), p. 19, quoted in Dawisha, *Syria and the Lebanese Crisis,* pp. 147-8.

13. This was the theme of Assad's statements to Radio Damascus on 27 August 1979 and again, on 23 April 1980.

14. See contribution by Rabinovich in previous chapter, esp. pp. 179-82 above.

15. On Syrian-PLO relations following the Reagan initiative of 1 September 1982, see Avner Yaniv and Robert J. Lieber, 'Reagan and the Middle East', *The Washington Quarterly* (Fall, 1983). See also Godfrey Jansen, 'Arafat and Assad: The Inevitable Clash', *Middle East International,* no. 203 (5 July 1983).

PART III

SYRIA AND THE SUPERPOWERS

12 WASHINGTON, DAMASCUS AND THE LEBANON CRISIS

Yair Evron

Introduction

American policy towards Syria has witnessed over the past few years sudden shifts in different directions: from deep mutual suspicion to what could be described as normal diplomatic dialogue and then, again, to frustration and hostility and even the use of military force. These turnabouts have been the result of the dramatic and bloody events in Lebanon since the mid-1970s. Whereas American-Syrian relations evolved primarily in other contexts — superpower rivalry and the festering Arab-Israeli conflict — since 1981, and more so since 1982, they have been inseparably intertwined with political and strategic developments in Lebanon. Paradoxically it was precisely Syrian involvement in Lebanon since 1975 which created bridges between the two countries and helped, to a limited extent, to smooth relations between Washington and Damascus, but from 1982 onwards led to a straining of relations. Lebanon, and Syria's involvement there, eventually forced the US to face some disturbing and always frustrating dilemmas regarding the use of American force as an instrument of foreign policy. Yet, it is again the situation in Lebanon that, at the time of writing appears, ironically, to be recreating a new dialogue between the US and Syria. This convoluted interaction between the two countries is all the more fascinating, as it involves relations between a superpower and a small, regional power. As will be argued in this chapter, however, the power that has been more constrained in the use of its military capabilities was the United States.

American-Syrian relations before the 1973 Yom Kippur war had been extremely cool. The negotiations following that war created a new context for their inter-relationship. After long and exhausting deliberations, US Secretary of State Henry Kissinger, shuttling between Syria and Israel while negotiating with the Israeli leadership, on the one hand, and Syria's President Hafez al-Assad, on the other, succeeded in working out a formula delineating the new cease-fire lines and providing for the signing of a disengagement agreement, which took place in 1974. Thereafter, the United States and Syria went through a slow process of thawing out their relations, which included the renewal of diplomatic contacts broken off in 1967 and the initiation of a diplomatic dialogue between the two countries.

Syria was at the time seeking ways to reduce dependence on the Soviet Union, as well as to create for itself new foreign policy options. The American assessment was that a constructive dialogue with Syria might, indeed, lead the latter to change its international orientation. At the least, the Syrian relationship with the Soviet Union would be weakened and perhaps its position on the Arab-Israeli conflict moderated. Certainly, similar moves regarding Egypt had achieved positive results; and there appeared to be no fundamental reason why they should not have the same effect on Syria, even though the process might be more prolonged.

This type of approach was certainly a well-tested Kissinger tactic. Indeed, in his dealings with the parties at the time, the then Secretary of State had been so well impressed by Assad's shrewdness, realism and pragmatism that he hoped to see further positive developments in American-Syrian relations.[1] As a manifestation of this hope, the US, in 1975, began extending financial aid to Syria. Though modest — only US $60-100 million a year — it was nevertheless viewed as another step in the drawn-out process of accommodation. But it was the American-Syrian dialogue concerning Lebanon in 1975-6 which proved that the process had borne some fruit. Before this dialogue is discussed in detail, American policy concerning Lebanon should be examined.

American Policy on Lebanon and Syria's Role[2]

One after the other, American administrations have perceived the Lebanese situation as an issue of secondary importance. Until the outbreak of civil war in Lebanon in 1975 (and except for the brief intermezzo of the 1958 American intervention), Lebanon played a negligible role in American considerations. It was only in the wake of the escalation of the civil war and, especially, the increased threat of a military confrontation between Israel and Syria, that Lebanon assumed a higher priority in American calculations. It is instructive to note that the main reason for the initial growth of American interest was not the internal affairs or fate of Lebanon *per se* but rather the threat of another Arab-Israeli war. Indeed, until 1982, Lebanon and its related problems continued to be treated by Washington as secondary to the larger issues of the Middle East: the Soviet encroachment, developments in the Gulf area and Israel's relations with the leading Arab states. Only with the deepening American commitment to Amin Jumayyil's regime did Lebanon itself become worthy of a major American initiative.

In the first stages of the Lebanese civil war, which began in April 1975, the Ford administration kept a low profile, with the obvious intention of maintaining the *status quo* in Lebanon. Because of the marginality of Lebanon in the American assessment of Middle Eastern problems, there was no readiness to get actively involved in resolving the difficult situation developing there. To be sure, the *status quo* forces, remembering the 1958 intervention, were hoping to involve the US in the crisis, but it refused to be drawn in. Thus, for example, although Kissinger reaffirmed US 'interest in Lebanon' in a letter to Prime Minister Rashid Karami on 6 November 1975, his phrasing clearly indicated America's disinclination to become directly involved.

American concern began to increase in September 1975, when there were indications that Syria and Israel might intervene militarily in Lebanon. These signs prompted the US to make clear its strong objection to any military moves by these other parties. On 30 September 1975, after a meeting between Kissinger and Foreign Minister Takla of Lebanon, the State Department issued this communiqué '....the Secretary noted that Lebanon is one of our closest friends in the Middle East and that we have a special interest in the independence and territorial integrity of that country, and in the national unity and cohesion of Lebanon.'[3] That statement obviously clarified US preferences regarding the internal situation in Lebanon. More importantly, however, it served as a warning to both Israel and Syria to refrain from military intervention.

The United States, however, was preoccupied with far more important issues regarding the Middle East during 1975, the primary one being the search for further improvement in the Israeli-Egyptian relationship. After an initial failure in March-April 1975, the US succeeded in September in bringing the two to sign the Sinai 2 Agreement. That major move stabilised relations between Israel and Egypt and — as became clear only years later — created, together with Sinai 1, the foundation for Sadat's peace initiative in late 1977. It also led to a deeper division in the Arab world and to great concern in Syria, which felt isolated *vis-à-vis* Israel. Indeed, Syrian reaction to the agreement, to Egypt and to the US was very hostile, which initially appeared to make the American-Syrian dialogue that had commenced a short time earlier that much more difficult.

Interestingly enough, however, the US and Syria found ways soon afterwards of reaching some understanding with regard to Lebanon. This was accomplished by two complementary strategies: first, a parallel decision in both Damascus and Washington to 'decouple' the Lebanese complex from the overall American-Syrian relationship; second, a shared effort to prevent the Sinai 2 Agreement from putting a halt to their general diplomatic dialogue. Thus, it appears, a Syrian compromise proposal presented to the Lebanese warring factions in December 1975 received tacit or even explicit backing from the US.[4]

January 1976 became a critical month in the Lebanese civil war after the Christian leadership had rejected Syria's proposal. There was a major escalation in military activity, accompanied by Christian threats to partition the country. As seen in other chapters in this volume, the deteriorating situation forced Syria to become even more active in attempting to manage the situation. First, Syrian Foreign Minister Khaddam threatened intervention; subsequently, intensive Syrian diplomatic activity took place in Beirut. Syria worked out a new formula with Lebanon's President Faranjiyyah, for political reform that accommodated some of the demands of the Muslim-radical Palestinian coalition (the National Front) while basically maintaining the political system of the country. By late January, the Christian forces that were co-operating within the framework of the Lebanese Front accepted this proposal.

Khaddam's threats of intervention raised concern in Israel, which had by then developed a strategy of deterrence against Syrian military intervention in Lebanon.[5] To forestall the danger of direct military confrontation between the two regional powers, the United States adopted a complex strategy: on the one hand, Washington kept signalling its opposition to hasty and extreme moves by either Syria or Israel. On the other hand, the administration tried to delineate areas of shared interest in Lebanon between the two regional powers. Thus, a complex three-actor game developed: Syria, diplomatically active in Lebanon, also kept signalling the possibility of military intervention, yet sought indirect or tacit endorsement by the US for such a move. That endorsement, though, had to include Israel's 'acceptance'. Israel, on its part, issued deterrence threats against any Syrian military intervention, yet began signalling its readiness to accept some Syrian military move, provided it was conducted within specific limits.[6] The United States became one of the main channels through which Israel and Syria communicated their intentions.

Israeli readiness to 'accept' some Syrian intervention crystallised once it became apparent in February–April 1976 that, frustrated by Muslim-Palestinian opposition to its diplomatic efforts, Syria had turned against the latter and sided with the Christians. The United States communicated to Syria the Israeli 'red lines' defining the limits of Syrian intervention.[7]

It appears that much of the American diplomatic activity during that period was directly co-ordinated by Kissinger, with Richard Murphy, the US ambassador in Damascus, providing the crucial link with President Assad. From April, an additional important role was played by Dean Brown, who was despatched to Lebanon on a special mission.

The Syrian invasion of Lebanon that began on the night of 31 May until 1 June (fighting continued until October) certainly succeeded in constraining the National Front and in imposing some order in the country. A state of controlled semi-anarchy persisted, but there was no recurrence of the civil war. Thus, one American objective had been secured: the instability in Lebanon was reduced and there appeared to be no threat of a new round of escalation. This impressed upon the administration in Washington the view that Syrian activity in Lebanon was basically of a stabilising nature. More important from the American point of view was the success of the Israeli-Syrian tacit understanding about the deployment and use of force in Lebanon. To be sure, that success was due in the first place to the coincidental recognition by both regional powers that the costs involved in a military confrontation far outweighed the benefits. Nevertheless, the US was active in contributing to that calculus and came to view it as an important asset.

Throughout the Carter presidency (1977–80), the United States continued to see Syria's role in Lebanon as a stabilising one. There was some hesitancy in the American view as a result of the Syrian bombardment of East Beirut in late 1978 and the growing co-operation between Syria and the PLO. But the basic American perception remained unchanged. Syria, however, vehemently opposed the Camp David accord, regarding it as leading to its total isolation. There is no doubt that the forceful American role in the Camp David treaty exacerbated differences between Washington and Damascus. Carter's attempts to bring Syria into the peace process mitigated these difficulties, but did not remove them.

Reagan's Middle East Policy

A much more pronounced change in American-Syrian relations appeared with the coming to power of the Reagan administration in January 1981. From the outset, that administration adopted a strongly anti-Soviet posture. Indeed, the conflict with the USSR became the main organising principle of American policy in regard to the Middle East. To be sure, the Carter administration, under the impact of the fall of the Shah, the miserable episode of the hostages in Teheran, and the Soviet invasion of Afghanistan, had already begun to formulate a new Middle East policy. One element was the creation of the Rapid Deployment Force (RDF), (later to be renamed Rapid Joint Deployment Force — RJDF). Another, the formation of the Carter Doctrine for defending the Gulf area against a possible Soviet attack. There were also the beginnings of an attempt to create a new set of regional defence arrangements in co-ordination with America's regional friends. These initiatives characterised the last year of the Carter administration.

The Reagan administration strongly emphasised these policies and, in some respects, went beyond them. The first and guiding assumption of Reagan's Middle East policy was that the main danger faced by the United States in that region was the extension of Soviet influence in the Persian Gulf. Secondly, the Arab-Israeli conflict, now perceived as less salient and destabilising than had previously been assumed, was to receive less attention. American efforts were to focus on the more urgent problems in the Gulf. Reagan did not change past American principles for the ultimate resolution of the Arab-Israeli conflict — that is, an Israeli territorial withdrawal in exchange for peace; in this respect, the Camp David process remained important. But the Reagan administration perceived that momentum could be maintained with a lower investment of American effort.

The third element of the new US policy, directly related to the first two, consisted of a conceptual division between the Gulf area and the Arab-Israeli conflict. It was assumed that the systems of interaction among states in these two areas were separate and that there was little spill-over between them. Hence, the two areas lent themselves to separate American policies. Given this assumption and the assumed urgency of any threat to American interests in the Persian Gulf, it was decided that the United States could neglect the Arab-Israeli conflict area and concentrate instead on the Persian Gulf.

Fourth, the Reagan administration assumed that the foreign policies of regional powers were primarily organised around the question of

East-West relations. According to this conception, which to a certain extent underlay much of the Reagan approach, regional problems were of only secondary importance to Middle Eastern leaders: decision-makers in Riyadh, Cairo and Jerusalem were preoccupied with the Soviet threat. Conversely, Syria's behaviour was directed by the Soviet Union.

Finally, and in the specific context of the Arab-Israeli conflict, the administration harboured strong animosity towards the PLO. In contrast to the Carter approach, the Reagan administration was adamant in its condemnation of international terrorism: it viewed the PLO as a threat, not only within the Middle East, but also in the world at large.

The main operational conclusion from these assumptions was the attempt to build a new regional defence organisation oriented to the West. This policy, which had been initiated under Carter, was christened the 'strategic consensus', and its main objective was to defend the Gulf region. The policy seemed to the Americans to possess great potential: it promised to free American foreign policy from involvement in the entangling complexities of intra-regional disputes and, at the same time, to catch all client states in the inclusive sweep of an anti-Soviet axis. A second operational conclusion, which again was a continuation of a Carter initiative, was the accelerated build-up of the RJDF. Finally, in direct contrast to the Carter approach, there emerged a certain neglect of the Arab-Israeli issue and, primarily, of the Camp David process.

The US policy soon ran into major problems. Haig's visit to the Middle East in April 1981, which was supposed to lay the foundations of the 'strategic consensus', led to a series of disappointments. Regional leaders, although concerned about the Soviet threat, emphasised nevertheless problems of a more regional nature. The Saudis talked about the Palestinian problem and the dangers emanating from revolutionary Iran. Israeli leaders were primarily concerned with Syrian behaviour in Lebanon. In addition, the Americans witnessed in this period a series of Israeli actions, some of them provocative, that seemed to demonstrate the potency of the Arab-Israeli conflict. Of importance in this context were the Israeli, Maronite and Syrian actions and over-reactions in the April 1981 missile crisis, Israel's limited incursion into Lebanon in the summer of 1981, the attack on the Iraqi nuclear reactor and the Israeli annexation of the Golan Heights.

By early 1982, it had become clear that the sweeping 'strategic consensus' could not in itself obtain all of Washington's regional goals for the Middle East: there remained the necessity for a more traditional, if more complex, approach in dealing with the intrinsic conflicts and problems of the region. In particular, the Arab-Israeli conflict required more attention. Furthermore, the distinction that had been drawn between the Persian Gulf and the Arab-Israeli conflict zones now seemed to be less valid. The operational outcome of these conceptual readjustments was to devote energy to the Camp David accord and, most urgent of all, to secure the last phase of the Israeli withdrawal from Sinai. Indeed, Haig's visit to the Middle East in early 1982 was designed to underline America's continued interest in the Camp David process. The American views had certainly undergone a change; however, they remained in flux and lacked focus and coherence.

American-Syrian Relations and the 1982 War [8]

The Reagan administration's initial attempts to build a Middle Eastern 'strategic consensus' added to the growing animosity between Syria and the US. Even the successful American effort in April-May 1981 to stop Israel from attacking Syrian missiles in Lebanon's Beqaa valley did not improve Washington's worsening relations with Damascus. By early 1982, the situation was described by one American official as having reached its nadir since 1973. US policy on Lebanon, also, had developed an anti-Syrian strain in its emphasis on the need for the complete withdrawal of all foreign forces (meaning, also, Syrian) from Lebanon and the formation of a 'strong central government'. Indeed this tenet became the Reagan administration's main long-term objective in Lebanon.

The change in attitude should now be placed within the general context of American policy towards the Middle East. By 1982, two variants of that policy had developed, each sharing the same basic assumptions mentioned earlier regarding the Soviet threat and ways to handle it, but differing in its assessment of the relative importance of Israel and the Arab states to American interests. One group of decision makers, led by Secretary of Defence Caspar Weinberger, emphasise the importance of the moderate Arab States, primarily Saudi Arabia. The other group, led by Secretary of State Haig, emphasised Israel's role as an important asset for the US. To be sure, the difference here was more a question of emphasis than a manifestation of differen policies. Nevertheless, it had its impact on specific decisions during the evolving crisis in Lebanon.

It should be noted that below the level of decision-makers, most American officials who dealt specifically with Syria and Lebanon saw the solution to the Lebanese equation as lying firmly within an *Arab* context. They assumed that a concerted Arab effort, led by Saudi Arabia, would ultimately bring about Syria's withdrawal and the formation of a strong, independent Lebanese government.

While American views of the Syrian role in Lebanon were changing, the concern over an Israeli-Syrian military confrontation remained high, since such a conflict might result in uncontrolled escalation and possibly even lead to a superpower crisis. Notwithstanding the Reagan administration's firm anti-Soviet posture and rhetoric, a direct crisis with the Soviet Union was regarded as undesirable and dangerous. In this attitude, the Reagan administration was following the behaviour pattern of previous administrations: deterrence of Soviet military initiatives in the Middle East, coupled with caution and a 'crisis management' approach. Hence, the American efforts to dissuade Israel from striking at the Syrian missiles in the Beqaa valley in April 1981, and to stop Israel from invading Lebanon at several points in time between December 1981 and June 1982(*).

Once the war in Lebanon did break out, on 6 June 1982, the United State adopted a 'damage limitation' approach: limiting the cost of negative reactions from America's Arab allies, especially Saudi Arabia and Egypt; minimising Soviet inroads into the Arab world; and avoiding the danger of an American-Soviet crisis. Together with this strategy, there was also a recognition of the possible benefits of this war. Although the United States was not in collusion with Israel in regard to the latter's 'big plan' in Lebanon, the war presented the possibility of implementing American political objectives: withdrawal of all foreign forces — the Syrians and the PLO (and, of course the Israelis, as well) — and the establishment of a strong central government. Indeed, Haig defined these American objectives soon after the war started.[9] Another beneficial consequence seemed to be the blow to Soviet prestige in the Middle East resulting from a Syrian and PLO set-back. Thus, the notion of a solution to the Lebanese problem within an *Arab* context was now overshadowed by the possibility of more immediate benefits.

During the first few days of the war, an ambiguity persisted regarding

(*) US opposition to Israel military action, of course, stemmed also from its concern regarding reaction from the other Arab countries and — until April 1981 — from the possibility that such an action might jeopardise the final phase of Israel's withdrawal from the Sinai.

its scope. When Israel assured the US that it intended to implement only its 'little plan', a military confrontation between Israel and Syria appeared to be avoidable, giving American diplomacy room to manoeuvre. The US pursued its diplomacy in Lebanon primarily through the mediation of Philip Habib, who arrived in Israel on the second day of the war.[10] His first task was to mediate between Israel and Syria. On 8 June he carried an Israeli ultimatum to Damascus; but even before he met with President Assad, the Israelis had launched their strike against Syrian forces in the Beqaa.

Immediate American efforts ensued at the highest level to secure a cease-fire, prompted by the fear that the 'damage limitation' strategy might collapse because of Israeli-Syrian military escalation. A Soviet note delivered to President Reagan, though relatively moderate in tone, nevertheless injected a feeling of further grave consequences, at the superpower level. Moreover, Arab criticism of the Israeli operation and what appeared to be American acquiescence to it was mounting. By Friday, 11 June, the US succeeded in forcing Israel to accept a general cease-fire. In fact, however, fighting ended only in the eastern sector, where the main Syrian units had been engaged by Israel. Battles continued in the western and central sectors, where Israel fought both PLO and Syrian units; these were areas not directly affecting the area always considered strategically crucial to Syria — the Beqaa valley.

After mediation lasting about ten weeks and conducted against the background of the Israeli siege of Beirut, the US succeeded in securing an agreement for the withdrawal of PLO and Syrian forces from Beirut. The negotiations were conducted with the participation of many parties, Syria being one of the main actors. At the time of the negotiations, the Syrian position was relatively weak. Syria had suffered a limited military defeat (primarily in the air); it had failed to mobilise meaningful Arab support; and its political allies in Lebanon had either suffered military defeat or, as in the case of Lebanon's President Sarkis and part of the Maronite community, lowered the profile of their relationship. Against that background, Syria became more flexible and eventually agreed to the American plan. Indeed, one of the possible benefits for Syria was that the PLO, never a convenient or co-operative ally, was crushed, and part of what was left of that organisation would become far more dependent on it than previously.

Prior to the Beirut agreement, American-Syrian negotiations seemed to have created a somewhat more relaxed medium for overall American-Syrian relations. Yet subsequent events changed that mistaken perception. The United States became involved in a series of policy steps and initiatives that appeared threatening to Syrian decision-makers. At the same time, Syria gradually strengthened its position in Lebanon and *vis-à-vis* Israel. The combination of these developments precluded, for the time being, the possibility of a meeting of purpose between the US and Syria.

The Beirut agreement created a new peace-keeping force — the Multinational Force — of which the American contingent was the largest. Deployed in Beirut, the MNF withdrew after a while, but returned following the massacre in September by Phalangist troops of Palestinians in the Sabra and Shatilla refugee camps and the Israeli withdrawal from West Beirut. At that time, the US assumed a posture of deep commitment to a specific policy regarding Lebanon. As mentioned earlier, the US had never considered Lebanon to be of much intrinsic political or strategic interest. By autumn 1982, that position had changed. The US now became involved in Lebanon *per se* and developed a commitment to the new regime headed by Amin Jumayyil. The new policy was not the result of a change in the relative strategic importance of Lebanon, rather it was a combination of external factors and the dynamics of intervention and commitment. By that time, American-Syrian relations had become completely dependent on developments in Lebanon.

The position of the United States was that Syrian forces should withdraw from Lebanon as part of a general plan for the withdrawal of all foreign troops. Next, the US assumed the role of the main external backer of Amin Jumayyil's regime in Beirut. In order to accomplish its new objectives in Lebanon, the US pressed ahead with negotiations to secure an agreement between Israel and Lebanon. It was assumed — wrongly as it turned out — that following such an agreement, negotiations would begin with Syria and that Syria would be ready to withdraw, as well. The American diplomats relied on several rationales for this assumption. For one thing, Syria had repeatedly declared a willingness to withdraw once Israel had done so and given a request of the Lebanese government. Second, it seemed that the Syrian presence in Lebanon involved Syria in high costs, especially after the Israeli deployment along the Lebanese-Syrian border at a distance of only 20-odd kilometres from Damascus. Since the Syrians were apprehensive over the possibility of an Israeli shelling of Damascus, a symmetrical Israeli-Syrian withdrawal would seem to offer Syria a clear dividend. Finally, the US trusted Saudi Arabia to exploit its position as Syria's main financial backer in persuading the Syrians to evacuate Lebanon.

The Americans decided, therefore, that priority should be given to negotiations between Israel and Lebanon and that its own negotiations with Syria be postponed to a later stage. This proved to be a grave tactical mistake. The Israeli-Lebanese talks finally culminated in the agreement of 17 May 1983, and it appeared as if the next stage would be relatively easy to accomplish. And indeed, Israel declared its readiness to withdraw completely from Lebanon. Syria was now expected to follow suit, in consonance with previous declarations. But here lay a fundamental misunderstanding of Syrian interests.

By mid-1983, it had become clear that for Israel the costs of deployment in Lebanon were beginning to outweigh by far the benefits. Syria was keenly aware of this change. In addition, Syria's perceived need of maintaining a military presence in the Beqaa valley, and the considerable political influence it enjoyed throughout Lebanon as a result, made Syrian willingness to withdraw fully less and less keen. Finally, the Israeli-Lebanese agreement included several elements that clearly affected Syrian interests adversely. The Syrians, consequently, became convinced that the United States was backing a strategy that would allow Israel a prominent position in Lebanon. Unable to tolerate this possibility, Damascus proceeded to frustrate its negotiations with Washington by delay tactics, and maintaining persistent ambiguity. These tactics, in turn, only deepened American suspicions concerning Syria's true objectives in Lebanon.

The obstinate Syrian position was also influenced by the internal situation in Lebanon itself. The Lebanese opposition, made up of Shi'ites, Druzes, the Sunni elite of the Tripoli area and even some Christian notables (most prominently, Faranjiyyah), refused to accept Amin Jumayyil's plans. Frustrated by his inability to bring about political reform, they formed a tactical alliance. Their natural external backer was Syria. In addition, the deployment of a Soviet-manned air-defence system increased Syrian deterrence against any military move by Israel, and thus boosted Syria's self-confidence.

The change in the Syrian position on withdrawal, together with the aid it extended to groups opposing Jumayyil's government, led, in mid 1983, to a change in the American perception of the Israeli role in Lebanon. Washington had seen the potential Israeli threat to Syria a an important bargaining card in the negotiations with Assad. But by the summer of 1983, it had also become clear that the Israeli withdrawa from parts of Lebanon would enable the opposition forces in thes regions to coalesce and turn against the central government. An ironi paradox now emerged: Israel, becoming less and less enchanted with it role in the area, was anxious to withdraw, at least from the Shouf moun tains. On the other hand, both Jumayyil and the US were eager for Israel to extend its stay there.

The Dilemma of the Use of Force

When Israel eventually withdrew from the Shouf in September 1983 and Druze and Shi'ite units subsequently began pushing towards Beirut, the United States was forced to contemplate the possibility of the direct use of force in defence of the Lebanese government. By that time, the Americans had assembled a considerable force off the shores of Lebanon to back up its MNF contingent of marines in Beirut. The political-strategic impact of the US military presence was primarily bound up with the Reagan administration's commitment to the Jumayyil government. Washington's high military profile was intended to signal American commitment and resolve. It was, however, a passive military posture and soon proved untenable. When Druze units, backed by PLO fighters and Syrian artillery, attacked Souk al-Garb, the suburb controlling the south-eastern entrance to Beirut, it placed Lebanese army units in a precarious situation, and the US then decided to use limited force. American naval units opened fire and helped block the advance on Beirut.

The United States attempted to delineate parameters for its use of force: the basic posture was one of defence and deterrence; accordingly, direct attacks on the marines or infringement of a 'red line' around Beirut would be met with measured responses. Major problems arose in the application of this policy. Military actions against the American forces, such as the bombing of marine headquarters in Beirut that killed 240 men, aroused the urge for revenge beyond the measured pursuit of defence and deterrence. The problem was that the identity of factions acting against the marines was often difficult to establish; similarly, Syrian involvement in these attacks was indirect and seemed not to provide grounds for retaliation. Furthermore, whereas operations against the Syrians might perhaps be helpful in the negotiations, their political cost would be considerable. Consequently, the American response was primarily periodic heavy naval shelling of areas from which fire had been directed at Beirut or at the American units themselves. The targets were mainly Druze and Shi'ite militia units or, in rare instances, Syrian artillery. In only one case did American aircraft go on the attack, striking at Syrian SAM deployments.

In the final analysis, it seemed that American military force would be

unable to obtain Washington's objectives in Lebanon. Amin Jumayy
proved inept in bringing about national reconciliation, and Syria
backing of opposition groups undermined the government. In such ci
cumstances, the rapid translation of American force into politic
assets seemed impossible. Washington was forced, once again, *
reconsider its interests and strategy in Lebanon.

The starting point for the Reagan administration's reconsideratio
was the recognition that whereas the American military presence i
Beirut served as a guarantee that the Jumayyil government would n
fall, the actual application of military force could not coerce th
majority of Lebanese to back the central government. This goal cou
be secured, if at all, only by means of a new political formula that depe
ded to a large extent on the political behaviour of Jumayyil himse
Moreover, as unpalatable as the thought was, the US had to recogni
the painful fact that Syria could play a useful role in the slow and to
tuous process of reaching an accommodation among Lebanon's wa
ring communities. This recognition developed only gradually again
the background of US public displeasure at the uncertainty of purpos
surrounding the deployment of the marines in Beirut. Perhaps eve
more important than the sway of public opinion was the old-ne
recognition that Lebanon was not an important interest for the Unite
States. There was no point in shedding blood and being involved in
messy and sordid domestic situation, when no clear advantage in term
of hard interests could be secured.

Thus, the United States decided to pull its contingent of marines o
of Beirut and to lower the profile of her commitment to Jumayyil. Th
development contributed to and was in turn affected by Jumayyil
decision to renew the old alliance between the Maronites and th
Syrians.

Therefore, from mid-1984 the US returned, at least partly, to h
1976 policy. American officials reached the conclusion that Syr
could contribute more to the stability of the central regime in Beirut tha
an American military presence. So much so, that one official went as f
as to suggest that the Syrian role could be considered 'helpful' within th
context of Lebanon.

American-Syrian relations will probably be affected by th
Lebanese context for some time to come. But with the decline in impo
tance of Lebanon in American considerations about the Middle Eas
Syria will probably increasingly be perceived within more importa
contexts: superpower competition and the future of the Arab-Israe
conflict.

Notes

1. See Henry Kissinger, *Years of Upheaval,* (Little Brown Co., Boston, 1982), chs. XXI and XXIII.

2. This analysis is partly based on chapter 6 of Yair Evron, *War and Intervention in Lebanon: 'Israel-Syrian Conflict and Superpower Rivalry* (forthcoming).

3. US Department of State, Bureau of Public Affairs, *US Policy in the Middle East: November 1974, February 1976,* Selected Documents, No. 4 (Washington, October 1976) p. 95.

4. For details of Syrian mediation in Lebanon see *inter alia*, Itamar Rabinovich, *The War for Lebanon 1970-1983* (Cornell University Press, Ithaca, NY, 1984), chapter 2; Itamar Rabinovich and Hanna Zamir, *War and Crisis in Lebanon 1975-1981* (Hakib-Butz HaMeuchad, Tel-Aviv, 1982) (in Hebrew), Adeed I. Dawisha, *Syria and the Lebanese Crisis* (MacMillan, London, 1980); Evron, *The Lebanese Crises,* chs. 2, 3.

5. For details of the Israeli-Syrian 'Dialogue', see Evron, *War and Intervention in Lebanon,* ch. 2.

6. These included a geographical restriction on the movement of Syrian forces as well as a restriction on the size of forces and their weapon systems. Israel also demanded limitations on Syrian air force activity in the skies of Lebanon and vetoed the deployment of Syrian ground-to-air missiles in Lebanon.

7. Interview with an ex-American official in Washington, April 1982. For further details see Evron, *War and Intervention in Lebanon,* ch. 2.

8. My analysis is compatible with much of the criticism of American policy included in William Quandt's article, 'Reagan's Lebanon Policy: Trial and Error', *The Middle East Journal,* vol. 38, no. 2 (Spring 1984). My paper was initially written before I had the opportunity of reading Quandt's article.

9. This was done in the programme 'This Week' on ABC. See *Washington Post* and *The New York Times* reports of 14 June 1982.

10. The decision on Habib's mission was taken before the war began. Indeed, it has been suggested that initially Habib went to the Middle East with a new plan aimed at stabilising the situation in Lebanon. See Alexander Haig, *Caveat* (MacMillan, New York, 1984), pp. 336-8.

13 MOSCOW, DAMASCUS AND THE LEBANON CRISIS

Robert O. Freedman

Introduction

One of the most striking features of Syria's rise to the status of an important regional power has been its success in exploiting its relations with the Soviet Union for advancing its own interests. The Soviets are not averse to Syria's ascent, since in broad terms, any gain in stature and influence by their ally would also be regarded as a gain for themselves. Nevertheless, the march of the Syrians towards a position of regional power has occasionally faced the Soviets with exceedingly difficult situations.

The growing Syrian involvement in the Lebanese imbroglio in the course of the 1970s is a good case in point. Moscow was not at all opposed to the increase in Syria's influence in Lebanon. When, however, the situation there brought the Syrians into open conflict with Israel, the United States and the PLO, the Soviet Union at times faced the difficult prospect of a major confrontation that could harm not only its own position in the region, but also its global standing. Even the well-being of the Soviets in the most immediate sense could have been affected. On these occasions, the Soviets must have wondered whether or not their great investment in Syria has made them capable of stopping the Syrians from moving ahead. The answer in the discussion that follows is that there were severe limitations on their ability to do so.

The Soviets, the Syrians and the Middle East

Observers of Soviet policy in the oil-rich and strategically located Middle East are generally divided into two schools of thought. While both schools agree that the Soviet Union wants to be considered a major factor in Middle Eastern affairs, if only because of its propinquity, they differ on the ultimate Soviet goals in the region. One school of thought sees Soviet Middle East policy as being primarily defensive in nature: that is directed towards preventing the region from being used as a base for military attack or political subversion against the USSR. The other school of thought sees Soviet policy as offensive, aimed at limiting and ultimately excluding Western influence from the region and replacing it with Soviet influence. It is the opinion of the author that Soviet goals in the Middle East, at least since the mid-1960s, have been primarily offensive in nature; and that in the Arab segment of the Middle East, the Soviet Union appears to have been engaged in a zero-sum-game competition for influence with the United States. A brief discussion of the tactics and overall strategy employed by Moscow in its quest for influence in the region will serve as a background to the subsequent analysis of Soviet policy during the Lebanon crisis.[1]

In its efforts to weaken and ultimately eliminate Western influence from the Middle East, and particularly from the Arab world, while promoting Soviet influence, the Soviet leadership has employed a number of tactics. First and foremost has been the supply of military aid to its regional clients.[2] Next in importance comes economic aid: the Aswan Dam in Egypt and the Euphrates Dam in Syria are prominent examples of Soviet economic assistance, although each project has had serious problems. In recent years, Moscow has also sought to solidify its influence through the conclusion of long-term friendship and co-operation treaties, such as the ones with Egypt (1971), Iraq (1972), Somalia (1974), Ethiopia (1978), Afghanistan (1978), the People's Democratic Republic of Yemen (1979), Syria (1980) and the Yemen Arab Republic (1984). Repudiations of the treaties by Egypt (1976) and Somalia (1977) indicate that this has not always been too successful a tactic. Moscow has also attempted to exploit both the lingering memories of Western colonialism and Western threats against Arab oil producers. Another tactic has been the establishment of party-to-party relations between the CPSU (Communist Party of the Soviet Union) and the ruling parties in a number of Middle Eastern one-party states. Moscow has provided assistance in developing a security apparatus and other elements of political infrastructure to selected states in the region. It has offered the Arabs diplomatic support at such international forums as the United Nations and the Geneva conference (on an Arab-Israeli peace settlement). Finally, Moscow has given the Arabs direct military aid for use against Israel. This last, though, has been limited in scope because Moscow continues to support Israel's right to exist both for fear of unduly alienating the United States, with whom the Russians desire additional SALT agreements and improved trade relations, and for maintaining Israel as a convenient rallying point for potentially anti-Western forces in the Arab world.[3]

All these tactics have been employed, to a greater or lesser degree of success, over the last two decades; nevertheless, the USSR has run into serious problems in its quest for influence in the Middle East. The numerous inter-Arab and regional conflicts (Syria-Iraq, North Yemen-South Yemen, Ethiopia-Somalia, Algeria-Morocco, Iran-Iraq, etc.) have usually meant that when the USSR has favoured one party, it has alienated the other, often driving it over to the West. Secondly, the existence of communist parties in the Middle East has proved to be a handicap for the USSR, as communist activities have, on occasion, caused a sharp deterioration in relations between Moscow and the country in which the communist party has operated.[4] The communist-supported *coup d'état* in Sudan in 1971, communist efforts to organise cells in the Iraqi army in the mid and late-1970s and the activities of the Tudeh Party in Iran against the Khomeini regime are recent examples of this problem. Third, the wealth which flowed to the Arab world (or at least to its major oil producers) since the quadrupling of oil prices beginning in late 1973 has enabled the Arabs to buy quality technology from the West and Japan, and this has helped weaken the economic bond between the USSR and a number of Arab states, such as Iraq. Fourth, since 1967, and particularly since the 1973 Arab-Israeli war, Islam has been resurgent throughout the Arab world. The USSR, identified in the Arab world with atheism, has been hampered as a result.[5] Finally, the United States and, to a lesser extent, France and China have actively opposed Soviet efforts to achieve predominant influence in the region. This opposition has frequently enabled Middle Eastern states to play the extra-regional powers off against each other and, thereby, prevent any of them from securing predominant influence.

To overcome these difficulties, Moscow has evolved an overall strategy — the development of an 'anti-imperialist' bloc of states in the Arab world. In Moscow's view, these states should bury their internecine rivalries and join together, along with such political organisations as the Arab communist parties and the PLO, in a united front against what the USSR has called the 'linchpin' of Western imperialism in the Middle East — Israel. Under such circumstances, the Soviets hope that the Arab states would use their collective pressure against Israel's supporters, especially the United States. The ideal scenario for Moscow, and one which Soviet commentators have frequently referred to, was the situation during the 1973 Arab-Israeli war when virtually all the Arab states supported the war effort against Israel while also imposing an oil embargo against the United States. As is well known, not only did the oil embargo create domestic difficulties for the United States, it also caused serious problems in the NATO alliance, a development that was warmly welcomed by Moscow. Unfortunately for the USSR, however, the 'anti-imperialist' Arab unity was created not by Soviet efforts, but by the diplomacy of Egypt's president, Anwar Sadat. When Sadat changed his policies and turned towards the United States, this unity fell apart. None the less, so long as Soviet leaders think in terms of Leninist categories like 'united fronts' ('anti-imperialist' Arab unity, in Soviet parlance, is merely another way of describing a united front of Arab governmental and non-governmental forces) and so long as there is a deep underlying psychological drive for unity in the Arab world, Moscow can be expected to continue to pursue this strategy as a long-term goal. It is in this context that Soviet policy during the Lebanon crisis can best be understood.

For its part, Syria has primarily viewed Moscow as a supplier of military equipment and diplomatic assistance both to enhance Syria's prestige in the Arab world and to aid the Syrians in confrontation with their main regional enemy, Israel. Relations between the USSR and Syria first became close in 1966, with the advent of the left-wing Ba'athist regime. During this period, though, there was a disagreement within the Syrian regime between Salah Jedid and Hafez al-Assad on how close to draw to Moscow. When Assad, who favoured a more limited relationship, overthrew Jedid in November 1970, a marked cooling of Soviet-Syrian relations took place. Soviet support for Syria during the 1973 war helped to warm relations again; however, Syria's refusal to attend the Soviet-co-sponsored Geneva peace conference in December 1973 and US Secretary of State Henry Kissinger's successful shuttle diplomacy, which brought about a Syrian-Israeli disengagement agreement, again chilled Soviet-Syrian ties. Yet another change in relations occurred when in 1975 Syria again turned to the USSR after the Israel-Egypt Sinai 2 agreement, only to clash violently with Moscow the following year, when the USSR both criticised Syria's military intervention in Lebanon and delayed promised shipments of arms.[6]

Interestingly enough, it was the Syrian intervention in Lebanon, coupled with Sadat's decision to sign a peace agreement with Israel, which once again turned Syria back to Moscow. As has been seen elsewhere in this volume, Assad's decision to intervene on the side of the Christians in the Lebanese civil war was not popular in Syria. In addition, as Islamic fundamentalism began to rise in the Middle East in the aftermath of the 1973 war, the secular, Alawi-dominated Ba'athist regime, already widely accused of widespread corruption, came in for increasing criticism. The end result was the rise of Muslim Brotherhood opposition to the regime.[7] Compounding this domestic problem for

Assad was a difficult foreign policy situation. On his eastern front was a hostile Iraq (see chapter 7 by Amazia Baram). In the west, the Syrian army, although *ex post facto* under the mandate of the Arab League, was badly bogged down in Lebanon (by the autumn of 1978, Syria had changed sides and was aiding the PLO and Muslim forces against the Christians). On the south-west lay an increasingly powerful Israel, now recovered militarily from the 1973 war and led by a hard-liner, Menachem Begin. Only to the south was there an ally, Jordan, to which Syria offered a military alliance in 1975 and with which co-operation reached the point of joint staff exercises in 1976.

For the Syrians to have any hope in a confrontation with Israel, Egyptian participation on the side of Syria was an imperative. Yet Sadat's willingness to sign the Camp David accord in September 1978 and a peace treaty with Israel in March 1979 removed Egypt, the most powerful Arab state, out of the Arab ranks. Assad denounced the agreement, thereby taking a position coinciding with that of the USSR, which also greeted Camp David with hostility. The Soviets feared it to be a major blow against the 'anti-imperialist' Arab unity they had long sought. While Moscow was encouraged by the Arab unity in opposing Camp David, and especially by the *rapprochement* between Syria and Iraq, which made possible the formation of a large anti-Egyptian bloc in the Arab world, the anti-Egyptian unity was very short-lived. The renewal of the Syrian-Iraqi confrontation after the accession to power of Saddam Hussein in July 1979 (Jordan's decision to ally itself with Iraq in the renewed conflict further isolated Syria), the Soviet invasion of Afghanistan in December 1979, and the Iraqi invasion of Iran in September 1980 served to split the Arab world once again.[8]

By the time of the Israeli invasion of Lebanon in June 1982, it appeared as though the Arab world had become divided into three major groupings. First, there was what might be called the 'peace' camp, consisting of Egypt, Sudan, Oman and Somalia, all of which were pro-Western (to the point of providing facilities for the US Rapid Deployment Force and being committed, to a greater or lesser degree, to peace with Israel) and were backing Iraq in the Iran-Iraq war. At the other extreme was the so-called Front of Steadfastness and Confrontation, composed of Syria, Libya, the People's Democratic Republic of Yemen, Algeria and the PLO, which were all, at least on paper, opposed to any kind of peace with Israel: all were following a pro-Soviet line on such issues as the Soviet invasion of Afghanistan, while Syria and Libya were outspoken in their support of Iran in the Iran-Iraq war. Located between the 'peace' camp and the 'Steadfastness' Front were the 'centrists', an amorphous group that had indicated a willingness to live in peace with Israel (albeit under very stringent terms), had denounced both Camp David and the Soviet invasion of Afghanistan, and were backing Iraq. The 'centrists' were composed of states that ran the spectrum from being mildly pro-Western (such as Morocco, Saudi Arabia and the United Arab Emirates) to neutral (as in the cases of the Yemen Arab Republic [North Yemen] and Kuwait). Even Iraq, before 1978 among the most hostile to Israel of Arab states, had moderated its position and could now be considered part of the centrist bloc, both for this reason and for its improved relationship with the United States.

Given this situation, Moscow's goal was to try to move the centrist Arab states back towards the Front of Steadfastness and Confrontation into an 'anti-imperialistic' bloc, much as had existed immediately after Camp David. On the other hand, the Soviet leadership was concerned about a *rapprochement* between the Egyptian camp and the centrists, since this would leave the pro-Soviet Steadfastness Front in an isolated position in the Arab world, with its individual components engaged in their own intra-Arab and regional confrontations (i.e. Algeria-Morocco, PDRY-Oman, Libya-Egypt, Syria-Iraq, Syria-Jordan, Syria-Israel and PLO-Israel). Such a development would also exacerbate internal strains within the Steadfastness Front, especially the conflict between Assad and Arafat, of the PLO.

Syria — because of its backing of Iran, its renewed confrontation with Iraq, its continuing confrontation with Israel, its poor relations with Egypt and its hostility to Jordan (owing to the latter's support of Iraq) — was now extremely isolated in the Arab world. It could no longer count on Arab support for its confrontation with Israel. By 1980, therefore it had begun to appeal to the USSR to give it the military assistance to match Israel's power. In return, Assad became one of the few Arab leaders to support the Soviet invasion of Afghanistan. Even more important, Assad agreed to sign a Friendship and Co-operation treaty with Moscow, which he did in October 1980, after a decade of resisting such a move.[9]

For Moscow, the signing of the treaty with Assad and the provision of additional military aid posed a number of problems. In the first place, the Soviets had to be concerned lest Assad, beset by internal and external difficulties, provoke an international crisis, either with Israel or with one of his Arab enemies, and then drag in the USSR. Second, Assad, who had demonstrated his independence of Moscow on a number of occasions in the past, might do so again, thus complicating Soviet Middle East policy at a time when, because of the Iran-Iraq war, this policy was already in a state of disarray. Indeed, in the crisis with Jordan in late November 1980 and in the Syrian 'missile crisis' with Israel, April-June 1981, Assad demonstrated just such an independent turn.[10]

In the year between the Syrian missile crisis and the Israeli invasion of Lebanon, there was evident strain in the Soviet-Syrian relationship, one complicating factor being a clash between Assad and the Syrian communist party which attacked Assad's domestic policies in a front page article in the party newspaper.[11] As Israel and the United States began to talk about 'strategic co-operation',[12] Syria redoubled its efforts to obtain increased military equipment from the Soviets. The USSR, however, appeared reluctant to meet Syrian requests, perhaps remembering Syria's previous efforts to embroil Moscow in its adventures. Thus a military delegation led by Syria's Defence Minister Mustafa Tlas which visited Moscow in September 1981 reportedly did not get all it wanted.[13] Even after Israel annexed the Golan Heights on 13 December 1981 (an event which led the US to suspend the Memorandum of Strategic Understanding concluded with Israel two weeks earlier), Moscow did not move to step up assistance to Damascus although the USSR strongly denounced the Israeli move. Similarly, when Foreign Minister Khaddam journeyed to Moscow in January 1982 in an apparent effort to gain increased Soviet support following the Golan annexation, he did not have a great deal of success. The Soviets pointedly avoided any specific commitment to Syria, merely reiterating their three-point peace plan, which included Israel's right to exist. The talks were described as having taken place in 'an atmosphere of friendship and mutual understanding' — an indication that serious disagreements remained between the two countries.[14]

In the aftermath of Khaddam's visit, both Moscow and Damascus encountered increasing problems in their Middle East policies. Moscow's hopes for Arab unity on an 'anti-imperialist' basis deteriorated further as the Morocco-Algerian confrontation over the former Spanish Sahara intensified. Furthermore, Morocco signed a major military agreement with the US that provided for transit facilities for the US Rapid Deployment Force (RDF) in an apparent quid pro quo for increased shipments of military equipment.[15] In addition, Morocco boycotted meetings of the Organisation of African Unity, a Pan-African organisation that Moscow also wanted to see unified on an 'anti-imperialist' basis (some OAU members recognised the Algerian-backed Polisario rebels). As for Syria, there was an anti-regime uprising by the Muslim Brotherhood in the city of Hama in February 1982 in which as many as 12,000 people were reported to have been killed.

Two months later, Syria blocked the Iraqi oil pipeline that ran through Syria, an event that weakened Iraq, but made Moscow's hopes for an 'anti-imperialist' Arab unity dim further. Meanwhile, the Lebanese-based PLO, already under heavy Syrian pressure, found itself fighting against Shi'ite forces in southern Lebanon which were protesting against PLO activities in their section of the country. This conflict was of particular concern to Moscow both because the Shi'ites, as the poorest element in the Lebanese population, were a prime recruiting ground for the Lebanese communist party and other leftist Lebanese elements allied with the PLO and also because the Shi'ite militia, Amal, was now fighting against leftist forces.[16]

Perhaps the greatest problem for Moscow, however, was the gradual *rapprochement* between Egypt and the centrist Arabs. Induced in part by the Israeli withdrawal from the last part of the Sinai on 25 April 1982, the *rapprochement* was accelerated by Iran's successes in the war with Iraq. As the Iranians took the offensive and threatened Iraqi territory in the late spring, the frightened Gulf states turned to both the United States and Egypt for support. The Gulf states now wanted to move in the same direction as Iraq, which soon after the outbreak of the war had become a recipient of Egyptian military equipment and had moderated its position towards Egypt as a result.[17] In addition, the warm official greetings by Jordan and Morocco to Egypt after the final Israeli Sinai withdrawal also appeared to signal their interest in improved ties with Egypt.[18] Thus, by the time of the Israeli invasion of Lebanon, there was movement towards a *rapprochement* between Egypt and the centrists. Indeed, a special meeting of the Steadfastness Front took place at the end of May 1982 to try to reverse this trend.[19]

In sum, it was a badly disunited Arab world, whose pro-Soviet members were isloated and whose centrist states were gradually moving towards a reconciliation with Egypt, which faced Soviet policy-makers on the eve of Israel's invasion of Lebanon.

From the Israeli Invasion until the Death of Brezhnev (June-November 1982)

Soviet inactivity during the period from the Israeli invasion of Lebanon until the exodus of the PLO from Beirut in August 1982 has already been discussed by this author and others elsewhere and need only be summarised here.[20] Contrary to its behaviour during the 1973 Yom

Kippur war, Moscow provided no military help during the course of the fighting. Its verbal warnings to Israel and to the United States were only of a very general nature — and very ineffectual — until the announcement of the possible deployment of US troops in Beirut. Even then, Brezhnev quickly backed down from his warning after it became clear that the US was going ahead with the deployment. Moscow did mount a resupply effort to Syria once the fighting had ended. As soon as it became clear, however, that Israel was not going to invade Syria and was restricting its efforts to destroying the PLO infrastructure in Lebanon (although battering Syrian troops stationed in Lebanon in the process), the Soviets took no other substantive actions, thus demonstrating once again that the Soviet-Syrian treaty did not cover Syrian activities in Lebanon. To be sure, Moscow appealed to the Arabs to unite to confront Israel and to use their oil weapon against the United States; but the badly divided Arab world, threatened on the east by Iran, took neither action. Indeed, the Arab states were unable even to convene a summit conference until after the PLO had left Beirut.

Although there was a spate of Arab criticism of Moscow for its lack of assistance to the PLO and Syria,[21] Syria itself held aloof from joining in. Instead, Syrian Information Minister Ahmad Iskander told a press conference in Damascus that the Soviet Union was a 'sincere friend', which had 'helped us defend our lands, wives and children'; he also called for a strategic alliance with the Soviet Union.[22] While the Syrians appeared to be using their battle losses against Israel and Iskander's press conference in yet another effort to obtain such an alliance, Moscow utilised this press conference, which was given prominent coverage by Tass, to demonstrate its continuing importance in Arab affairs and the major role it had already played in aiding Arab defence efforts.

None the less, it was Washington, not Moscow, that controlled the pace of events in the Middle East during the period leading up to the exodus of the PLO from Beirut. The Soviet leadership could do little but sit on the diplomatic sidelines as the American-mediated exodus took place on 20 August. The US moved to keep the diplomatic momentum in its favour on 1 September, when President Reagan issued his plan for a Middle East settlement.[23] The Arab states, finally convening their long-postponed summit in Fez, issued their peace plan one week later.[24] With the US and Arab peace plans on the table, the USSR hastened to issue its plan, which came in a speech delivered by Brezhnev in mid-September. Although a number of points were repetitions of previous Soviet proposals, others seem to have been added to emphasise the similarity between the Fez and Soviet plans.[25] The elements of the Soviet plan that repeated earlier proposals were a call for the withdrawal of Israeli forces from the Golan Heights, the West Bank, the Gaza strip and Lebanon to the lines which existed before the June 1967 war; the establishment of a Palestinian state on the West Bank and Gaza; the right of all states in the region to a secure and independent existence; and the termination of the state of war between Israel and the Arab states. These points in many ways resembled the Fez plan, except for Moscow's more explicit call for Israel's right to exist and an end to the state of war between Israel and the Arab world. The new elements in the Brezhnev peace plan seemed to be virtually modelled on the Fez plan. Thus, Moscow called for the Palestinian refugees to be given the right to return to their homes or to receive compensation for their abandoned property; for the return of East Jerusalem to the Arabs and its incorporation into the Palestinian state, for freedom of access to the sacred places of the three religions throughout Jerusalem, and for Security Council guarantees for the final settlement. Brezhnev also took the opportunity to repeat the long-standing Soviet call for an international conference on the Middle East, with all interested parties to participate, including the PLO, which the Soviet leader again characterised as 'the sole legitimate representative of the Arab People of Palestine'.

In modelling the Soviet peace plan on Fez, Brezhnev evidently sought to prevent the Arabs from moving to embrace the Reagan plan. Nonetheless, with the United States clearly possessing the diplomatic initiative in the Middle East after the PLO pull-out from Beirut and with both Arafat and Jordan's King Hussein, along with other Arab leaders, expressing interest in the Reagan plan, Moscow was on the diplomatic defensive. Given this situation, it is not surprising that Brezhnev seized upon the massacres in the Sabra and Shatilla refugee camps to point out to Arafat that 'if anyone had any illusions that Washington was going to support the Arabs ... these illusions have now been drowned in streams of blood in the Palestinian camps...'[26]

Nonetheless, despite the massacres, Arafat evidently felt that there was value in pursuing the Reagan plan, and he began to meet with his erstwhile enemy, King Hussein, to work out a joint approach to the United States. Such manoeuvring infuriated Syria, which sought to use pro-Syrian elements within the PLO to pressure Arafat into abandoning his new policy, a development which further exacerbated relations between Assad and Arafat. In addition, evidently fearing the weakening of the Steadfastness Front and the possibility of the PLO (or at least

Arafat's followers) defecting from it, Moscow continued to warn the Arabs about purported efforts by the US to split the PLO and to draw Jordan and Saudi Arabia into supporting the Reagan plan, which the USSR termed a cover for Camp David.

In mid-November 1982 Brezhnev passed from the scene. His successor, Yuri Andropov, had the task of rebuilding the Soviet position in the Middle East, which had suffered a major blow as a result of the Israeli invasion of Lebanon.

From Andropov's Accession to the 1983 War Scares

Andropov had to face the fact that the Soviet Union's position had deteriorated in three major areas. In the first place, Soviet credibility had suffered a major blow because its frequent warnings to the United States and Israel during the course of the war had proved to be ineffectual. Second, the quality of Soviet military equipment supplied to Syria and, to a lesser degree, of Soviet training had been called into question by the overwhelming victory of US-supplied Israeli weaponry. Finally, the United States had the diplomatic initiative in the Middle East; not only was the Reagan plan — and not the Soviet peace plan — the central factor in Middle East diplomatic discussions, but Arafat and King Hussein had begun to meet regularly and the governments of Israel and Lebanon had begun talks on a Lebanese-Israeli peace accord. Under these circumstances, the new Soviet leader, although preoccupied with consolidating his power and trying to block the installation of US Pershing II and cruise missiles in Western Europe, evidently felt that Moscow had to move before Soviet influence in the Middle East fell any further.

Andropov moved both militarily and diplomatically. On the military front, he dispatched several batteries of SAM-5 missiles to Syria in January 1983 — along with Soviet soldiers to operate and guard them.[27] This move went far beyond the Soviet resupply effort of tanks and planes to Syria that had been going on since the end of the Israeli-Syrian fighting in 1982 because the SAM-5 was a weapons system that had never been deployed outside the USSR itself. The system had the capability of engaging Israel's EC-2 aircraft system, which had proved so effective during Israeli-Syrian air battles in the first week of the Israeli invasion of Lebanon. Moscow was thus demonstrating to the Arab world — and especially to Syria — that it was willing to stand by its allies.[28] None the less, by manning the missiles with Soviet soldiers,

Moscow was also signalling that it, and not Syria, would determine when the missiles would be fired. Given the fact that in both November 1980 and April 1981 Assad had tried to involve the USSR in his military adventures,[29] this was probably a sensible precaution — especially when Assad and other Syrian officials began to issue bellicose statements several months later. Yet another cautionary element in the dispatch of the SAM-5 batteries was that Moscow never formally announced that its own troops were involved in guarding the missiles, thus enabling the USSR to avoid a direct confrontation with Israel (and possibly the United States) should Israel decide to attack the missile sites.

Diplomatically, Andropov at the same time was benefiting from developments in the PLO that challenged Arafat's opening to Washington. Moscow's interest in preventing a PLO turn to the United States was shared by both Syria and Libya, which actively moved to undermine Arafat's position. The efforts of the anti-Arafat forces proved successful, as the Palestine National Council, which after a number of postponements finally convened in Algiers in mid-February, formally stated its refusal to consider the Reagan plan 'as a sound basis for a just and lasting solution to the Palestine problem and the Arab-Israeli conflict'.[30] Moscow's obvious satisfaction with this development was reflected in the praise given by *Pravda* correspondent Yuri Vladimirov to the Council's policy document, terming it a reaffirmation of the organisation's determination to continue the struggle against imperialism and Zionism.[31] As the Reagan plan was faltering, a development which weakened US influence in the Middle East, Moscow was seeking to underscore its improved position in the region by issuing a public warning to Israel not to attack Syria. The Soviet warning, issued on 30 March, came after a series of Syrian warnings, yet was limited in nature. Although Moscow warned that Israel was 'playing with fire' by preparing to attack Syria, it made no mention of the Soviet-Syrian treaty. Indeed, in listing those on Syria's side in the confrontation with Israel, the Soviet statement merely noted: 'On the side of the Syrian people are Arab patriots, the Socialist countries, and all who cherish the cause of peace, justice and honour.' The statement also emphasised the need to settle the Arab-Israeli conflict politically, not through war.[32]

The rather curious Soviet warning can perhaps be understood if one assumes that Moscow did not seriously expect an Israeli attack on Syria. With the more cautious Moshe Arens as Israel's new Defence Minister and with rising opposition to Israel's presence in Lebanon being felt in Israel's domestic political scene, it appeared unlikely that Israel would attack Syria, even to take out the newly installed SAM-5 missiles. Even the hawkish Israeli chief-of-staff, General Raphael Eitan, in an interview on Israeli armed forces radio, stated that Israel had no intentions of starting a war.[33] If, therefore, Moscow basically assumed that Israel would not go to war, then why the warning? If it assumed that Israel would not attack Syria, Moscow could now take credit for the 'non-attack' and thereby demonstrate to the Arab world that Soviet diplomacy was effective *vis-à-vis* Israel, at least as a deterrent. If this, in fact, was Moscow's thinking, not all the Arabs were convinced. The Saudi paper *Ar-Riyad* expressed a lack of trust in the Soviet warning, noting that the limited value of Soviet statements had been proved during the Israeli invasion of Lebanon, 'which dealt a sharp and severe blow to the Kremlin when the Soviet missiles became no more than timber towers in the face of the sophisticated weapons the United States had unconditionally supplied to Israel'.[34]

Three days after the Soviet warning to Israel, Andrei Gromyko, who had recently been promoted to Deputy Prime Minister, held a major press conference in Moscow,[35] the main emphasis of which was on strategic arms issues. He also took the opportunity to make two major points about the Middle Eastern situation. In response to a question from a correspondent of the Syrian newspaper *Al-Ba'ath,* Gromyko stated that 'the Soviet Union is in favour of the withdrawal of all foreign troops from the territory of Lebanon, all of them. Syria is in favour of this.'[36] Second, Gromyko noted, once again, that the USSR was in favour of Israel's existing as a state: 'We do not share the point of view of extremist Arab circles that Israel should be eliminated. This is an unrealistic and unjust point of view.'[37] The thrust of Gromyko's remarks were clear. By urging the withdrawal of all foreign troops from Lebanon — including Syrian troops — and re-emphasising the Soviet commitment to Israel's existence, the Soviet leadership seemed to be telling Syria that Moscow was not desirous of being dragged into a war in Lebanon on Syria's behalf, despite the provision of SAM-5 missiles.

The rapid pace of events in the Middle East, however, was soon to pose additional problems for the Soviet strategy. One week after King Hussein had announced his refusal to enter into peace negotiations, the US embassy in Beirut was blown up by a car bomb, with a large loss of life. Reacting to both events, President Reagan despatched his Secretary of State, George Shultz, to salvage the stalled Israeli-Lebanese talks and regain the momentum for the United States in Middle Eastern diplomacy. As Shultz toured the region and shuttled back and forth between Beirut and Jerusalem, prospects for a Lebanese-Israeli agreement began to improve. Both Moscow and Damascus, though for different reasons, wanted to see the Shultz mission fail. The USSR did not want to see any more Arab states following in Egypt's footsteps and agreeing to a US plan for a Middle East peace settlement. Syria, which had long sought the dominant position in Lebanon, feared that any Lebanese-Israeli agreement would strengthen Israel's position at Syria's expense. In addition, Syria did not wish to see any more Arab states moving to make peace with Israel, since this would leave Syria increasingly isolated as an Arab confrontation state facing Israel. The end result was a rise in tension and yet another war scare in which Moscow was to play a role, albeit perhaps a somewhat unwilling one.

Less than a week after King Hussein refused to enter the peace talks, the Syrian government raised its price for a troop withdrawal from Lebanon. As late as March, Syria appeared to have been willing to have a simultaneous withdrawal of Israeli, Syrian and PLO forces. On 16 April, the Syrian government, strengthened both by its new Soviet weapons and by the Soviet warning to Israel, stated that Syria would not even discuss the withdrawal of its troops until all Israeli forces had left the country.[38] The United States sought to assuage Syrian opposition in a letter from Reagan to Assad in which the US president indicated that the United States was still pressing for an Israeli withdrawal from the Golan Heights.[39] The US ploy was not successful. Indeed, Syria appeared to step up tension by allowing guerrillas to infiltrate Israeli lines to attack Israeli troops. Simultaneously, it accused the Israeli government of reinforcing its troops in Lebanon's Beqaa valley and of staging 'provocative' military exercises on the Golan Heights.[40] Israel's Foreign Minister Yitzhak Shamir called the Syrian-induced tension 'artificial'.[41] Defence Minister Arens, however, was concerned about Soviet and Syrian intentions, and put Israeli troops on alert, indicating that Israel would not leave Lebanon until Syria did.[41] Syria then stepped up the pressure when on 26 April its forces fired on an Israeli bulldozer near the cease-fire line.[43]

Despite the rise in tension between Syria and Israel, US Secretary of State Shultz continued to work for an Israeli troop-withdrawal agreement. On 6 May, his efforts were crowned with success as the Israeli government accepted, in principle, a plan that had already been agreed to by Lebanon.[44] The next US goal was to try to gain Arab support for the agreement so as to pressure Syria into withdrawing its forces from

Lebanon as well. As might be expected, neither Moscow nor Syria was in favour of a rapid Syrian exodus. Although interested in Syria ultimately quitting Lebanon, Moscow did not want any precipitate withdrawal in the aftermath of the Israeli-Lebanese agreement lest the United States reap the diplomatic benefit. Syria complained that Israel had received too much from the treaty, that Lebanon had 'capitulated to the Israeli aggressor'.[45] It was unclear at the time, however, whether Syria opposed the withdrawal of its own troops on principle or whether President Assad was posturing so as to improve his bargaining position *vis-à-vis* Lebanon (so as to obtain a better deal than Israel did); *vis-à-vis* the Arab world (long isolated because of its support for Iran, Syria was now openly confronting Israel and, therefore, merited Arab support); and *vis-à-vis* the United States (so as to have the US pressure Israel for a withdrawal from the Golan Heights). As the crisis was played out until the end of May, with military manoeuvres and threats of war (almost all from the Syrians), it appeared as though Assad was enjoying the opportunity to play a major role once again in Middle Eastern events.

As Syria was exploiting the Lebanese situation for its own ends, Moscow was cautiously supporting its Arab ally. On 9 May, three days after Israel had agreed in principle to withdraw, the Soviet Union issued an official statement denouncing the agreement. In a gesture of support for Syria, Moscow demanded that 'first and foremost' Israeli troops must withdraw from Lebanon. The statement added, however, that 'American and other foreign troops staying in Lebanon also must be withdrawn from it', an oblique reference to Moscow's continuing desire to see Syrian troops leave, too.[46] Perhaps to enhance the atmosphere of crisis, Soviet dependants were withdrawn from Beirut although the Soviet ambassador to Lebanon attributed the departure to the beginning of summer camp in the USSR.[47] Moscow's act may have been a means of returning from the diplomatic sidelines to a role in the Middle East peace process. Indeed, on 10 May, Shultz openly urged Moscow to use its influence to 'get Syria to withdraw its troops.[49] Shultz also indicated, though, that the United States was not yet ready for an international conference on the Middle East, which was still a goal of Soviet diplomacy.[49]

By giving Syria even a limited degree of support, Moscow had to be concerned about the possibility of war erupting, especially as Syria began to issue increasingly bellicose threats. The threats, moreover, involved Soviet support for Syria in case of war.[50] Syria's bellicosity, however, may have overstepped the bounds of propriety in so far as

Moscow was concerned. The Soviet ambassador to Lebanon would not reply to 'such hypothetical questions', when asked about the assertion by Syria's Foreign Minister that Moscow would fully support Syria in a war with Israel, and added that the USSR continued to support the withdrawal of all foreign forces from Lebanon.[51] These themes of caution were repeated during the visit of a Soviet delegation to Israel in mid-May to attend ceremonies marking the 38th anniversary of the defeat of Nazi Germany. Upon arrival at Ben Gurion airport, one of the leaders of the delegation, a well-known Soviet journalist, Igor Belayev, took the opportunity to state that Syria's recent military moves in the Beqaa valley were purely defensive and that Syria had no aggressive intent towards Israel.[52] Similarly, Karen Khachaturev, deputy director of the *Novosti* news agency, noted that the USSR favoured a peace treaty between Israel and Lebanon — but only after all Israeli soldiers departed — and reiterated Moscow's support of Israel's right to live in peace and security.[53]

Syria continued to escalate the political and military pressure to undermine the Israeli-Lebanese agreement. It formed an alignment with a group of Lebanese leaders opposed to the agreement. These included former premier Rashid Karami, former president Sulayman Faranjiyyah, Druze leader Walid Jumblatt, and Lebanese communist party first secretary George Hawi.[54]

Assad then stepped up the military pressure in the Beqaa. After refusing to see US envoy Philip Habib, he predicted a new war with Israel in which Syria would lose 20,000 men.[55] Two days later, Syrian planes fired air-to-air missiles against Israeli jets flying over the Beqaa — the first such encounter since the 1982 war.[56] Assad followed up this action by conducting military exercises both on the Golan and in the Beqaa, and the danger of war appeared to heighten.[57] Israel kept very cool during the crisis with only a limited counter-mobilisation. For its part, Moscow kept a very low profile (although it did send a new aircraft carrier into the Mediterranean), supporting Syria politically but issuing no threats against the United States or Israel and again appealing for a full withdrawal of all foreign forces from Lebanon. By the end of May, the crisis had subsided and the dangers of a Syrian-Israeli war in Lebanon had been replaced in the headlines by the growing revolt within the PLO against Arafat's leadership. This development, too, was engineered by Assad, as the Syrian leader appeared to want to bring the PLO under Syrian control once and for all.[58]

The revolt against Arafat underlined the PLO leader's weakened position in the aftermath of the Israeli invasion of Lebanon, which had eliminated his main base of operations. Although supported by the bulk of Palestinians living outside Syria and Syrian-controlled regions in Lebanon, and receiving support from both Iraq and Algeria, Arafat had no real power to resist Syria's crackdown. As the summer wore on, the positions of Arafat's supporters in the Beqaa were overrun, and Arafat himself was expelled from Syria. In early August, the Palestine Central Council, meeting in Tunis, called for an 'immediate dialogue' to rebuild relations with Syria.[59] This effort, along with others attempted during the summer, proved of no avail; in early September, Arafat, who had once again begun to meet with Jordanian officials, admitted that all attempts at negotiations with Syria had failed.[60]

The dissension within the PLO faced Moscow with another of its serious problems of choice. On the one hand, a victory for the PLO hard-liners would make it even more difficult for Moscow to succeed in pro-moting its Middle East peace plan. In addition the very split within the PLO and the fact that Iraq and Algeria were backing Arafat against the Syrian-supported opposition further underlined the disunity in the Arab world. This was one more obstacle in the way of the 'anti-imperialist' Arab unity that Moscow had sought for so long. On the other hand, Moscow could not have been too unhappy with the fact that Arafat was being punished for his flirtation with the Reagan plan. In any showdown between Assad and Arafat, *realpolitik* impelled Moscow to side with Assad. In the aftermath of the Israeli invasion of Lebanon, Syria was the main Arab state opposing US diplomacy in the Middle East, and Assad had granted Moscow the use of Syrian naval and air force facilities.[61]

In addition to bringing Arafat's forces in the Beqaa under his control, Assad was profiting from the growing war-weariness of Israel, which was planning a unilateral withdrawal from the Shouf mountains and seemed in no mood to go to war to throw the Syrians out of Lebanon. On 1 June Prime Minister Begin stated that Israel was not preparing to attack Syria,[62] and a week later Israel's Deputy Foreign Minister, Yehuda Ben-Meir, also ruled out military action to remove Syrian forces from Lebanon.[63] One month later, US Secretary Shultz stated that American marines would not fill any vacuum created by any Israeli unilateral withdrawal.[64]

Under these circumstances, Assad was able to fill the vacuum with Syrian-backed forces, in large part because of mistakes by the Lebanese government. By July, the government of Amin Jumayyil had alienated two of the major forces within Lebanon: the Druzes and the Shi'ites. In part because Jumayyil did not establish an equitable power sharing system and in part because Phalangist policies in both the Shouf and the Shi'ite areas of Beirut angered the Druzes and Shi'ites, the latter entered into an alignment with Syria. Walid Jumblatt, the Druze leader, did so explicitly, by leading a newly proclaimed 'National Salvation Front' (which included as members Rashid Karami, a Sunni Muslim, and Sulayman Faranjiyyah, a Christian opponent of Jumayyil). The Shi'ite leader, Nabih Berri, gave tacit support to the organisation.[65]

The strengthening of the Syrian position in Lebanon was, on balance, a plus for Moscow, since US diplomatic efforts to secure a troop-withdrawal agreement from Lebanon had all but collapsed by the end of August. Moscow again raised the possibility of a joint US-Soviet effort to bring about a Middle East peace settlement.[66] Yet the situation also had its dangers for Moscow. As Israel stepped up planning to withdraw its troops from the Shouf mountains, the possibility that new fighting would erupt became increasingly strong, particularly since no agreement had been reached between the Druzes and Jumayyil about deploying the Lebanese army in the Shouf to replace the departing Israelis. Exacerbating the situation was the statement of the Syrian government on 27 August that it would defend its allies against the Lebanese army.[67] Since the United States was backing the Jumayyil government, a direct US-Syrian confrontation could occur, and then Moscow would again be faced with the problem of how to react to a military conflict in which its principal Arab ally was involved. This time, however, the opponent would most likely not be Israel, backed by the United States, but the United States itself. In short, Moscow faced the prospect of a superpower confrontation over Lebanon. When in the event the crisis did occur, the USSR adopted a very cautious policy so as to avoid any direct involvement.

US involvement in the crisis had actually begun before the Israeli withdrawal, but escalated during the fighting in the Shouf in September 1983, partly in support of the Lebanese army, which it was training. Moscow expressed its concern over the US armed intervention, but balanced its lack of threats with support of Syria's right to remain in Lebanon — which was a change from earlier Soviet policy. Increasingly, though, Moscow faced the dilemma of whether or not it should get directly involved, particularly as Syrian positions came under American fire. Nevertheless, during the entire crisis, it failed to mention publicly the Soviet-Syria treaty. It is not surprising, then, that the USSR, which feared a superpower confrontation over Lebanon — an area of only tertiary interest to the USSR — warmly welcomed the cease-fire that ended the crisis.[68] For its part, Syria had refrained from public complaints about the lack of Soviet aid (repeating the strategy it followed in June 1982).

The Soviet Union now adopted what appeared to be a contradictory policy: despatching to Syria accurate, 70-mile-range SS-21 ground-to-ground missiles, on the one hand, and down-playing its military relationship to Syria, on the other.[69] In October, the US marine headquarters in Beirut were blown up with a very large loss of life. Accusing Syria of at least indirect responsibility and threatening retaliation, the US began flying reconnaissance missions over Syrian lines in Lebanon. Moscow disassociated itself from intervening, but did feel constrained to issue a (very limited) warning to the US, if only to show support of the 'progressive' Lebanese forces backed by Syria.[70] On 8 November, Assad mobilised his army, despite both American and Israeli statements that they were not going to attack Syria. A week later, Syrian forces fired on American reconnaissance planes.[71]

Moscow, none too pleased with Syrian claims to Soviet aid in case of a widened conflict[72] or with Assad's crackdown on Arafat's forces both in the Beqaa and in the Tripoli area, continued to call for increased Arab unity.[73] It still wished to see the PLO as an independent actor who would need Soviet support, rather than as a dependent element of the Syrian army. The Soviets did not succeed, however, in getting Syria either to moderate its presssure on Arafat or to cease stressing the possibility of a Soviet-US confrontation if the Americans resumed fighting the Syrians.[74] In Tripoli, an uneasy cease-fire was at last achieved, and Moscow moved again to champion Syria by issuing a low-key warning to the US.[75] When on 4 December US planes openly attacked Syrian forces, Moscow was again faced with the dilemma of either supporting its client — and running the risk of a confrontation with the US — or losing some of its diplomatic credibility. Once again, caution won out, and Syria learned that it could not expect more than Soviet moral support against the US so long as the confrontation was limited to Lebanon.

Although Moscow did seek to utilise the American attack on Syria to undermine the US position in the Middle East, it seems clear that it had resorted to its primary course of action pursued since the September crisis — an appeal to the Arabs to help Syria themselves. Unfortunately for the USSR, which had hoped that the US attack would force the centrist Arabs to again rally around Syria and what was left of the Steadfastness Front, this was not to happen. With Syria's ally Iran threatening to close the Straits of Hormuz, the centrist Arabs, and particularly the members of the Gulf Co-operation Council, had no choice but to rely on the US for help. To its apparent bitter disappointment, the end result was that Syria, without Soviet or Arab support against the US and with its efforts to topple Arafat only moderately successful (the PLO leader, who continued to command widespread Palestinian support, left Tripoli under the UN flag), moved to de-escalate the tension. Thus, Syria not only returned the body of a dead US airman, it then made a major concession by releasing the captured airman. Yet in the final analysis, these gestures paid off from the Syrian point of view: they ultimately enabled President Reagan to take the difficult decision of withdrawing the marines from Lebanon altogether. In turn, Syria scored an impressive victory, which could not but enhance the Soviet position, too, although Syria was to have considerable difficulty consolidating its position in Lebanon.

Conclusion

Syria's involvement in the Lebanese crisis faced Moscow with a number of critical dilemmas. The Soviets, powerless to limit this involvement, were forced to back their Syrian allies up in order to defend their credibility. Yet by doing so, the Soviets were led uncomfortably close to a confrontation with the United States. Moreover, in the later stages of the conflict, when Syria pursued the PLO, the Soviets were forced to make a choice between backing the Syrians and backing the PLO.

Given this complexity, the Soviets have not done too badly. Their alliance with Syria was preserved and even strengthened, without being involved in a confrontation with the United States. Their success, though, was far more in damage limitation than in an actual advancement of their position. Indeed, in the final analysis, the Lebanese crisis underlined once again what has increasingly become a familiar notion: the Soviets, much like their American rivals, and perhaps even more so, do not control their Middle Eastern clients. They are constrained by their global interests to such an extent that they have little choice but to play to the tune of their far weaker allies.

Notes

1. For recent studies of Soviet policy in the Middle East, see Robert O. Freedman, *Soviet Policy Toward the Middle East Since 1970,* 3rd edn. (Praeger, New York, 1982); John D. Glassman, *Arms for the Arabs: The Soviet Union and War in the Middle East* (Johns Hopkins, University Press, Baltimore, 1975); Galia Golan, *Yom Kippur and After: The Soviet Union and the Middle East Crisis* (Cambridge University Press, London, 1977); Yaacov Ro'i (ed.), *The Limits to Power: Soviet Policy in the Middle East* (Croom Helm, London, 1979); and Adeed Dawisha and Karen Dawisha (eds.), *The Soviet Union in the Middle East: Policies and Perspectives* (Holmes and Meier, New York, 1982).

For an Arab viewpoint, see Mohamed Heikal, *The Sphinx and the Commissar* (Harper and Row, New York, 1978). For a recent Soviet view, see E.M. Primakov, *Anatomila Blizhnevostochnogo Konflikta* (Mysl', Moscow, 1978).

2. For studies of Soviet military aid, see Glassman, *Arms for the Arabs;* George Lenczowski, *Soviet Advances in the Middle East* (American Enterprise Institute, Washington, 1972); and Amnon Sella, 'Changes in Soviet Political-Military Policy in the Middle East after 1973', in Ro'i (ed.), *The Limits to Power,* pp. 32-64.

3. For a view of the role of Israel in Soviet Middle East strategy, see Freedman, *Soviet Policy Toward the Middle East,* ch. 8.

4. For a study of Soviet policy towards the communist parties of the Arab world, see Robert O. Freedman, 'The Soviet Union and the Communist Parties of the Arab World: An Uncertain Relationship', in Roger E. Kanet and Donna Bahry (eds.), *Soviet Economic and Political Relations with the Developing World* (Praeger, New York, 1975), pp. 100-34; and John K. Cooley, 'The Shifting Sands of Arab Communism', *Problems of Communism,* vol. 24, no. 2, (1975), pp. 22-42.

5. For an analysis of the Islamic revival, see Daniel Pipes, 'The World is Political: The Islamic Revival of the Seventies', *Orbis,* vol. 24, no. 1 (Spring 1980), pp. 9-41.

6. For analyses of Soviet-Syrian relations up to Camp David, see Freedman, Soviet Policy Toward the Middle East and Galia Golan, 'Syria and the Soviet Union Since the Yom Kippur War', *Orbis,* vol. 21, no. 4 (Winter 1978), pp. 777-801. For an analysis sympathetic to the Syrian role in Lebanon, see Adeed I. Dawisha, *Syria and the Lebanese Crisis* (MacMillan, London, 1980).

For other anlayses of Syrian politics and foreign policy, see John Devlin's studies 'Syria Since Camp David', in Robert O. Freedman (ed.) *The Middle East Since Camp David,* (Westview Press, Boulder, 1984), and *Syria: Modern State in an Ancient Land* (Westview Press, Boulder, 1983). See also David Pryce-Jones, 'Bloody Assad', *New Republic,* (30 January 1984), pp. 20-5.

7. For analyses of the domestic situation in Syria, see the contribution of Moshe Maoz in this book as well as N. Van Dam, *The Struggle for Power in Syria* (Croom Helm, London, 1979); Stanley Reed III, 'Dateline Syria: Fin de Régime?', *Foreign Policy,* no. 39 (Summer 1980), pp. 176-90; and Chris Kutscheria, 'Sticks and Carrots', *The Middle East,* no. 80 (June 1981), pp. 8-9.

8. These events are discussed in Freedman, *Soviet Policy Toward the Middle East,* ch. 9 and 10.

9. Ibid., pp. 395-6. See also Amiram Nir, *The Soviet-Syrian Friendship and Co-operation Treaty: Unfulfilled Expectations* (Jaffee Center for Strategic Studies, Tel-Aviv, 1983).

10. These two crises are discussed in Robert O. Freedman, 'Soviet Policy Toward Syria Since Camp David', *Middle East Review* (Fall-Winter 1982), pp. 31-42.

11. Ibid., p. 20; interview with Hanna Batatu, Washington, DC, 19 December 1983.

12. For a Soviet view of US-Israeli strategic co-operation, see *Pravda,* 15 September 1981.

13. Nir, *The Soviet-Syrian Friendship and Co-operation Treaty,* p. 19.

14. Khaddam was reported to have stated 'we are convinced the Soviet Union, the countries of the Socialist commonwealth, and all progressive forces' would support Syria in its struggle. The joint communiqué released upon his departure, however, noted only that 'both sides reaffirmed their desire to continue to strengthen co-operation between the Soviet Union and Syria in all fields, including the military field'. See *Pravda,* 16 and 17 January 1982.

15. For Moscow's highly negative reaction to this development, see the Moscow Radio Arab language broadcast on 28 May 1982 (Foreign Broadcast Information Service Daily Report: The Soviet Union [hereafter *FBIS: USSR*], 1 June 1982, p. H-3).

16. For a description of the increasingly severe problems facing the PLO in Lebanon on the eve of the war, see David Butler, 'In the Same Trench', *The Middle East,* (June 1982), p. 6. See also his report, 'Shi'ites in Beirut Clashes', *The Middle East,* (February 1982), p. 14.

17. See remarks by Taha Ramadan, First Deputy Prime Minister of Iraq, Baghdad Radio, 1 June 1982 (*FBIS: ME,* 2 June 1981, p. E-2).

18. The visit by Moroccan Foreign Minister Mohammed Boucetta to Cairo on 7 June 1982 further ended Egypt's ostracism, as did Egyptian President Mubarak's attendance at the funeral of King Khalid of Saudi Arabia later that month.

19. The Front proclaimed its opposition to any normalisation of relations with Egypt until it renounced Camp David. See *Pravda,* 26 May 1982.

20. The central reasons for Soviet inactivity during the Israeli invasion would appear to be (1) the failure of the other Arab states to aid Syria and the PLO; (2) Israeli air supremacy in the region; and (3) uncertainty over the possible US reaction to Soviet intervention. These reasons are discussed in Robert O. Freedman, 'The Soviet Union and the Middle East: Failure to Match the United States as a Regional Power', in Collin Legum, Haim Shaked and Daniel Dishon (eds.), *Middle East Contemporary Survey,* vol. 6, 1981-82 (Holmes and Meier, New York, 1984), pp. 40-8 and Karen Dawisha, 'The USSR in the Middle East: Super Power in Eclipse', *Foreign Affairs* (Winter 1982-83), pp. 438-52.

21. Libya's Muammar Kaddafi went so far as to berate a group of Soviet ambassadors, complaining that Arab friendship with the socialist countries was almost ready to go up in flames, the way Beirut is going up in flames, see JANA, (Tripoli), 26 June 1982 *(FBIS: ME,* 26 June 1982, pp. Q-2, Q-3).

22. Tass, 22 June 1982 (*FBIS: USSR,* 22 June 1982, p. H-3).

23. For a description of the Reagan plan, see Barry Rubin, 'The United States and the Middle East from Camp David to the Reagan Plan', *Middle East Contemporary Survey, 1981-82,* pp. 30-1.

24. For a description of the Fez Plan, see *The Middle East Journal,* vol. 37, no. 1 (Winter 1983), p. 71.

25. *Pravda,* 16 September 1982. For an analysis of the status of the Soviet Middle East peace plan on the eve of the Israeli invasion of Lebanon, see Robert O. Freedman, 'Moscow, Washington and the Gulf', *American-Arab Affairs,* no. 1 (Summer 1982), pp. 132-4.

26. *Pravda,* 11 September 1982.

27. See reports by Edward Walsh, *Washington Post,* 5 January 1983, and Thomas L. Friedman, *New York Times,* 21 March 1983.

28. It is also possible that the Soviet move was in part a response to the emplacement of US troops in Beirut, as well as a means of hampering US air operations in the eastern Mediterranean near Lebanon.

29. Freedman, 'Soviet Policy Toward Syria Since Camp David'.

30. Cited in report by Thomas L. Friedman, *New York Times,* 23 February 1983. The fact that Issam Sartawi, a PLO moderate who publicly advocated a compromise between Israel and the PLO, was forbidden to speak at the meeting was a further indication of the

erosion of Arafat's position. Sartawi was subsequently assassinated in April while attending the Socialist International Congress in Portugal. For general discussions of the PNC council session, see Judith Perera, 'Hammering Out a Compromise', *The Middle East,* no. 101 (March 1983), pp. 8-9, and Cheryl A. Rubenbery, 'The PNC and the Reagan Initiative', *American-Arab Affairs,* vol. 4 (Spring 1983), pp. 53-69. For an analysis of trends within the PLO, see Aaron David Miller, 'Palestinians in the 1980's', *Current History,* (January 1984), pp. 17-20, 34-6, and 'The PLO since Camp David', in Robert O. Freedman (ed.), *The Middle East Since Camp David.*

31. *Pravda,* 25 February 1983.

32. *Pravda,* 31 March 1983.

33. Cited in *Christian Science Monitor,* 30 March 1983.

34. *SPA* (Riyadh), 2 April 1983 *(FBIS: ME,* 4 April 1983, p. C-6).

35. The text of Gromyko's press conference may be found in *FBIS: USSR,* 4 April 1983, pp. AA-1 - AA-17.

36. Ibid., p. AA-15.

37. Ibid., AA-16.

38. Cited in Reuters report, *The New York Times,* 17 April 1983.

39. See report by David Landau, *Jerusalem Post,* 20 April 1983.

40. See report by Herbert Denton, *Washington Post,* 22 April 1983.

41. Cited in *Jerusalem Post,* 24 April 1983.

42. See *Jerusalem Post,* 26 April 1983.

43. Cited in *Jerusalem Post,* 27 April 1983.

44. For an analysis of the dynamics of the process leading to the Israel-Lebanon agreement, see the report by Bernard Gwertzman, *The New York Times,* 10 May 1983.

45. See report by Herbert Denton, *Washington Post,* 7 May 1983.

46. Tass report, 9 May 1983 *(FBIS: USSR,* 10 May 1983, p. H-1).

47. See reports by Thomas Friedman, *The New York Times,* 10 May 1983, and Nora Boustary, *Washington Post,* 10 May 1983.

48. See report by Bernard Gwertzman, *The New York Times,* 11 May 1983.

49. See report by John Goshko, *Washington Post,* 11 May 1983.

50. Syrian Foreign Minister Khaddam noted in an interview that in case war broke out between Israel and Syria, 'We believe that the USSR will fulfill its commitments in accordance with the (Soviet-Syria) treaty'. The next day, 10 May, Syrian radio warned that any Israeli attack against Syrian forces anywhere, even in Lebanon, would mean an 'unlimited war'. SANA (Damascus), 9 May 1983 *(FBIS: ME,* 9 May 1983, p. H-2); and Reuters report, *The New York Times,* 11 May 1983.

51. Beirut Domestic Service in Arabic, 10 May 1983 *(FBIS: ME,* 16 May 1983, p. H-8).

52. Cited in *Jerusalem Post,* 15 May 1983.

53. Ibid.

54. See Report by Robin Wright, *Christian Science Monitor,* 17 May 1983.

55. See report in *Jerusalem Post,* 24 May 1983.

56. See report by William E. Farrell, *The New York Times,* 26 May 1983.

57. See report by Hirsh Goodman, *Jerusalem Post,* 27 May 1983.

58. For an analysis of Syrian-PLO relations at this time, see the article by Eric Rouleau, *Manchester Guardian Weekly,* (15 May 1983).

59. See *FBIS: ME,* 5 August 1983, p. A-1.

60. See *Al-Watan Al-Arabi,* cited by INA *(FBIS: ME,* 2 September 1983, p. A-1).

61. For a description of Soviet military facilities in Syria, see *Near East Report,* vol. 27, no. 23 (June 1983), p. 2.

62. Cited in report by David Shipler, *The New York Times,* 2 June 1983.

63. Reuters report, *Baltimore Sun,* 8 June 1983.

64. Cited in report by Don Oberdorfer, *Washington Post,* 8 July 1983.

65. See report by Nora Bustany, *Washington Post,* 24 July 1983.

66. *Novosti* article by Pavel Demchenko, cited in AP report in the *Jerusalem Post,* 3 August 1983. *Novosti* reports are often used as a direct means of trying to influence Western nations.

67. *Tishrin* editorial, cited in Reuters report, *Washington Post,* 28 August 1983.

68. Andropov himself praised the cease-fire (*Pravda,* 30 September 1983) in a front page report of his meeting with PDRY leader Ali Nasser Mohammed. A Tass statement published in *Pravda* on 29 September, which noted that the cease-fire had been 'favorably received' in the Soviet Union, opposed both the Israeli and American troop presence in Lebanon and the 17 May Israeli-Lebanese agreement.

69. Moscow Radio in Arabic, commentary by Alexander Timoshkin, 6 October 1983 (*FBIS: USSR,* 7 October 1983, pp. H-2, H-3).

70. Moscow Radio Arabic, Rafael Artonov Commentary, 3 November 1983 (*FBIS: USSR,* 4 November 1983, p. H-3).

71. See report by Thomas Friedman, *The New York Times,* 11 November 1983.

72. For example, Syria's ambassador to London stated in a TV interview that a conflict caused by US 'aggression' against Syria would not be confined to one area, but would be 'large scale because of the help which we are supposed to get from our brothers and friends', *FBIS: ME,* 9 November 1983, p. i.

73. *FBIS: USSR,* 15 November 1983, p. H-2.

74. Damascus TV, 15 November 1983 (*FBIS: ME,* 16 November 1983, p. H-1).

75. Cited in AP report, *The New York Times,* 27 November 1983.

PART IV

THE SYRIAN PARADOX

14 THE SYRIAN PARADOX

Moshe Ma'oz and Avner Yaniv

Rich as most of the foregoing articles are in historical material and in analytical insights, they do not offer all the pieces of the Syrian puzzle. They mention many crucial Syrian decisions but do not provide a clear picture of Syrian decision-making procedures. Most of them make frequent references to Egypt, but the volume as a whole does not produce a comprehensive, sustained analysis of Syria's relationship with that country. They contain a certain amount of data on Syria's strategy but no comprehensive evaluation of the Syrian armed forces. Finally, although this collection of articles occasionally refers to Syria's policy towards and position in the Third World, it does not present a vivid description in this regard.

These issue areas of Syrian policy had to be left out both because of limits of space and because some of them are difficult to research in sufficient depth. A companion volume covering these and other topics is therefore begged by the present one and may be prepared in due course. Nevertheless, there are sufficient data in this book to facilitate an educated answer to the key questions that were posed in the introduction: namely, What makes Syria tick domestically and, more important still, as an actor on the Middle Eastern scene? The answers to these questions will be presented in this section under four headings: Syria's *goals,* the *constraints* it faces in trying to achieve these goals, the over-all *strategy* it has employed for this purpose and, finally, the *accomplishments* it can claim.

Goals

The standard articulation of Syria's long-term aspirations, be it by President Assad, one of his more prominent colleagues or through the official organs of the Ba'ath Party, suggests limitless or at least exceedingly far-reaching goals. Syria, according to such proclamations, wishes to consolidate its society, its economy and its political structure, with a view to casting a long shadow over the entire Middle East. Such statements of the country's goals imply a relentless drive towards the creation of a Greater Syria, to include Lebanon, the Alexandretta area, Jordan and Israel. If such aspirations, which are normally presented as if they are not a matter of either choice or necessity but something amounting to a historical and moral imperative, were realised, Syria would become the single most important factor in Middle Eastern regional politics. It would dominate the Arab League. It would succeed in off-setting the overbearing influence of Egypt and Iraq. It would be in an excellent position to realise the dreams of Pan-Arabism, and it would advance the Arab world towards the grandeur and status that it has always sought in the world arena.

Whether such a grand design really exists or whether it is merely an aspirational image, kept in the corner until an opportunity to implement it presents itself, is impossible to say. The Syrian decision-making 'black box' is sealed so effectively that what the Syrian elite, not to speak of President Assad himself, dreams of remains, and will probably continue to remain, an enigma shrouded in mystery.

Nevertheless, none of the areas of Syrian activity discussed in this volume offers any evidence that such a grandiose dream is an accurate representation of Syria's *operational* goals. There is, on the other hand, ample evidence o suggest that the Assad regime has taken the need for his country's economic and social modernisation very seriously. The vigour and determination with which a succession of 'five year' plans and other comprehensive reforms in agriculture, education, transportation and industrialisation have been implemented attest to the regime's genuine commitment to the overhauling of Syria's socio-economic structure. There is also resounding proof to the effect that Assad and his colleagues are determined to provide their country with a powerful military instrument, capable of resisting Israel, deterring Turkey and Iraq and holding at bay weaker actors, such as Jordan, Lebanon and the PLO. It is equally clear that this regime is not inclined to become a Soviet client, is not disposed to look kindly upon American pressures, is not likely to permit the Arab League in particular and the Arab political scene more generally to be dominated by Syria's opponents, least of all by Egypt. Nor does Syria seem inclined to accept a secondary role in transnational Ba'athist politics.

But none of these tendencies and dispositions is sufficient in itself to be held up as evidence of the existence of a Syrian grand design. Assad's Syria, in short, is not Nasser's Egypt. Syria may talk about Arab unity, but what seems to motivate it above all is a pervasive nationalist and particularist impulse. Assad and his colleagues are most probably driven by an all-consuming ambition of relatively modest proportions. They seek security and well-being for themselves, for the Alawi community of which most of them are a part, for the geographic part of Syria from which they come, and for Syria, in its present borders, as a larger entity. Their preferences are, it seems, graded in that order, forming a chain of concentric circles beginning with their own immediate interests and ending with an emerging Syrian national interest as they subjectively view it.

What they want is precisely what nationalists have always wanted in every part of the world: an integrated (Syrian) society, which is industrialised, modernised, centralised, socialised and populated by proud and spirited masses; which enjoys the benefits of economic prowess; and which is capable of sustaining its independence in the anarchic, chronically unstable, pervasively violent and breathtakingly convulsive Middle East. Assad's predecessors in Syria, especially leaders such as Adib Shishaqli, may have ultimately shared the same vision. But under Hafez al-Assad, this vague and distant dream seems to have been converted, with dogged determination and impressive skill, into a tangible, operationally palpable agenda, which, in spite of formidable constraints, has already begun to be implemented.

Constraints

The constraints with which the Alawi Ba'ath have had to contend have been formidable. Internally the goals of integration and nation-building entail a basic dilemma. Nation-building boils, down in the first place, to state-building: namely, the creation of capabilities with which to reshape the economy and social services of a state, change its occupational structure, set up industries, restructure the countryside, and constantly expand the absorptive capacities of cities facing the influx of rural population. All this must be accomplished with meagre resources and the minimum of tensions and dislocations.

Such an immense task can only be performed by a highly centralised and very stable state machinery. This type of top-heavy system was not created by the factionalised Sunni majority, which had attempted unsuccessfully to rule Syria before the advent of the Ba'ath. The Alawi inner circle of the New Ba'ath, which has ruled Syria since February 1966, provided precisely the kind of determined, coherent cadre that was needed to succeed in creating the necessary state machinary, especially after the removal of Jedid in November 1970. The advantages of unprecedented cohesion, however, seem to have been severely undercut by one major disadvantage: the distinct ethnic identity of this cadre. Differently stated, the special coherence of the leading Alawi elite was at once their chief source of strength and their Achilles' heel.

To solve the problem, Assad and his colleagues (and relatives) could do only one thing: make a special effort to cultivate the allegiance of the non-Alawi population, especially of other ethnic and religious elites, both in the towns and in the country. Yet such a policy of deliberate, calculated co-operation carries its own hazards. To succeed, it requires that a regime bend over backwards to please its rivals and win their confidence. That course, however, may demand more than any regime can do, at least in the short run, and may easily create schisms, suspicions and rivalries within the ruling elite itself. Finding the right balance between the two critical desiderata — namely, maximum co-optation of outsiders in order to broaden the regime's base and maintaining the inner cohesion of the ruling group — must have been one of the greatest challenges that the Assad regime has faced from its inception.

A related and not dissimilar problem must have been faced by Assad within the narrower confines of his own ruling elite. The 1966-70 period showed very clearly that Alawi predominance in itself was no guarantee for cohesion and a sense of purpose. In fact, the Jedid-Assad rivalry must have greatly diminished the effectiveness of the regime. The removal of Jedid was, in these terms, a net gain for Syria, as it facilitated for the first time in Syrian history the combination of a cohesive elite and a powerful leader at its top. The trouble, however, is that such a personification of power undercuts processes of institutionalisation and creates, by its very nature, an acute problem of succession and continuity. Assad may have been very effective. But he is reportedly in poor health, and there are already signs of a bitter power struggle among the 'diadochs' (to invoke a term from Syria's history during the Hellenistic era), those who wish to take the leader's place. This struggle could have a disruptive effect even before the departure of Assad and will most probably have an even worse impact after his retirement (or death).

Another critical constraint with which Syria has had to contend stems from the very success of Ba'athist economic programmes. As both Chapter 2 and Chapter 3 demonstrate, the net growth of the Syrian population has been remarkable. So has been the rate of urbanisation. What normally accompanies such structural changes is a revolution in expectations. Yet the ability of the economy to continue to grow synchronously is in doubt. The result, it may be deduced, may well be a great deal of pent-up frustration, which sooner or later could erupt into major challenges to the regime.

Such elements of weakness in the very fabric of the Syrian system create another constraining paradox. An insecure regime, conscious of its particularist image and ruling over a society experiencing a rapid and, presumably, disruptive process of change, faces a pervasive problem of legitimacy. In order to cope, such a regime has to couple repression, on the one hand, and selective co-operation, on the other hand, with an emphatic appeal to long-held and widely shared national aspirations. Both the 'Old' and the 'New' Ba'athist regimes acted in this fashion, and thus increasingly committed themselves (internally) and their country (externally) to a far-reaching, militant, dogmatic and dangerous set of goals. Assad has in practice acted in a distinctly cautious and prudent manner, presumably for the purpose of buttressing his regime's legitimacy. However, he, too, has not been able to escape the trap of open-ended rhetoric. The result has been a built-in schizophrenia in the over-all posture of the Assad regime. Seemingly, this regime seeks to lower Syria's sights and to make significant strides forward in practical terms; simultaneously, it has clung to a rhetoric suggesting ambitious regional as well as internal goals. In turn, though Assad's prudence is widely observed, Syria's proclaimed ambitions became the yardstick by which the regime is judged both inside Syria and by its neighbours. The suspicion that the Assad regime really means what its spokesmen say is reinforced by what it says; therefore, Syria is often treated as if its declared aspirations are also its real operational goals. Assad may have hoped to steer Syria gradually in a more pragmatic direction, but his regime has reinforced and perpetuated Syria's militant predisposition.

This built-in paradox is particularly important given the complexity of the international environment in which Syria operates. How can Syria develop a close and beneficial relationship with the Soviet Union and, at the same time, normalise and consolidate its relations with Turkey? How can Syria cultivate close relations with Khomeini's Iran and, at the same time, maintain equally close relations with Saudi Arabia, Kuwait and the rest of the Gulf states? How can Syria move forcefully towards strategic parity with Israel without increasing the latter's temptation to resort to a pre-emptive strike? How can Syria improve its ability to face Israel alone without stimulating suspicions and fears among Syria's other neighbours, which cannot remain indifferent to its growing military might? How can Syria, without weakening both its military posture and its domestic cohesion, manage Lebanon without occupying that country? How can Syria exert control over the PLO, and prevent it from moving towards accommodation with Israel, without exposing itself to charges of duplicity? How can a narrowly-based Alawi regime build an armed force large enough to deal with

Israel without outside help and without exposing itself to the danger of an attempt by that army to take over the country? How can sufficient resources be allocated for military purposes without compromising the regime's ambitious social and economic programmes while, at the same time, avoiding excessive dependence on the Soviet Union? How can a close alliance with the Soviet Union be compatible in the long run with the need for a dialogue with the United States and for a respectable position among the non-aligned nations? All these are formidable dilemmas that Assad and his followers have been facing *simultaneously* and over an extended period of time. If in spite of this combination of complexity and overload they have scored impressive successes, it has been largely due to their subtle, imaginative, flexible and forceful strategy.

Strategy

The cautious steady-handed style of the Assad regime suggests that it has not operated from a rigid, fully articulated dogma, nor from a detailed doctrine or strategy, rather it has followed pragmatically a set of more or less clear, yet probably unwritten, maxims. The first of these has undoubtedly been to maintain stability in Syria while moving steadily towards greater economic and social development. This required, first and foremost, tight control over the armed forces. To achieve this control, the inner circle of defence decision-makers has been based exclusively on the regime's loyalists — primarily, but not exclusively, Alawis. In addition, the regime promoted two alternative mechanisms of control: the internal security machinery (under Rif'at Assad) and the Ba'ath Party and the bureaucracy.

Supported by such instruments, the Assad regime set out to erode systematically the social and economic status and power of its internal rivals. This could be done through the visible improvement of the standard of living, through the use of the armed forces as a mechanism of integration and indoctrination and, last but not least, through direct repression. To the best of its ability the regime has tried to avoid direct coercion; but when repression became unavoidable, it was administered with an iron fist in order to create a lasting, deterrent effect. Finally, while seeking actively to co-opt the Sunni clergy, while co-operating with Iran and while attempting to underline the legitimate religious status of the Alawi community, the Assad regime has not hesitated to persecute ruthlessly the Muslim Brotherhood.

A similar admixture of ruthlessness and pragmatic accommodation is also evident in Syria's external relations. The fact that Syria is surrounded by five different neighbours makes it impossible for the Assad regime to engage in conflict with all of them at once. Hence, it seems to have attempted a selective and discerning attitude towards its neighbours. It has overlooked specific causes of friction with those with which it wished to avoid a confrontation, whereas it has turned comparable issues into much advertised causes for a policy of confrontation with other neighbours. Syria has played, in short, a game of accommodation, co-operation and restraint where it could, but also a forceful game of confrontation when larger, more pressing issues were at stake.

Co-operation and accommodation with Turkey and Iran were both essential and feasible. Turkey has close relations with Iraq, and, internal problems notwithstanding, the former country remains a force with which Syria could not pick a quarrel. There are a number of issues — Alexandretta, the Euphrates, the Kurds, terrorism, relations with other parts of the Arab world and, to an extent, relations with the Soviet Union — on which Turkey and Syria do not see eye to eye. But the need to avoid friction with Turkey has weighed far more heavily on Syrian calculations in the past two decades than the need to gain satisfaction on these other issues. The result has been a noticeable attempt by Syria to keep relations with Turkey within the bounds of cordiality and patience and not to allow differences over outstanding issues to turn into sources of escalating friction.

Iran is not a comparable source of threat to Syria, for the simple reason that the two countries do not have a common border. But Iran could have created difficulties through its influence over the conduct of the Shi'ites in Lebanon. The Assad regime, therefore, has evidently decided to ignore the ideological contradictions between Ba'athism and Khomeinism and seeks instead to cultivate cordial, co-operative relations with Iran. The fact that Iran has been engaged in a massive confrontation with Iraq has been a boon to the Syrian national interest, which had been troubled by Saddam Hussein's rampant self-confidence in the years immediately preceding the Iraqi invasion of Iran.

This advantage to Syria of the Iran-Iraq war, however, has been offset somewhat by one major disadvantage, the fact that the war forced Iraq to mend fences with the Gulf states, with Jordan, with the United States and, above all, with Egypt. As a result, the return of Egypt to a preponderant position in the Arab world, a position which Egypt lost when Sadat went to Jerusalem, has increasingly become a distinct possibility. Syria could see a new bloc formation in the Arab world in which Egypt, Syria's ultimate rival, would lead Sudan, Tunisia, Morocco, Oman, Somalia, the Gulf states, Iraq, Jordan and the Fatah-based PLO in the direction of close relations with the United States and accommodation, though not necessarily comprehensive peace, with Israel. In such an event, Syria would be isolated externally — and the Assad regime would become more beleaguered domestically.

The implications for Syria were quite clear. It had to keep up the ideological campaign against Iraq. It would have to keep alive the historic and ideological tensions between Iraq and the Gulf states through a co-operative policty towards the latter. It would have to mount pressures against Jordan as a means of deterring the Hashemite monarchy from moving into the Egyptian orbit (not to speak of forming a Cairo-Baghdad-Riyadh triangle). Finally, it would have to prevent Fatah, through propaganda, subversion, threats, suppression and terrorism, from jumping on the Egyptian-led bandwagon.

One factor that made it easier for Syria to pursue such a policy was the fact that, since 1980, it alone had maintained some momentum in the Arabs' conflict with Israel. By continuing to carry the banner of the conflict with the historic enemy of the Arabs, Syria in general and Alawi Ba'athism in particular could rightfully claim title to being the only genuine custodian of cherished Arab values. It is a claim that, despite the decline of Pan-Arabism, no Arab state can as yet challenge openly. Syria thus can charge Iraq with betraying the cause, level a similar accusation at Jordan and proceed to repress any sign of PLO 'deviationism'. In itself, this strategy is not evidence of the fact that Assad and his colleagues take Syria's claim as seriously as they say. It simply means that they can employ this ideology for the purpose of advancing their own, and hence Syria's, interests.

Nor is its strategy of creating an ideological *cordon sanitaire* shielding Syria from unwelcome political mutations in the Arab world, and thus protecting the Ba'athist regime at home, too, incompatible with the Syrian desiderata *vis-à-vis* Israel. It appears highly unlikely that the Assad regime, well prepared as it may be, still earnestly believes that the Jewish state can be destroyed in a military campaign. Indeed, actual Syrian conduct towards Israel and even some official statements in recent years suggest that Syria has been acting on the assumption that the Jewish state is there to stay, at least in the foreseeable future. Nevertheless, the Israeli involvement in Lebanon in the course of the

1970s, the Israeli invasion of that country in June 1982, the Egyptian-Israeli peace and Israel's traditional (though tacit) understanding with the Hashemites add up for Syria to a ubiquitous menace. It is not that Israel has at any time threatened Syria directly; rather it is that these Israeli activities can contribute, and have done so significantly, to the creation of the kind of regional order that the Assad regime wishes to prevent.

A permanent Israeli role in Lebanon threatens Syria's strategic underbelly. The Israeli-Egyptian peace bestowed on Egypt evidence of success in its retrieving of lost territories, and thus restored, at least potentially, Egypt's freedom of action and influence in the Arab world, which Nasser's policies had lost. Turned to a position of pre-eminence in Arab councils but anxious to preserve close relations with the United States and a *modus vivendi* with Israel, Egypt cannot but be impelled to extend the zone of peace created by its separate agreement. Specifically this implies that Egypt has a vested interest in drawing Jordan and perhaps other Arab actors into the settlement with Israel. The United States has a similar interest, and so does Israel. Ultimately all this could lead to an overall Middle Eastern settlement from which Syria would be excluded, unless of course it accepts what from its own point of view are most humiliating terms.

Preventing the realisation of this scenario entails, as has been said, a policy designed to keep Jordan, the PLO and Lebanon under varying degrees of Syrian control. The other side of the coin is Syria's need to maintain, and further enhance, a position of strength *vis-à-vis* Israel. Syria, in short, has to build the most formidable military force that its war potential permits. Paradoxically such a goal leads in the short run to a relatively low Syrian profile in the context of the conflict with Israel, for achieving a significant strengthening of the Syrian army will take several years, during which time Syria cannot afford major hostilities with the Jewish state. Therefore, although anxious to see Israeli forces withdraw from Lebanon, Syria has been exceedingly careful to avoid any military confrontation, not only on the Golan but also in Lebanon.

An interesting question is: what will Syria do once strategic parity with Israel, at least quantitatively, becomes a reality? Will Syria then go to war, and if not what else can it do? If the regime promises to carry on the struggle but advocates restraint until such time as it is 'ready', then once it is 'ready' it cannot afford not to act. The cautious, pragmatic style of Assad's regime suggests, however, that Syria will not initiate war, certainly not alone, against Israel in the foreseeable future. A more likely strategy is that Syria will cash in on its military might in terms of its position in the region. If it succeeds in building a wider coalition, Syria would not only reduce the risks inevitably involved in a war with Israel, but also *ipso facto* lessen Egypt's influence.

In addition, such a strategy might present Syria with opportunities for engaging Israel in wars of attrition along a wide front in which Israel's civilian hinterland would be exposed. If Israel then tried to escalate such a war in order to force Syria to de-escalate, the very occurrence of hostilities might strain Egypt's ability to maintain its cold peace with Israel.

Alternatively, but less likely, Syria might attempt to use a position of comparable strength *vis-à-vis* Israel as a basis for a negotiated settlement. The Soviet Union, on whose support Syria depends, would not necessarily be adverse to the idea (provided, of course, that it does not lead to the exclusion of the Soviets from the picture). A Syrian-Israeli understanding would lessen the dangers from the Soviet point of view. On the other hand, a Syrian move towards *détente* with Israel might turn the Soviets into a liability; at the least, they would cease to be an asset from the Syrian point of view. Indeed, as Sadat discovered a decade and a half ago, the key to a settlement with Israel is Washington, and not Moscow. Differently stated, a Syrian about-face *vis-à-vis* Israel will require, simultaneously, a significant modification of Syrian rhetoric, domestic positions and posture *vis-à-vis* the Arab world and a *renversement des alliances* with the superpowers. This entails a change of colossal magnitude, which Sadat could manage because of the different domestic setting in which he operated but which no Syrian leader to date, and apparently not even Assad, can hope to carry out. The alternative scenario — namely, building up strength, forming a solid bloc of support in the Arab world and then engaging Israel in limited but irritating hostilities — appears more likely, at least as a prelude to a quest for *détente* with Israel.

Whereas the dilemmas outlined above concern the long-term future, the situation in Lebanon presents Syria with far more pressing problems. Syria's strategy there appears to be the following. Syria does not wish to become more deeply entangled than it already is, but it cannot simply extricate itself, concerned as it is with preventing the penetration of Lebanon by others and, just as much, with obviating Lebanon's transformation into a hostile factor towards Syria itself. The maximum Syria can realistically hope for is the creation of an equilibrium more or less, among the Phalangists, the Druzes and the Shi'ites that would facilitate a modicum of stability under vicarious Syrian influence.

Hence, while supporting the Druzes and the Shi'ites in their struggle with the Phalangists, Syria has not allowed, and will not allow, these two parts of the Lebanese equation to vanquish the third factor altogether. Syria has in the past, and will again do so in the future, played off any two of these forces against the third, while it acts more as a final arbiter than as an occupying force (except for small parts of Lebanon that are immediately adjacent to Syria itself).

Accomplishments

Every article presented in this volume underlines important Syrian accomplishments. Moshe Ma'oz is impressed with the regime's success in arresting internal power struggles and with its governing ability. Kais Firro shows how substantially the Syrian economy has grown in the years of Assad's rule. Zeev Ma'oz demonstrates that Syria's power has increased on the whole more substantially than that of its reference group. David Kushner points out that Syrian-Turkish relations have completely recovered from the tensions that marred them until two and a half decades ago. Yair Hirschfeld shows how Syria has succeeded in collecting the greater pay-offs from its alliance with Iran. Amazia Baram provides a clear picture of Syria's success in managing the ideological and political feud with Iraq. Joseph Nevo underlines the fact that Syrian-Jordanian relations have undergone a virtual reversal, from intimidation by an ambitious Hashemite monarch to Jordanian fears of subversion by Syria. Avner Yaniv emphasises how prudent and meticulously controlled the Syrian strategic posture has been *vis-à-vis* Israel. Itamar Rabinovich argues convincingly that for Syria, the crisis in Lebanon has offered an opportunity for demonstrating power, influence and control. Moshe Ma'oz and Avner Yaniv stress the ruthless, consistent manner in which Syria has controlled the PLO. Yair Evron points out how Syria has succeeded in implanting in the Americans a great deal of respect towards it and Robert O. Freedman shows Syria's succeess in managing a most beneficial alliance with the Soviet Union.

Until less than a decade ago, Syria was hardly considered a pivotal Middle Eastern power. What this summarised catalogue of Syrian accomplishments very clearly suggests is that Syria's position in the region has been altered beyond recognition. Bluntly, it is no longer possible to ignore Syria or to treat it as a secondary or passive by-stander in a larger scene. Syria has become the key to any solution in

Lebanon and a dead-weight on the Arab-Israeli peace process. It may not be an established fact that Syria can prevent any serious move towards an Arab-Israeli settlement, but it is no longer a fantasy to argue that this is so.

And yet, this assessment does not represent the overall balance sheet of Syria's accomplishments, which is far from being decidedly favourable. An important lesson that emerges from the chapters of this volume is that the Syrian regime has to perform a heroic balancing act among numerous constraints. The extent to which it can succeed in all these diverse tasks depends, in the final analysis, on the continuation of stability within the Syrian state itself. If a leadership like Assad's continues to hold the reins of power, Syria can be expected to achieve a high proportion of its goals. It can continue to enhance its position as a countervailing force to Egypt and Iraq. It can continue to hold at bay both the Jordanians and the PLO and certainly the Lebanese. It can continue to derive significant benefits from its alliance with the Soviet Union without necessarily damaging its dialogue with the United States. Finally, and most important of all, this leadership can continue the internal process of nation-building.

But is this a realistic forecast? An unequivocal answer is impossible because everything hinges so much on personalities. No one knows how long Hafez al-Assad will live. No one outside the ruling circle in Damascus can really tell whether a successor has already been chosen. No one, indeed, can really say whether Assad's successor, even if he gains the approval of all his rivals, will be as astute as Assad. In this sense, the accomplishments of Assad's reign remain quite inadequate. The greatest success this regime could claim would be continuity in stability, in goals and in the ability to attain them. And since this attainment remains so unclear, it would be premature to declare the Alawi Ba'ath a success story. Indeed, if continuity is not maintained and if everything depends on the presence of Assad himself, Syria's future is highly uncertain. Assad's pending departure could well trigger off a power struggle at the top that would quickly spill over into the wider Syrian scene and possibly lead, not just to the diminution of Syria's power, but conceivably even to an internal war and, ultimately, the break-up of Syria's fragile political superstructure into its ethnic and religious component parts.

From the Syrian point of view, such a 'Lebanese' scenario is probably a haunting nightmare, a worst-case anlaysis that should be avoided almost at all costs. Even if such a cataclysm does not materialise, however, Syria's achievements would still remain mixed.

The Syrian state may have exhibited a dramatic ascent in its international stature, but the thrust of its domestic politics and foreign policy alike leads in a direction that seems out of step with the rest of the Middle East. For all its military power and for all its subversive capacities, Syria may be ultimately incapable of preventing Egypt, Jordan, Iraq, the Gulf states and even the PLO from heading towards amicable relations with the West and some accommodation with Israel. None of these powers would move in these directions if it were not in its interests. If it were in its interests, on the other hand, none of them would stop entirely simply because Syria objected.

Can Syria join such a throng? The answer seems to be negative. The stern, militant stance *vis-à-vis* Israel, the deepening reliance on the Soviet Union and the pervasively repressive nature of the regime all seem to be so solidly woven into the fabric of the Syrian system that it will take a long while before a change in course becomes a realistic proposition. Assad's Syria, then, presents an intriguing paradox. If it were not for its staunchly realistic operational goals and a robust pragmatism in execution, Syria would not have risen to its present status. Yet the same realism has also forced the regime to perpetuate a loud commitment to aspirations that turn Syria into a menace to its neighbours and, ultimately, into its own worst enemy.

INDEX

Note: 1. References are to Syria unless otherwise stated.
2. Sub-entries are in alphabetical order except where chronological order is significant.

Abdallah, King 141-2, 146, 147, 148, 149, 151, 153
Abu Mussa rebellion 203
accomplishments and Syrian paradox 261-3
administrative institutions, lack of 41
Afghanistan 225
invaded 228, 229
Aflag, Michel 23, 24, 228, 126, 127-8
agriculture 37, 38, 45-50, 62, 72, 132
see also irrigation; land
aid, foreign 44-5, 51, 54, 58, 62, 210
see also under military
air space, Jordan's use of Syria's 149-50
Al-Ghab valley project 46-7, 95
Alawi-Ba'athist rule
consolidated 25-30
Muslim opposition to 30-4
see also Ba'athist
Alawis 1, 10, 11, 19, 253
army members 23-5, 28
controlled 21, 22
migration 38
politics and 22-3, 32-3
Shi'ites and 180
Alexandretta (Hatay) problem 15, 85, 87, 99, 102-3
Algeria 228, 230
Iran and 110, 118
Iraq and 133
PLO in 203
Algiers agreement (1975) 120
Allon, Yigal 166, 169
Ammam summit conference 109-10
anarchists, Turkish 93, 97-8
see also terrorists
Andropov, Yuri 234, 235
'anti-imperialist bloc' 226-7, 229, 230
Arab League 151, 164, 172, 228
Arab Parliamentary Union conference 119
Arab Socialist Resurrection Party 18, 29
see also Ba'ath

Arab Union 108-10
Arabic language 12, 13
Arafat, Yassir 9
Assad and 147, 182, 195, 198-200, 234, 242-3
Hussein and 146, 187, 204, 234
Israel and 202
Jedid and 194
Maronites and 182
revolt against 239-40
Suwydani and 192
trail 173
West and 201, 233, 235
Arens, Moshe 157, 236, 237
Arif, Abd al-Salam 127
Armenians 38, 98-9
arms see army; military; missiles
army, Syrian
Ba'athist regime and 127-8
Border disputes and 93
elite units 27, 28
French rule in 11
officers 18, 19, 23
powers of 24-5
see also military; wars
Asi (Orontes) river 46-7, 95-6
Assad, Hafez al- 3, 9, 127, 251-63
and Egypt 134, 228
and Iran 118-19, 122
and Iraq 132-4
and Israel 157, 166, 171, 175
and Jordan 145, 147, 152
and Lebanon 179-85, 188-9, 238-40, 242
and PLO 192, 194-6, 198-201, 235
and religion 116
and Soviet Union 227, 229-30, 235
and Turkey 89-90, 97
and USA 209, 218
in power 25-32, 37, 128
personality 26
role 31
see also Syria under Assad
Assad, Rif'at 3, 27-8, 33, 145, 157, 256

264

268   Index